Microsoft Word 5 for the Macintosh Made Easy

Microsoft Word 5 for the Macintosh Made Easy

Paul Hoffman

Osborne **McGraw-Hill**

Berkeley New York St. Louis San Francisco
Auckland Bogotá Hamburg London Madrid
Mexico City Milan Montreal New Delhi Panama City
Paris São Paulo Singapore Sydney
Tokyo Toronto

Osborne **McGraw-Hill**
2600 Tenth Street
Berkeley, California 94710
U.S.A.

For information on translations or book distributors outside of the U.S.A., please write to Osborne **McGraw-Hill** at the above address.

Microsoft Word 5 for the Macintosh Made Easy

234567890 DOC 998765432

ISBN 0-07-881769-2

Publisher

Kenna S. Wood

Acquisitions Editor

Frances Stack

Associate Editor

Jill Pisoni

Project Editor

Judith Brown

Technical Reviewer

Bob Kermish

Copy Editor

Paul Medoff

Proofreading Coordinator

Kelly Barr

Proofreaders

Mick Arellano
Audrey Johnson

Indexer

Paul Hoffman

Director of Electronic Publishing

Deborah Wilson

Production Supervisor

Barry Michael Bergin

Production Assistant

George Anderson

Computer Designer

Peter F. Hancik

Typesetting

Jani Beckwith
Helena Charm
J. E. Christgau
Marcela Hancik
Susie Kim
Fred Lass
Bob Myren
Mickey Salinaro
Stefany Otis

Technical Illustrator

Lance Ravella

Cover Design

Bay Graphic Design, Inc.
Mason Fong

Contents

Introduction

Microsoft Word 5 for the Macintosh Made Easy will help you master Microsoft Word version 5. It discusses both the essential and unique features of Word and provides practical suggestions for putting Word to work for you. This book supplements Word's documentation, the Microsoft Word reference manual, by showing you, in step-by-step fashion, how to use Word.

Even though a few of Word's features appear complex, they are relatively easy to master once you understand the concepts behind them. This book is arranged to teach you these concepts in a natural order, and it reinforces the concepts with many practical examples. The examples demonstrate the numerous word processing functions performed in a typical business office, although they are just as useful in any situation that requires word processing capabilities.

Each chapter is divided into lessons, which are fully illustrated with pictures of the Macintosh screen so you will know what to expect as you use the program. There are also review exercises at the end of each chapter.

For those of you who have never used a word processing program before, this book explains basic concepts when they first appear in the text. Even if you have used other word processing programs, you will find that some of Word's features are unique (for example, it can display several parts of a file simultaneously). These, too, are explained in full, so you can completely understand the power of Word. You only need to know the basics of using the Macintosh to use this book; you do not need to be familiar with any other word processing program.

If you already have Microsoft Word or are thinking of buying it, this book is for you. As a beginning user, you will find that the lessons are easy to follow, and succeeding lessons build on concepts learned earlier in the book. If you are an intermediate user, you will find that topics mentioned only briefly in different parts of the reference manual are described fully in one source in this book. All users will also find that the real-world examples in this book are more helpful than the terse step-lists in the Word manual.

If you are using an earlier version of Word than 5, you should upgrade your copy. Version 5 has many significant new features and improvements to the user interface. Like every program, Word had some bugs in its earlier versions, and most of these have been fixed in version 5. Contact Microsoft to determine how you can upgrade to version 5.

What Is Microsoft Word?

A *word processing* program is a computer program that lets you type and save any text (such as memos, letters, reports, and books). Word processing programs such as Microsoft Word let you easily enter text for a document, revise the text once it has been entered (called *editing*), and print the text out on your printer in a professional form (called *formatting*).

There is a wide variety of word processing software available for many different computers. Some software gives you the bare minimum of capabilities, while other programs, such as Word, give you many more useful features that make word processing easier.

Word is useful for all types of word processing, such as writing short memos, business letters, financial statements, articles, books, and long reports. It is generally easy to use, and has many advanced features that you can use or ignore, depending on the type of document you are writing. For example, many people use Word for creating brochures and advertisements. The more you use Word, the less you need to worry about what your text will look like, so you can spend more time concentrating on what you want to say.

Advantages of Using Word

If you have compared Word to other word processing packages, you know that it has many features that others do not. Of course, having a plethora of features does not make a word processor good: you have to be able to use these features easily. Three outstanding features of Word are mentioned briefly here and described fully in the rest of the book.

Undo Feature

Since it is common to make mistakes when you edit text, Word has an "undo" feature that lets you take out your last change. This means that if you do something you didn't intend to do, you can tell Word to undo it. This feature can save you a great deal of typing and frustration.

Help Feature

If you are ever unsure of what you are doing in Word, the program can always offer help. This prevents you from having to look up information in the reference manual (or in this book) when you just want to know a small bit of information. The help that Word gives you is often more useful than the help you get from other programs, since it first gives you help on what you are currently doing, and then makes it easy to ask for more information if you need it.

Windows

One problem with many word processing programs is that you can only see a small portion of your document at a time. With Word, you can see many parts of the text at the same time in different windows. You can also see two parts of a document in one window. This feature is very useful when you are writing a long document, since you can look at what you wrote earlier while you write new text. You can even use Word to look at different files on the screen at the same time, and to move text between files.

Using Word in Business

You have probably heard of the many advantages that word processing offers over normal typing for a business. Since Word has many more features than most other word processing programs, it lets you do more work more easily. For example:

- Most businesses have form letters (standard letters for which the computer fills in a different name and address), and many word processing packages let you write simple form letters. Word allows you to integrate other information into your form letters, so that the letters look more personalized. Word can also read the names and addresses from data files stored by other programs, such as data management systems, and integrate these names and addresses into letters. This feature is often called *mail merge*.
- Word's advanced formatting lets you make reports that look professionally typeset. With Word, you can design each page to your specifications, and not worry about what it will look like if you change some of the text. Word works well with all printers that work with the Macintosh.
- With Word, newsletters and other bulletins can be printed with many columns on one page, giving your writing a more professional look. You can also use many different type styles (such as **boldface** or *italics*) and different type sizes so that your headlines stand out from your text.
- Many of Word's features are especially useful in certain professions. For example, Word's ability to number lines on a page is very helpful for lawyers' pleadings and depositions.
- You can use Word to make an outline, then use that outline to prepare a business document. You can have Word automatically number the headings in your outline and change those numbers as you move or delete headings.

As you read this book, remember that you can always try out the information that is presented to you. Use the files that the book tells you to type in, or create your own. The more you use Word for your own files, the more quickly you will master Microsoft Word.

New Features in Version 5

Microsoft Word version 5 has many features that did not appear in previous versions. These features make Word easier to use and allow you to prepare business documents in a more natural way.

- In addition to an improved spelling checker and thesaurus, Microsoft has added a grammar checker that looks for common mistakes in your document. For instance, it finds doubled words such as "the the" and wordy phrases such as "in the first place."
- You can quickly find and retrieve files from disk based on their contents. You can assign keywords to documents and look quickly for those words. You can also look for any words in a document.
- The Find and Replace commands now let you specify formats for finding and replacing. It is also much easier to find special characters with the new commands since you do not need to remember the cryptic character codes.
- The new *ribbon* allows you to format characters using buttons at the top of your document. The ribbon also has additional buttons for other Word features such as drawing.
- You can make simple drawings from within Word and include them in your documents. Even if you have a Macintosh drawing program, you will find that this feature lets you quickly generate graphics to embellish your work.
- With the new Symbol command, you can easily add symbols to your document in any font.
- Word version 5 works very well with Macintosh System 7. Word uses new System 7 features like Publish/Subscribe and balloon help, as well as advanced AppleEvents that help Word work well with other System 7 programs.

These features are described throughout this book. This book has been completely revised for these new features (as well as dozens of minor ones), so you should be running Version 5 if you intend to try all of the book's examples.

I

Word Basics

1

Getting Started

This chapter explains the few steps you need to follow before you can begin to use Word for your Macintosh and shows you how to start up the program. After following the installation instructions, you can start to edit and format documents immediately; in fact, you will start using Word in Chapter 2 to enter a business letter that is used throughout the next six chapters and in many other sections of the book as well.

If you have no word processing experience, the following section gives you a quick overview of many of the terms you will find in this book. If you are familiar with another word processor, you can probably skim the section.

Word Processing Terms

Word processing programs give you two major capabilities: editing and formatting of text. *Editing* is the ability to enter text into the program, make corrections, save the text on disk, and later change the text. *Formatting* is the ability to specify how the text will look when you print it out; for example, in boldface or italic in a specific type size and style. Formatting also allows you to add special features to the printout, such as page numbers on each page, and to specify the width of the left and right margins.

In order to make a word processing program work, you give it *commands*, which are instructions that tell the program what you want to do. In Word, you can give commands by using the mouse, or by pressing the ⌘ key (sometimes referred to as the *Command key*) and one or more other keys at the same time.

When you write a document, you *insert* text into a file. This is done by typing the text as you would on a typewriter. Once you have done this, you can use editing commands to correct mistakes or to rearrange the text. While you are editing, you can move around in the text so you can edit different parts. When you want to see text that is not on the screen, the word processing program *scrolls*, or moves, the screen to the desired location. When you are done with a file, you can *save* it on disk, and when you want to use the file later, you can tell the word processing program to *open* it from disk.

Preparing for Word

Microsoft Word comes on disks containing the programs and special files needed to run it. Since Word is such a large program, it takes up several disks. Most people run Word from hard disks, since it runs much faster there. In addition, running many of Word's utilities, such as the spelling checker, is tedious on a floppy-based system. If you do not have a hard disk, you must have at least two floppy drives in order to run Word.

Follow the directions in the installation guide that comes with Word to copy the files from the Word distribution disks to your hard disk or to other floppies. You should never run Word directly from the floppies that the program comes on since you might damage the floppies and then be unable to run Word at all.

After you have installed Word, it is a good idea to store the distribution floppies in a safe place, preferably away from your computer. (Many people even keep their distribution floppies in a different room.) If your copy of Word that you have made on your hard disk or other floppies later becomes damaged or lost, you can reinstall the program from these floppies.

Starting the Word Program

You start Word in much the same way you start other Macintosh applications. Start your Macintosh as you normally do. To start Word, open the folder in which it was installed by *double-clicking* it (clicking twice in rapid succession) and double-click the Word icon, which is shown here:

This is the method you will normally use for starting Word.

Another method for starting Word and editing an existing file is to double-click the icon for that file. When you double-click a Word document, the Macintosh operating system will start the Word program and open that file automatically.

The first time you run Word you are asked to personalize your copy. This puts your name and company name into the program; these names are shown each time you start the program. If you work for a company, they may have already personalized your copy for you.

When you start Word without opening a document, you see Word's main window, shown in Figure 1-1. The file is named "Untitled 1" until you save it to disk with a name of your choice. The next new file that you open during this session will be named "Untitled 2," and so on. As you can see, many of the features of the Word window are the same as in other Macintosh programs, but some are unique to Word. Those features that are only seen in Word are described throughout this book.

One mark on the window that may interest you now is the horizontal line near the top of the document window. This is called the *end-of-file marker* because it shows you where the end of your document is. All text in your document appears above this mark.

Entering Text

As soon as Word is loaded, it is ready for you to start entering text. Near the upper-left corner, the blinking vertical bar is where the first letters you

Figure 1-1. *Features of Word's main window*

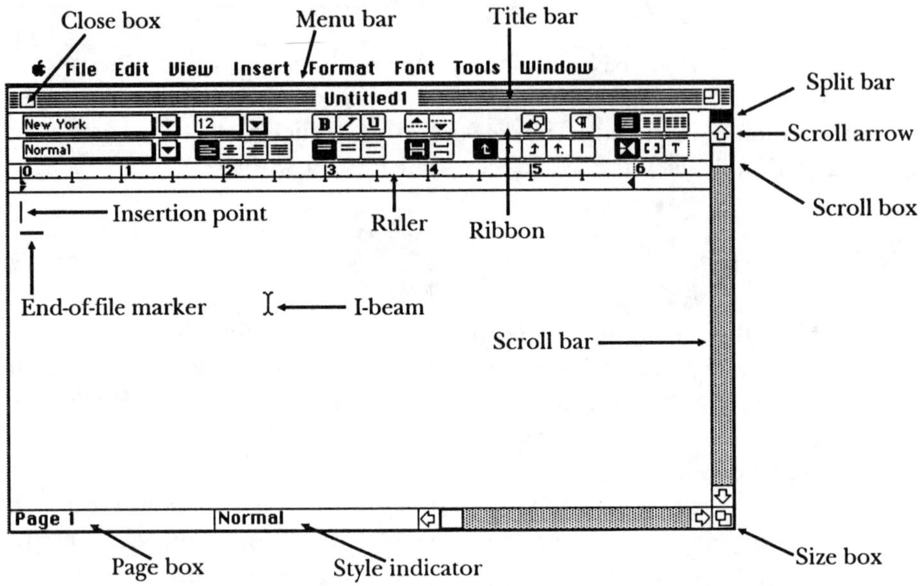

type appear. This bar is called the *insertion point,* just as in other Macintosh programs. It indicates where you are in text.

When you type text, you can correct typing mistakes by pressing the (DELETE) key in the upper-right corner of the main part of the keyboard to erase the character to the left of the insertion point.

You can type just as you would on a typewriter. To start experimenting, type **This is just like a typewriter**. If you make a mistake as you type, you can press (DELETE) to erase the letter (or letters) you just typed.

Selecting and Inserting Text

To tell Word to do something to some text in your document, you first indicate the text you want to work on; then indicate the action. To indicate the text on which you will work, you *select* the text with the mouse or the keyboard. If what you want to do is insert text, you set the *insertion point* to the position where you want to insert the new text.

While selecting and inserting text may sound easy, it is often one of the things that confuses beginning Word users, especially those who have not dealt much with computers. Even though selecting is basic to all Macintosh use, it requires you to use a few things at once and thus can be a bit daunting to beginners. Figure 1-2 shows the way your screen should look with the sentence that you just typed.

Note that there are two nontext items that appear as vertical bars. The blinking vertical bar that is at the end of your text is the insertion point that you were just introduced to. The other vertical bar, which moves when you move the mouse, is called the *I-beam.* The I-beam is one of a few shapes that the *mouse pointer* takes as you move it around the screen. The insertion point and the I-beam are very different and should not be confused.

The arrow pointer and the I-beam are both different aspects of the mouse pointer. They are used to point at menus and parts of your document. Their shape is totally dependent on where you move the mouse. As you move from a command or window control area to the text area, the pointer changes from the arrow to the I-beam. The insertion point, on the other hand, is a specific location in your document that remains the same even when you move the

Figure 1-2. *Screen after sentence is typed*

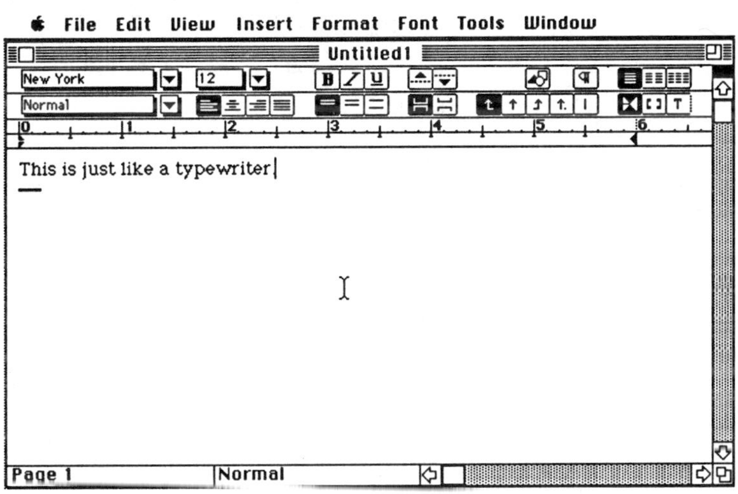

mouse pointer. You can see this by moving the I-beam around and noting that the blinking insertion point remains stationary.

When you begin to type, the Macintosh (not Word) makes the mouse pointer invisible. It becomes visible again when you move the mouse. This makes it easier to type because the mouse pointer is not obscuring the text you are typing.

This chapter shows you the basics of selecting and inserting text. You will see more ways to select and insert text in the next chapter.

Selecting Text with the Mouse

To select text, you click the I-beam at the beginning of the group of characters you want to select, hold down the button on the mouse, move the I-beam to the end of the group of characters, and release the mouse button. This is known as *dragging* the mouse across the text. As you select text, it becomes *highlighted,* meaning that it appears as white letters on a black or colored background.

For example, assume that you want to select the letter "j" in the word "just" in the sentence you typed. Move the I-beam to just before the "j", as shown here:

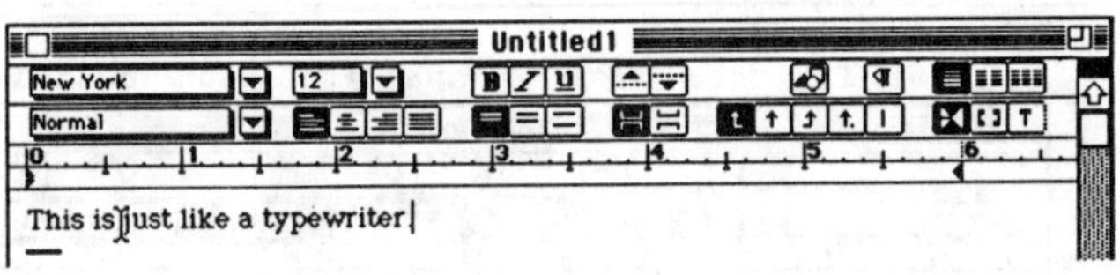

(If you see an arrow instead of an I-beam when you start to make a selection, you are pointing above the letters.) Hold down the mouse button; the blinking insertion point jumps to the location of the I-beam, but don't be concerned with that for now. While holding down the mouse button, drag the I-beam to the right until the "j" in "just" is highlighted, as shown here:

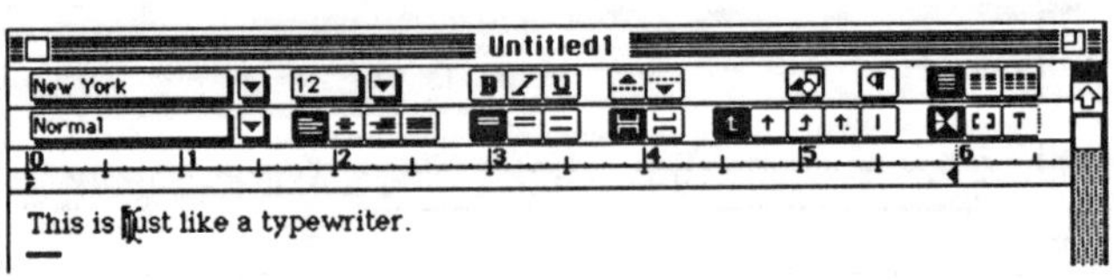

Release the mouse button, and you have selected the letter.

You have now created a selection. Whenever you give Word commands that have an effect on text in your file, the effect is only on the selected text. You can select from one character to the whole document at any time. The text that is highlighted is the text that is currently selected (in this case, the letter "j").

You have just seen how to select a single letter by dragging the mouse. You can also select more than one letter using the same technique. For example, to select the word "like" in the sentence, move the I-beam to just before the "l", hold down the mouse button, drag the I-beam to the right until the "e" is highlighted, and release the mouse button. You have now selected the entire word.

You can use the mouse to quickly select specific amounts of text. A common task is to select a whole word. Instead of having to drag over the word as you just did, you can double-click the word you want. To see this, move the I-beam to anywhere over the word "just" and double-click. The result is

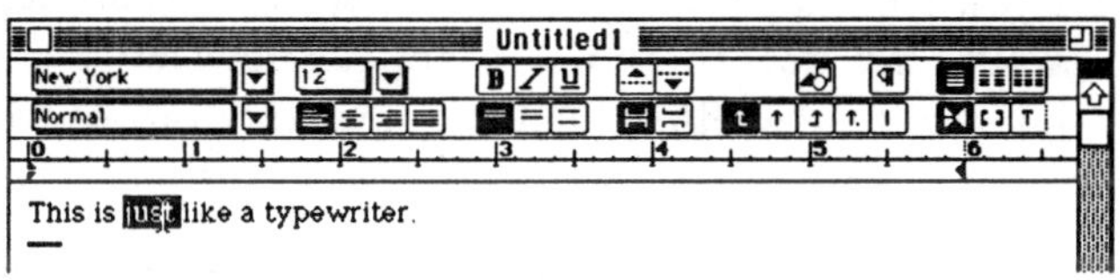

Note that Word also selects the space after the word.

You can also select a whole sentence quickly. If you hold down the ⌘ key at the same time as you click once anywhere on the sentence, Word selects the entire sentence, including the space after the period.

Inserting Text

You may be wondering, "If the insertion point disappears when I select text, why have an insertion point at all?" The insertion point tells you where the next letter that you type appears—in other words, "where you are." As you can imagine, that can be pretty important. It allows you to quickly change the place where you insert text.

When you click the I-beam in the text area, Word puts the insertion point in the place where you click. If anything is selected when you click the I-beam, it becomes deselected when the insertion point is placed. You can now see that you will never have both a selection and an insertion point on the screen at the same time.

To see this, first select the word "just" by double-clicking it. Next, put the I-beam between the letter "r" and the period at the end of the sentence. When you click the mouse button, "just" becomes deselected and the insertion point appears between the "r" and the period.

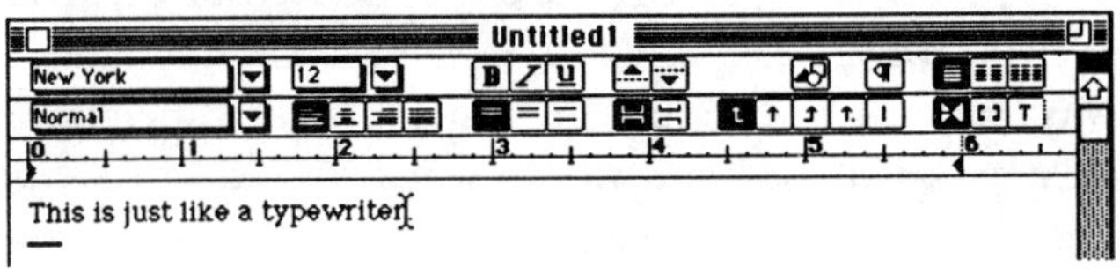

If you begin typing when the insertion point is between two characters, the text you type appears at that position. For example, type **but is much easier** and notice how these words appear between the "r" and the period. Every time you type a letter, the insertion point moves to the right.

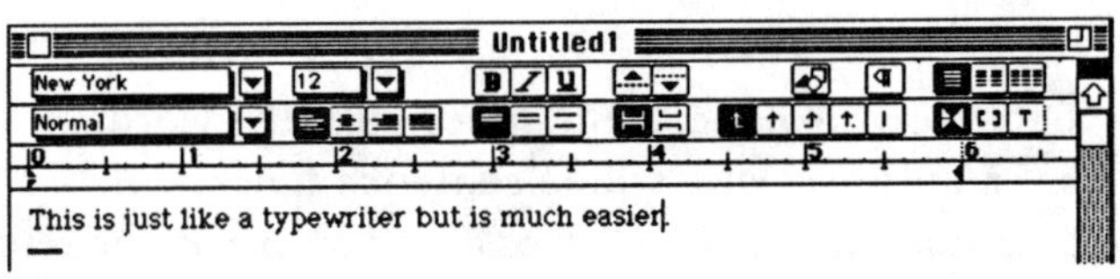

It may take some practice to get used to pointing with the mouse. A common mistake is to click the mouse button so hard that you move the mouse, with the result that the pointer is no longer exactly where you want it on the screen. If you press the mouse hard and move it as you are pressing, you make a selection instead of placing the insertion point. When you point at information on the screen, Word uses either the tip of the arrow or the middle of the I-beam (not the whole pointer) to determine what you are pointing at.

Selecting and Inserting Text with the Keyboard

So far, you have only seen how to use the mouse to create selections or place the insertion point. Some people prefer to use the keyboard, especially if they are already familiar with using other computers. Word lets you perform these tasks with the keyboard as easily as with the mouse.

To move the insertion point, use the arrow keys (a few older keyboards do not have arrow keys). These arrow keys, marked (←), (→), (↑), and (↓), almost always appear below the right (SHIFT) key or between the main part of the keyboard and the numeric keys on the far right. Experiment with these keys to see how the insertion point moves in the sentence you have typed.

Making selections with the keyboard is just as easy. You first move the insertion point to the beginning of the desired selection, hold down the (SHIFT) key, and use the arrow keys to move to the end of the desired selection. The selection (as indicated by the highlighting) moves as you press the arrow keys. Release the (SHIFT) key when you have finished making the selection.

For example, to select the word "typewriter" in the sentence you typed, use the (←) or (→) key to move the insertion point to the left of the first "t". Hold down the (SHIFT) key and press the (→) key until the entire word is selected.

Using Word Commands

Just as there are two ways to give commands in the Macintosh Finder, there are two ways to give Word commands: with the mouse and with the keyboard. Almost every command can be given with the mouse, and most can also be given with the keyboard. Some people strongly prefer the mouse over the keyboard; others, the opposite. Most Word users, however, find that they use a mixture of mouse and keyboard to give commands.

All Word commands appear in the *menus*, which are grouped in a *menu bar* at the top of the screen. The menus contain groups of similar commands and look like this:

 File Edit View Insert Format Font Tools Window

In this book, every command is named by the command name and the menu name so that you can find it easily. For example, the Ribbon command appears in the View menu. In this book, you would be told to "give the Ribbon command from the View menu." Note that the first menu on the left, marked with an apple symbol, is called the Apple menu.

To give a command with the mouse, you point at the desired menu, click and hold the mouse button, and then drag down to the desired command while still holding down the mouse button. When you release the button, the command executes. For example, give the Ruler command from the View menu. This command turns the *ruler* on and off.

Many Word commands also have *keyboard equivalents*—keystrokes you can press instead of having to use the mouse. The keyboard equivalents are various combinations of the ⌘ key, the OPTION key, the SHIFT key, and regular keyboard keys. The keyboard equivalents of commands are listed on the menu, to the right of the name of the command. The symbols for keyboard equivalents used in the menus are

Symbol	Meaning
⌘	⌘ key
⌥	OPTION key
⇧	SHIFT key
⌨	Key on the keypad

For example, here is the View menu:

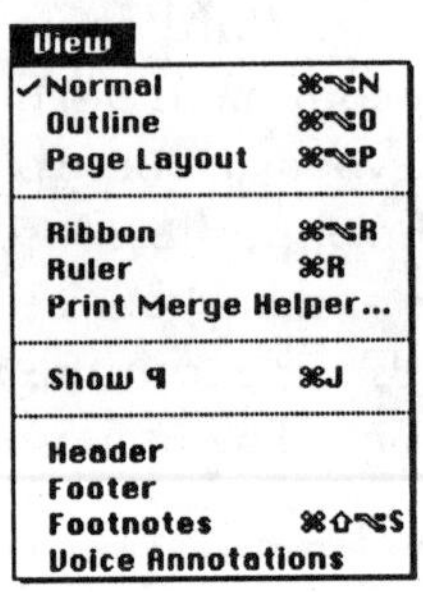

The keyboard equivalent for the Normal command from the View menu is ⌘-OPTION-N, for Outline it is ⌘-OPTION-O, and so on. To see how to use

keyboard equivalents, press ⌘-OPTION-R, the key combination for the Ribbon command. This turns on and off the *ribbon*. The top of your screen (without the ribbon and ruler) now looks like this:

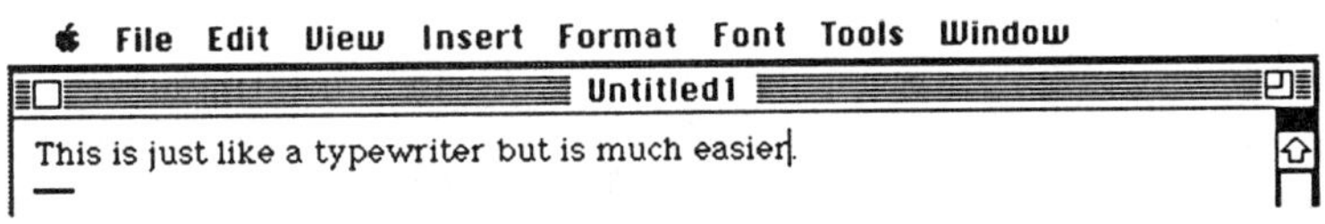

You can change the keys associated with any command, as you will see in Chapter 16. The keyboard equivalents discussed in this book are the ones that come assigned to the commands when you run Word for the first time. You can also add and remove commands from the menus. If you are using a copy of Word that someone else has used, the key equivalents and the commands that you see in the menus may be somewhat different from what you see in this book.

Many Word commands act on a part of a document you specify. For example, you may want to make a word in your text bold. When you want a command to act on some specific text, you always indicate the text first, then give the command. This is true of all Macintosh programs: specify what you want to work on first, then give the command.

Word is designed so you can use it without a mouse if you have a keyboard with a keypad, such as the one on the Macintosh Plus and all of the newer Macintoshes. (The *keypad* is a separate group of number and operation keys that looks like a set of calculator keys to the right of the typewriter keys.) However, the method you must use to do this is so convoluted that it is unlikely you will want to. If you are interested in using Word without a mouse, see the Keyboard section of the Word manual.

Making Paragraphs in Word

In your text, each set of lines that is grouped as a unit is called a *paragraph*. Unfortunately, this is easy to confuse with the definition of a paragraph that you learned in grammar school, which is a group of sentences developing an idea. In Word, a paragraph is really just a line or a group of lines that end with a press of the RETURN key. For instance, in a business letter, the line with the date, the lines that show the recipient's address, and the line with the salutation are all paragraphs, as is each group of sentences in the letter. When you see the word "paragraph" in this book and the Microsoft Word reference manual, it refers to Word's definition.

Word identifies the end of a paragraph by a special mark that it puts in your text when you press the RETURN key. For this reason, you do not use the RETURN key at the end of each line inside a paragraph, only at the end of the paragraph. One of Word's features that makes typing much easier is automatic *wordwrap*, which eliminates the need to decide where to end each line. As you type a paragraph, Word automatically figures out what will fit on a line and where to start a new line. You only press RETURN at the end of the paragraph.

For example, continue typing after the sentence you have already typed. Use the mouse or keyboard to move the insertion point to follow the period, and type a second sentence: **As I type in this second sentence, I notice that Word goes to the next line without my pressing the Return key.** Now press RETURN, and notice that the insertion point moves to the beginning of the next line after the text.

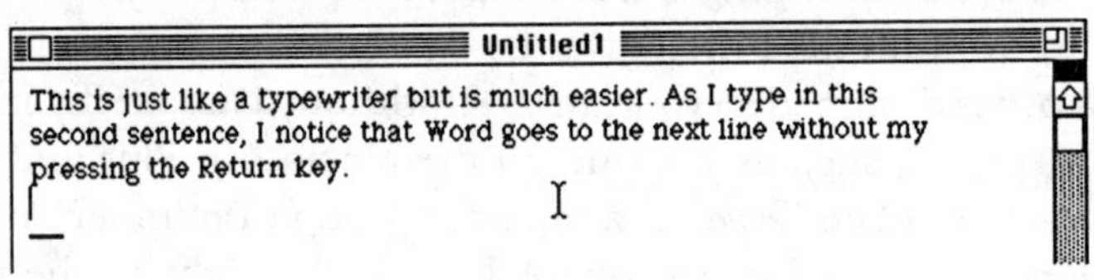

Getting Help

The Help command is a quick way to get information about a Word command or to figure out what is happening in the program. The Help command has a list of choices that you can use to get information about any command and all of its options.

To get help, give the Help command from the Window menu. You can select the topic you want help on from the list box, shown in Figure 1-3. When you are finished, click the Cancel button to continue with Word.

Figure 1-3. *Help dialog box*

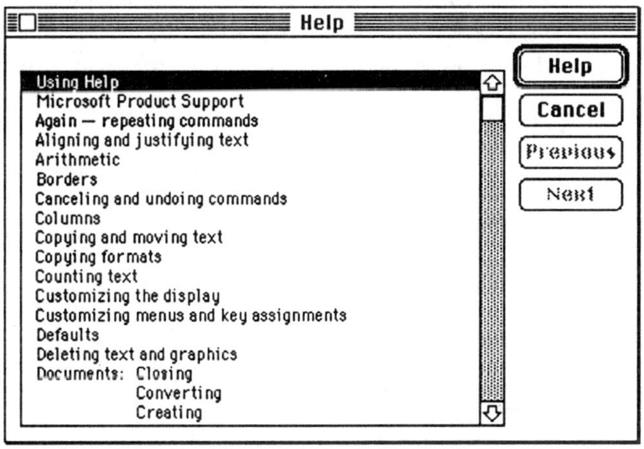

You can also get help on specific Word commands. To do this, press ⌘-?. (You do not need to use the SHIFT key for this.) The arrow pointer becomes a question mark, which you can use to select the command for which you want help. For example, to find out how to open files, press ⌘-?, and then pull down the File menu and select the Open command. You can also get help on particular dialog boxes by pressing ⌘-? when the dialog box is on the screen.

If you are running System 7 on your Macintosh, you can also get balloon help for Word's commands. Balloon help in Word works just like balloon help in all other System 7 programs.

Leaving Word

Since you have only entered practice text, it is unlikely that you want to save it in a file (don't worry; the real text comes at the beginning of the next chapter). When you leave Word, the program checks to see if you have saved your text in a file before it returns you to the Finder. It is easy, however, to tell Word not to bother.

When you want to exit from Word and return to the Finder, give the Quit command from the File menu or press ⌘-Q. If there is text that you have not saved on disk (you will learn how to save text in the next chapter), Word prompts

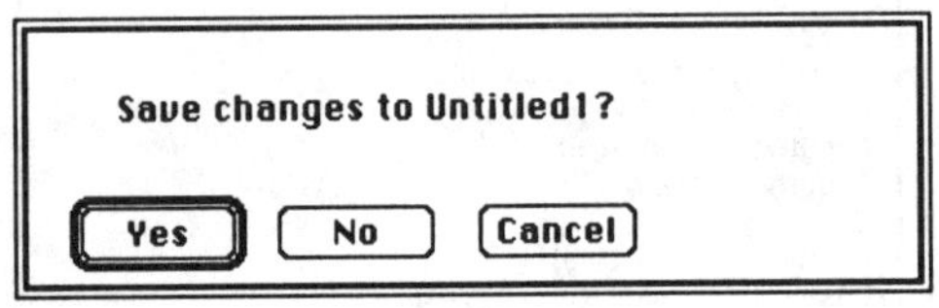

If you want to save your text under the filename Untitled 1, click the Yes button in the box. In this case, however, you can click the No button, since the material is just for practice. If you realize that you want to do more editing or would like to save the file under a different name, click the Cancel button. You can also quit from Word with the ⌘-Q key.

Review

Start a new document and copy any two sentences from this book into the document. Select the first sentence using the mouse. Then place the insertion point in the second sentence. Now select the first sentence using the keyboard.

Type another sentence between the first and second sentence. Note how the text moves to the right as you do this.

2

Basic Editing with Word

This and the next seven chapters show you how to enter and edit a variety of documents, from short memos to long reports. The lessons in this chapter use the sample business letter that you type in the first lesson.

Lesson 1: Typing Your First File

Now that you know how to start Word, how to enter text, and a bit about giving Word commands, you are ready to type your first exercise, the business letter in Figure 2-1. Type it using the rules you have learned so far; if you make mistakes, correct them with the DELETE key.

Note that this letter may be longer than one Macintosh screen, depending on the size of your monitor. If you reach the bottom of the screen as you are typing, just keep typing. Word scrolls the text up as you type.

Whenever you want to add text to the middle of text that you have already entered, simply move the I-beam to the desired location, click the mouse button to set the insertion point, and type.

Figure 2-1. *Text of Sample 1 file*

January 11, 1992

Chris Richford, Vice President
Manufacturer's Bank of the Northeast
1000 First Avenue
Millerton, CT 06492

Dear Ms. Richford:

I am pleased to send you the latest update on the results of our expanded product line. The enclosed summary documents our increased profit margin (7%) for the fourth quarter of 1991, which is largely due to the successful introduction of our new model, the DC50. In 1992 we expect to continue increasing our profitable inroads into this new area.

As you can see, we are well within the projections we outlined to you when you helped us obtain short-term financing. Thank you again for all your assistance. If you have any questions regarding this information, please feel free to call me.

Sincerely,

Thomas Mead, Controller
National Generators
1275 Oak Glen Industrial Park
Oak Glen, CT 06410

The next section explains how to save the letter you have just typed in a file on disk. This file will be used in many of the chapters in this book.

Lesson 2: Saving Your Text in a File

Now that you have text that you want to keep, you need to know how to tell Word to save it in a file. To do this, give the Save As command from the File menu. Word displays the dialog box shown in Figure 2-2. Type **Sample 1** and press RETURN (or type **Sample 1** and click the Save button).

Figure 2-2. *Save As dialog box*

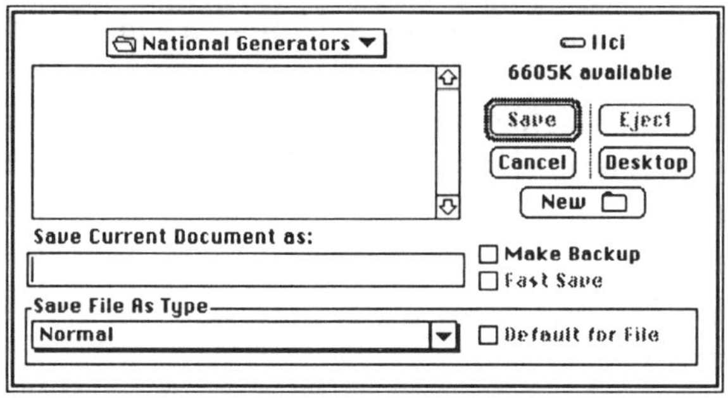

Word displays a dialog box for Summary Info. This contains any notes that you might want to make about the file for future reference. This optional information is not part of the letter itself, for example, but it could be useful to you when, in a few years, you come across the file and wonder what is in it. Summary information is described in Chapter 21. For this example, click the Cancel button to save without a summary.

Word saves the file on disk. You can continue to edit the file if you wish, or you can leave Word with the Quit command. If you are unfamiliar with dialog boxes, there is a lesson later in this chapter on that very subject.

You have other choices in the Save As command that you will not use yet, but that you should know about. The list in the Save File As Type section lets you select a type of file to save; for example, if you are creating a file to be read by another Macintosh program. This is described in much more detail in Chapter 22.

The Make Backup button tells Word to keep a copy of your file without any changes since the last time you saved it. Since this is a new file, this is not useful here. The Fast Save button can only be used some of the time and causes Word to save your file in a faster method, but in a way that takes up more disk space than a normal save.

The other buttons near the top right of the dialog box are for changing disks or folders. These are the same buttons you see in every program on your Macintosh. The Eject button is only available if you are saving to a disk that can be ejected, such as a floppy disk. The Desktop button (called the Drive button in versions before System 7) allows you to choose a different drive to save the file on.

It is a good idea to save your file in a different folder than the one in which Word is saved. Although you may be tempted just to save all your Word files in the Word folder, this leads to difficulty later. It is best to create folders for your various projects and keep files for those projects in those folders.

Lesson 3: Opening a File

If you want to edit this file again later (which you will, since it is used for examples throughout this book), you will open it with the Open command from the File menu. A list of files will appear. Either click the file you want (to select it) and click the Open button, or double-click the file you want.

If you make editing changes in a file and you do not want to save those changes (for example, if you are experimenting with some Word commands and do not want to change the file on disk), use the Close command from the File menu; when the command prompt asks if you want to save your changes, click the No button.

Word can open many types of files, not just ones that you created in Word. For instance, you can open graphics files, as described in Chapter 7. Chapter 22 gives more detail about the additional types of files you can open.

Lesson 4: Scrolling Around in Your Document

Word gives you many ways to move around in a file when you are editing. Since your file can be much longer than a single screenful of text, you need a way to find text that you want to change or add to. As you saw before, you always have either an insertion point or selection in your text. However, that insertion point or selection may not be visible if you are looking at a different part of your text.

To start this lesson, move to the beginning of the Sample 1 file. If you have closed the file, open it with the Open command. If you have quit from

Word, start Word and open the file automatically by double-clicking the file's icon in the Finder. If the insertion point is not already there, move to the beginning of the text by dragging the *scroll box* (on the right side of the screen) up to the top of the scroll bar. Click the I-beam before the first letter of the file to place the insertion point there.

Since you do not have any need for the ribbon or ruler until later in this book, you should hide them. Give the Ruler command and the Ribbon command from the View menu. Your screen should now look like Figure 2-3.

Scrolling with the Mouse

To see different parts of your text, use the scroll bar on the right border of the window. For example, to scroll the screen down one line, click the arrow that is pointing down at the bottom of the screen. If you point at this arrow and continue to hold down the button, the screen continues to scroll. The scroll bar on the bottom border of the window moves it left and right, which you rarely want to do.

Figure 2-3. *Top of Sample 1 document*

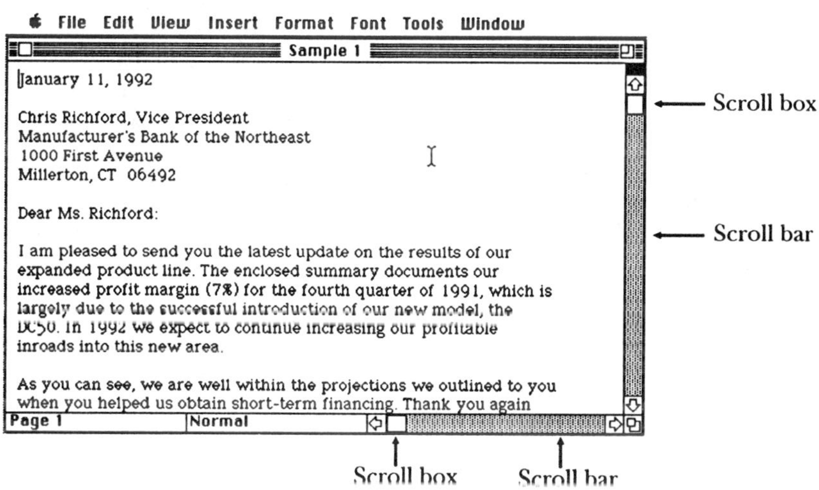

To jump to a particular place in your text, you can drag the scroll box up and down the scroll bar and then release the mouse. This is sometimes called *thumbing*, since it is like thumbing through a book. To get to the end of a file, drag the box to the bottom of the bar; drag it to the top to get to the beginning of the file.

If you click above or below the scroll box in the scroll bar, Word jumps up or down by a full screen. In this case, that is not very useful, since the Sample 1 letter is quite short. In longer documents, it is very handy to click in the scroll bar if you are looking for particular information or skimming the information in a file.

When you scroll or jump using the scroll box or the scroll bars, Word does not change the position of the insertion point or selection. You can see this by scrolling back to the top of the Sample 1 file. Notice that the insertion point is still blinking before the first letter. If you had made a selection and scrolled with the mouse, your selection would still be highlighted and in the same place.

Scrolling with the Keyboard

To scroll up or down a line at a time with the keyboard, press (↓) or (↑). To move up or down by a full page, press the (PAGE DOWN) or (PAGE UP) keys (if you have them) on your keyboard. You can also press the (3) or (9) key on the keypad to the right of the main keyboard. Scrolling with these keys differs from scrolling with the mouse because Word moves the insertion point when you scroll with the keyboard. When you give these keyboard scrolling commands, Word puts the insertion point at the top of the window that you see when you scroll.

You can also scroll line by line using the keyboard without moving the insertion point or selection by pressing the (+) and (*) keys on the keypad.

Lesson 5: Changing Text

You saw in Chapter 1 how to select text and how to insert text at the insertion point. As you were typing the text for the Sample 1 file earlier in this chapter, if you made a mistake, you had to correct it by pressing the DELETE key, character by character. However, there are faster ways of deleting text than backspacing over one character at a time. You can select all the text you want to delete (with either the mouse or keyboard) and press DELETE.

Deleting text is a common practice, but replacing text with new text is even more common. For example, as you review what you have written, you often think of better words to use. To replace some text in a document with new words, simply select the text and begin typing. Word deletes the first text and starts inserting at that point.

To see this, assume that you want to replace the word "pleased" with the word "happy" in the first full sentence. Select "pleased" and type **happy**. Notice that when you type the "h", Word removes the selected text, replaces it with "h", and puts the insertion point at that spot. It is as if you had pressed DELETE and started typing.

You can also delete text with some keyboard commands. To delete the character after the insertion point (instead of the one before it), press ⌘-OPTION-F. You can also delete whole words at a time. ⌘-OPTION-DELETE deletes the word before the insertion point, while ⌘-OPTION-G deletes the word after it.

Lesson 6: More Ways to Select Text

Most people prefer to use the mouse for moving the insertion point and selecting text. This is because using the mouse makes a very visual connection to the document; you do not have to remember which keys to use.

Selecting Text with the Mouse

You can choose from six different kinds of selections of fixed lengths: a character, a word, a sentence, a line, a paragraph, and the entire document. If you want to select a portion of text that is not included in the six choices (such as several words but not a sentence, several sentences but not a paragraph, or several paragraphs, but not an entire document), you can also make selections of varying lengths.

You already saw in the last chapter how to select a character, a word, and a sentence by dragging, double-clicking, and clicking with the ⌘ key, respectively. You also learned how to select varying amounts of text by clicking and dragging.

To review the steps, point at any letter in the word "update" in the first sentence. Click the button to set the insertion point, double-click to select the entire word, press the ⌘ key, and hold down the mouse button to select the entire sentence. Select a variable amount of text by clicking at the beginning of the desired selection and dragging to the end.

To select larger areas of text, move the mouse pointer into the *selection bar*, the blank column between the left window border and the text. When you point to the selection bar, the I-beam changes to an arrow that points up and to the right, instead of to the left (as in the command area). For example, point to the selection bar on the third line of the body of the letter, which begins with "increased profit margin", as in Figure 2-4.

Clicking in the selection bar has a different effect than clicking in the text. Clicking once selects the entire line, double-clicking selects the entire paragraph, and pressing both the ⌘ key and the button together selects the entire document. Experiment with each of these choices.

Figure 2-4. *Pointing in selection bar*

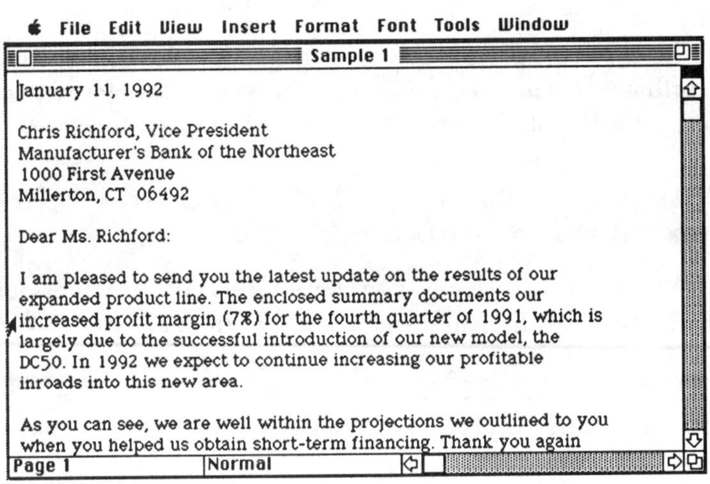

When selecting by dragging, if the text that you want to select is not completely on the screen, you can extend the selection by scrolling the screen. To do this, start your selection, hold down the mouse button, and briefly bring the pointer into the upper or lower screen border. Word then scrolls the screen, and you can continue to extend your selection. Sometimes Word scrolls more than you expect, so using this method takes a bit of practice. If you are still holding down the mouse button, you can back up to the proper spot and then release the button.

Selecting Text with the Keyboard

Word has many keyboard commands that allow you to move the insertion point and select parts of your document. The keyboard commands for selecting text are the same as the keyboard commands for moving the insertion point, except that the SHIFT key is held down. For example, the ↓ key moves the insertion point down a line, while SHIFT-↓ extends the selection down one line.

Table 2-1 shows the keys for moving the insertion point. In this table, "Keypad" indicates a key on the keypad to the right of the main keyboard.

You may have noticed that many of these key combinations use the keypad. Of course, you may want to use the keypad for its most obvious use, namely to type numbers. To do so, you must put Word in *numeric lock* mode by pressing the CLEAR key at the top of the keypad. When you are in numeric lock mode, you see that the indicator in the page box in the lower-left corner of the main window has changed from "Page 1" (or whatever page you are on) to "Num. Lock".

Note that pressing ⌘-A or ⌘-OPTION-M selects the entire document. These are the only keyboard commands that select without you having to press SHIFT.

Lesson 7: The Undo Command

Now that you know how to select any text you want, you can experiment with selecting different amounts of text and deleting or replacing them. You

Table 2-1. *Insertion Point Movement with the Keyboard*

To Move Insertion Point	Key
Right one character	(→) or (6)(keypad)
Left one character	(←) or (4)(keypad)
Up one line	(↑) or (8)(keypad)
Down one line	(↓) or (2)(keypad)
To end of line	(1)(keypad)
To beginning of line	(7)(keypad)
Up one page	(9)(keypad)
Down one page	(3)(keypad)
Left one word	(⌘)-(←) or (⌘)-(4)(keypad)
Right one word	(⌘)-(→) or (⌘)-(6)(keypad)
Next sentence	(⌘)-(1)(keypad)
Beginning of sentence	(⌘)-(7)(keypad)
Up one paragraph	(⌘)-(↑) or (⌘)-(8)(keypad)
Down one paragraph	(⌘)-(↓) or (⌘)-(2)(keypad)
To top of window	(HOME) or (⌘)-(5)(keypad)
To bottom of window	(END)
To beginning of document	(⌘)-(HOME) or (⌘)-(9)(keypad)
To end of document	(⌘)-(3)(keypad) or (⌘)-(3) or (⌘)-(END)

might hesitate to experiment with important information, fearing that when you delete information, it is gone forever. With Word, however, you can give the Undo command from the Edit menu to undo the last change and restore the text that you deleted, replaced, or changed.

The Undo command restores your text to the way it was before your last edit. For example, if you select a paragraph of text and then delete it by pressing (DELETE), you can use the Undo command from the Edit menu to bring the paragraph back, even if you have moved to a new selection. The Undo command only works to restore the last editing command that you have given, such as Cut, or Copy, or pressing (DELETE) a few times. It cannot restore earlier edits.

The Undo command can also undo your last Undo command. This may seem strange, but it is useful if you are not sure that you want to restore an edit you have made. For example, if you delete a sentence but are not sure that you deleted the correct sentence, you can undo the deletion; and if it turns out that you did delete the correct sentence, give the Undo command again to cause Word to delete it again.

To experiment with the Undo command, delete the date from the letter.

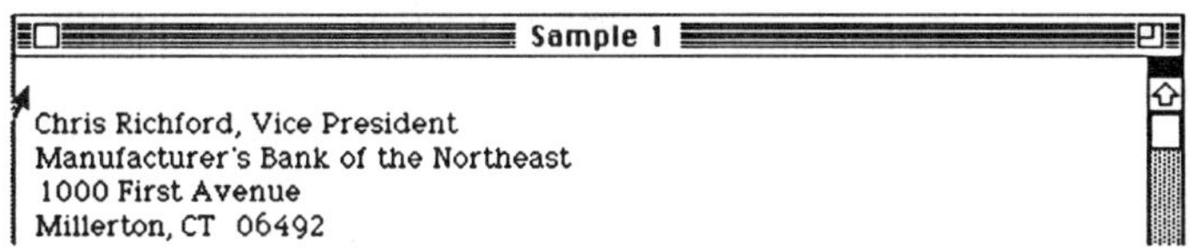

Now give the Undo command, and the date is restored.

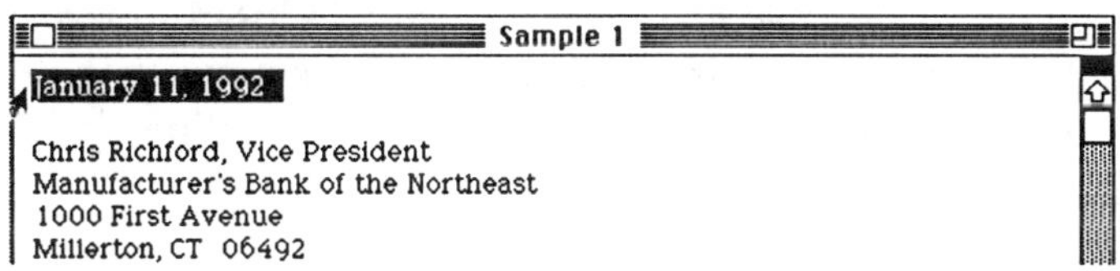

As you will see in later chapters, you can use the Undo command to reverse a number of different editing commands. You may well find it to be a safety net at a critical moment. Remember, however, that Undo can only restore your last edit; anything done before that cannot be undone.

Lesson 8: Making Choices in Dialog Boxes

The Word commands introduced so far have been quite simple. When you give some commands, however, you are offered a *dialog box* of items to choose from. Dialog boxes are common to all Macintosh programs. This lesson is a quick refresher on how to use the mouse and the keyboard to make dialog box choices.

The Character command from the Format menu is a good example of a command that has a dialog box with lots of choices. When you give the

Character command, Word presents you with the Character dialog box shown in Figure 2-5. Many of the dialog boxes that you see in the Finder have only one or two buttons, such as OK or Cancel. Here you see three sets of buttons, as well as four drop-down lists. One of the sets of buttons includes the familiar OK and Cancel.

The choices under Style allow you to set the type style for the selected characters. If you click one of the square boxes (such as Bold), an "X" appears in the box:

This indicates that the type style is selected. A list of square boxes, sometimes called *check boxes*, indicates that you can check more than one of the boxes at the same time. For example, both Bold and Outline options selected looks like this:

Round buttons (sometimes called *radio buttons*) under Position indicate that only one of the choices in the group of buttons can be selected at a time. For example, if you click the Superscript button, the Normal choice is deselected.

The choices under Font, Size, Underline, and Color are made with *drop-down lists*. You can select from the list by clicking the name or the arrow and scrolling up or down the list while holding down the mouse button.

Figure 2-5. *Character dialog box*

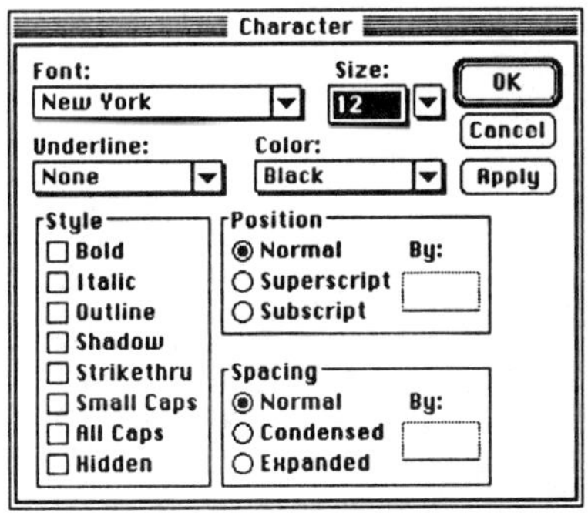

Some dialog boxes allow you to enter text or numbers; you have already seen this in the Save As command. In the Character dialog box shown in Figure 2-5, you can make a selection either by clicking the arrow next to the font size and selecting from the list or by selecting the indicated font size and typing in a new number.

Many Word dialog boxes can be moved around on the screen while they are open. This lets you look at your document before you make your choices. You can click the title bar of any dialog box with lines in its title bar (like the Character dialog box shown here) and drag it to a new location.

When you start Word, the program always turns on the ruler and ribbon. Since these won't be useful until later in this book, it is a good idea to tell Word that you do not want to see them automatically. You use the Preferences command from the Tools menu to tell Word how you want it to act. Give that command, and you see the Preferences dialog box, shown in Figure 2-6.

The Preferences command, described in detail in Chapter 16, lets you choose the settings for many different parts of Word. In this case, you want to make a View setting, so click the View icon, the second from the top on the left side of the dialog box. The dialog box changes to that shown in Figure 2-7.

Since you do not want to see the ruler or ribbon, click the With Ruler On and With Ribbon On choices in the Open Documents section. The Xs in the

Figure 2-6. *Preferences dialog box*

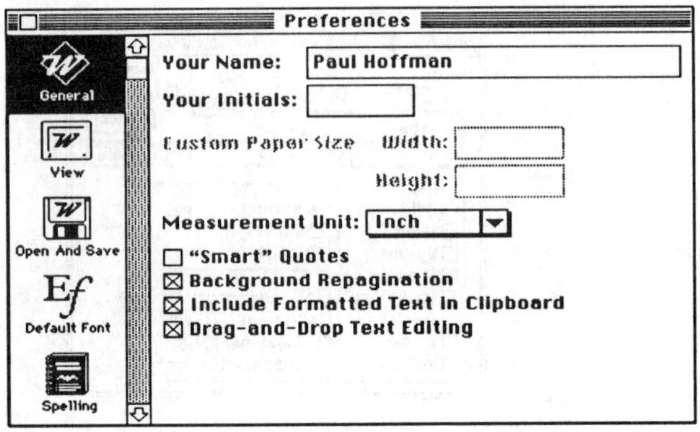

boxes disappear. Now click the close box in the upper-left corner of the dialog box. From now on, when you open documents, neither the ruler nor the ribbon will appear unless you select them.

Figure 2-7. *View preferences*

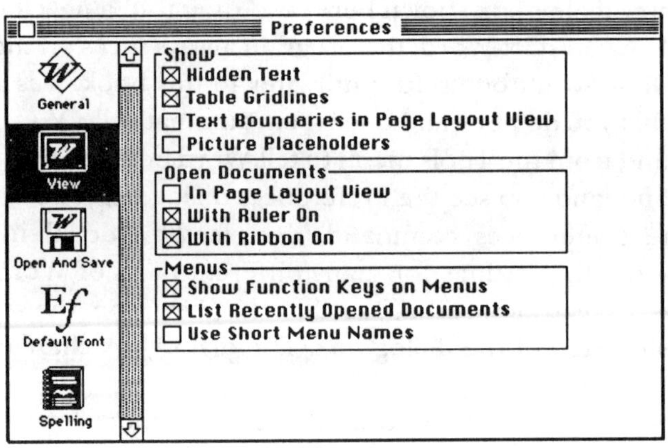

2

Making Dialog Choices with the Keyboard

Word is one of the few Macintosh programs that lets you make dialog box choices with the keyboard. Only die-hard keyboard enthusiasts will want to do so because the method is somewhat convoluted. Table 2-2 shows the keystrokes you can use to work in dialog boxes.

Lesson 9: Inserting Special Characters in Your Text

In Chapter 1, you saw how to type text into your document. You saw that to make paragraphs, you had to use the RETURN key and that Word inserted a special paragraph mark into your document. There are other special characters in Word for other purposes, which are described in this lesson.

Line Breaks Within Paragraphs

If you want to force Word to start a new line within a paragraph, but not start a new paragraph, hold down the SHIFT key while you press the RETURN key. This key combination is called a *newline*, and it lets you make lines of different lengths within a paragraph that are not like the lines of a paragraph

Table 2-2. *Keystrokes for Setting Dialog Boxes*

Action	Keystroke
Set currently selected choice	0 (keypad) or ⌘-SPACEBAR
Select item in list	↑ or ↓
Close list without selecting	ESC
Move to an option	⌘ plus the first letter of the option
Move to next option group	→
Move to previous option group	←
Next option	. (keypad) or ⌘-TAB
Previous option	SHIFT-. (keypad) or SHIFT-⌘-TAB
Next text box	TAB
Previous text box	SHIFT TAB

made with wordwrap—you can start a new line without starting a new paragraph. You would use newline instead of starting a new paragraph because many Word formatting commands pertain to the whole paragraph. If you signal a paragraph with (RETURN), you have to format it separately from the preceding lines; if you use newline, you only need to format the whole paragraph once.

A good example of using newline is in typing the recipient's address in a letter. In Chapter 11 you will see how to change (RETURN) characters into newlines.

Look again at the Sample 1 letter. You used (RETURN) characters at the end of each line. Instead, it is better to use a newline (the (SHIFT)-(RETURN) combination) in the two addresses since each address is really a single unit. You can change the (RETURN) characters to newline characters by selecting each one and pressing (SHIFT)-(RETURN). You can see the difference after you have made the changes by giving the commands to select whole paragraphs and noticing that the whole address is selected.

Nonbreaking Spaces

A *nonbreaking space* acts like a piece of glue between two words and prevents wordwrap from placing them on different lines. For example, it is common typing practice not to leave a short abbreviation at the end of a line. Instead of having text look like this,

> Please be sure that all of the samples are sent to Ms.
> Price as soon as possible.

you would want to move the abbreviation to the second line:

> Please be sure that all of the samples are sent to
> Ms. Price as soon as possible.

This is easy when you are typing on a typewriter. However, remember that Word wraps words for you automatically, sometimes splitting an abbreviation from what follows.

If you want to be sure that a space between words is never broken, use a nonbreaking space, which is typed as (⌘)-(SPACEBAR). The space looks identical to a normal space on your screen, but Word never uses that word break as a line break.

Inserting Other Characters

The Macintosh has many special characters that are directly accessible through the keyboard using the (OPTION) key. For example, many European languages use umlauts on some vowels, as in "ö". To type this character on the Macintosh, hold down the (OPTION) key, press (U), release the (OPTION) key, and press (O). It is often difficult to remember all of the key combinations, since each font can have up to 255 characters.

To make inserting these characters easier in Word, Microsoft included the Symbol command from the Insert menu. This command shows you a table of all the characters in the current font, such as in Figure 2-8. The table is in the order that the characters appear internally in the font.

To insert a particular character in your text, put the insertion point where you want the character, give the Symbol command, and click on the desired character. You can bring up the Symbol dialog box by pressing (⌘)-(OPTION)-(Q).

Figure 2-8. *Symbol dialog box*

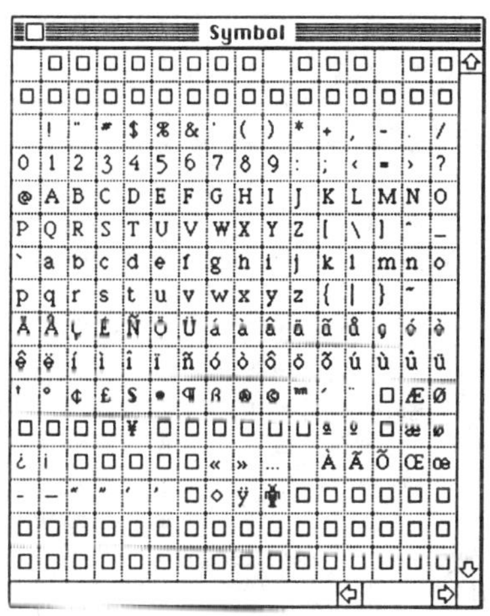

You can insert as many characters as you want this way, since the Symbol window stays open until you close it by clicking its close box in the upper-left corner or by pressing (⌘)-(W). You can also change the font when the Symbol window is open by using the Font menu.

The Symbol command is particularly useful with the fonts that are not alphanumeric. For instance, Figure 2-9 shows the Symbol dialog box for the Zapf Dingbats font, a font that comes with the Apple LaserWriter and other PostScript-compatible printers. As you can see, this font is made up of symbols that you might want to use to decorate your documents. Choosing the symbols with the Symbol command is much easier than looking them up in a table and pressing the corresponding keys.

Although the international characters can also be entered directly using the (⌘) and (SHIFT) keys, the Symbol command is much more efficient and requires less memorization. You can use the Key Caps desk accessory to determine the keystrokes necessary for the international characters.

Figure 2-9. *Symbol dialog box for the Zapf Dingbats font*

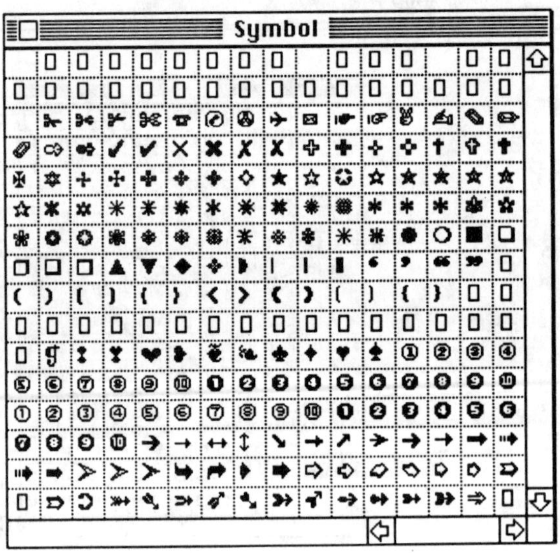

Lesson 10: Printing Your Document

Normally, the primary purpose of word processing is to obtain a finished printed document. At this point you have learned the basics of using Word to input and edit a document. Now that you have edited your text, it is likely that you want to see it on a printed page.

To print the file that you are editing, use the Print command from the File menu. When you give this command, you see a dialog box that is different for each type of printer. This dialog box is explained in detail in Chapter 8. For most Macintosh printers, to print a single copy of your document, you simply click the OK button to begin printing. You will also see in Chapter 8 how to use the Page Setup command, which helps you set up printing parameters.

Before printing, be sure that your printer is turned on and that it is properly connected to your Macintosh. If you want to stop the printer, press the ⌘-. key combination. It may take a while for the printer to stop printing because many printers store quite a bit of text before they print it out.

Review

Start a new document and type a few paragraphs from a magazine article you have read recently. Make sure you type in more than one screenful of text, and don't worry about spelling. Save this text on disk as "Magazine." You will use this file in the review sections for many other chapters.

Practice moving the insertion point with the keyboard and practice scrolling with the mouse.

Change the first word in the second sentence of your document to something else. Think about the many ways you can do this, and try them all. Each time you make a change, undo the change with the Undo command from the Edit menu.

3

Using Word's Windows

Using Word's windows effectively will probably save you more time than any of its editing features. Until now you have used only one window in Word. You can split the large window into two smaller ones with little effort. You can also have many separate windows in different files open at once. This may seem like a feature that only advanced users would want. However, it is possible to use windows in your everyday editing to meet a number of different needs.

For example, if you are editing the top of a letter and want to look at some information near the bottom, you do not need to take your attention away from either part if you split your window into two. If you are writing a memo and need to look at a report you wrote earlier, you can use one window for the memo and another window for the report.

Splitting windows and using multiple windows is especially useful if you have a large screen. Many Macintosh owners have *full-page displays*, which are screens that allow you to see the equivalent of a full sheet of paper at a time. With such a screen, or the even larger *two-page displays*, you can use multiple windows with ease.

Lesson 11: Splitting a Window in One File

To see how two windows can significantly help editing, start Word with the Sample 1 file in one window. You can now split the window horizontally to get two views of the file. When you are looking at two parts of one file, it is common to make a split about halfway down the screen.

The one feature of the Word window you may notice is different from those in most other Macintosh programs is the black bar near the top of the scroll bar, above the up scroll arrow on the right side of the window. This is called the *split bar* because you can use it to split a window.

Splitting a window is straightforward. Point at the split bar, and the mouse pointer becomes a *split icon*. Hold down the mouse button and drag the split bar down to where you want to divide the window; when you release the button, the window is split.

When you point to the split bar, the pointer changes shape, as shown here:

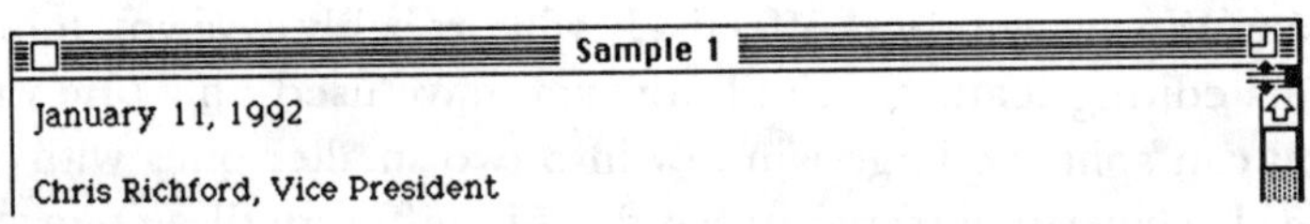

When you press the button, notice that Word draws a gray bar across the screen. It may be hard to see the bar at first. Look right below the title bar:

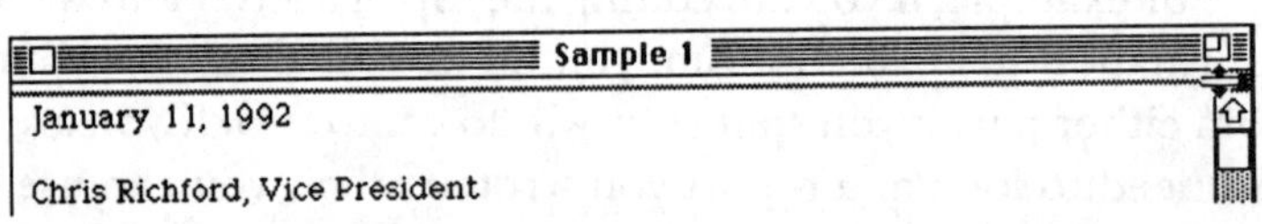

Now drag the split bar down until the gray bar is below the line that begins "I am pleased...", as in Figure 3-1. When you release the button, Word creates the two halves of the window, each with its own separate vertical scroll bar, as shown in Figure 3-2.

You also can split a window by pressing ⌘-OPTION-S. This splits the window exactly in half.

Figure 3-1. Gray bar positioned at desired point

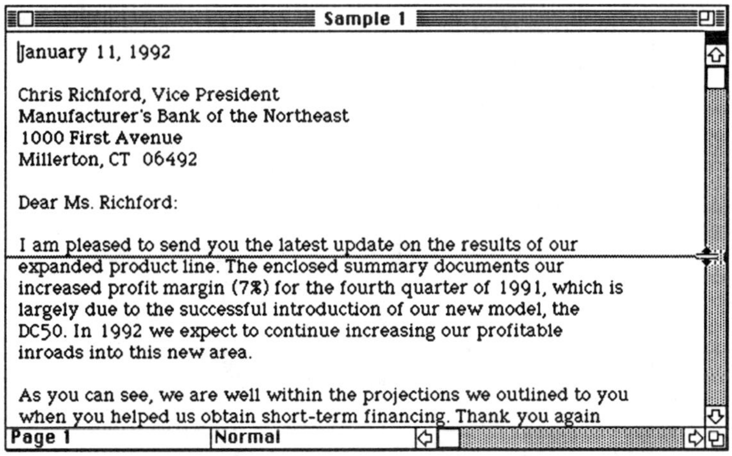

Figure 3-2. Window after splitting

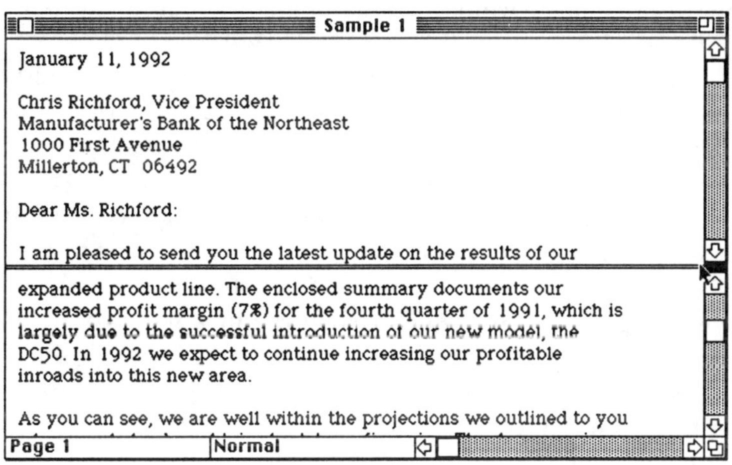

Figure 3-3. *Top and bottom part of file*

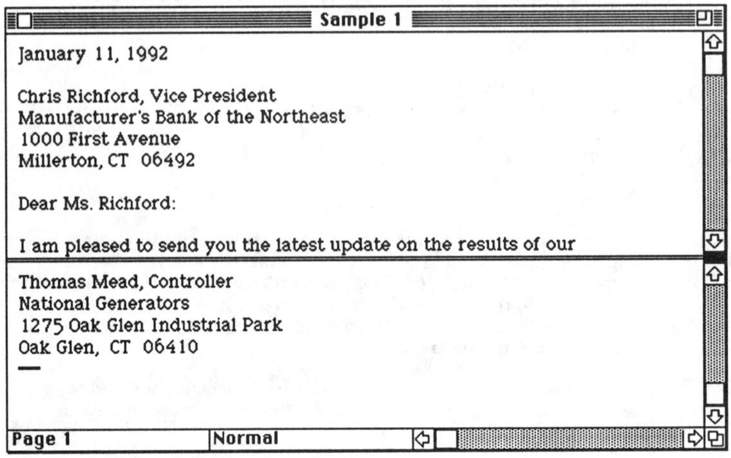

You can change the position of the split at any time by dragging the split bar to a new location. You cannot change the location with the keyboard. To go back to a single window, drag the split bar all the way to the top or bottom of the window or press ⌘-OPTION-S again.

Once you have split a window, you need only point to either part to move the insertion point from part to part. The text that you view in each part of a window can be scrolled independently. If you want, you can view the same text in both halves of the split window.

To see how you can view different parts of a document, split the window again (if you closed it) and move the insertion point to the bottom half by clicking in that part of the window. Click the down arrow in the scroll bar for the bottom half of the window. You can now scroll to the end of the file as shown in Figure 3-3.

Now move the insertion point to the beginning of the file in the lower half, so both windows show the same text. After the line "1000 First Avenue" in the top half, type **Suite 120** and notice that the second window is updated almost simultaneously.

Each half of a window can be used independently. You can use the Find command to find specific information in one part of the window without losing your place in the other. This is useful in finding related text in a long document. Other good uses for split windows are moving text, which you will see in Chapter 4, and comparing similar text.

Lesson 12: Moving and Sizing Windows

You can change the location of a window by dragging the title bar, and the size of a window by dragging its size box. As you will see in the next lesson, it is convenient to change the locations and sizes of windows when you have more than one window open on the screen.

To move a window, click its *title bar*—the striped area at the top of the window—and drag the window while still holding down the mouse button. This is exactly like moving windows in all Macintosh programs. Note that you can move a window so that part of the window disappears off the side or bottom of the screen.

To change the size of a window, click and drag the *size box* in the lower-right corner of the window. This allows you to make the window narrow or short. Again, this is like other Macintosh programs.

You also can change the size of Word windows by using the *zoom box* on the right side of the title bar. Clicking this box causes the window to grow to the full size of the screen or, if it is already enlarged, to shrink to its previous size. This is handy if you have many windows that you open only occasionally. After you close these less-used windows, instead of having to drag down the size box of your main window, you can simply click its zoom box or press ⌘-OPTION-].

The zoom box remembers the shape of the window that you last used. If you change the window, zoom to full screen, and then zoom back, your window is the same size and shape and in the same location as it was before you zoomed to full screen. For example, use the size box to shrink the Sample 1 window to the middle of the screen, as in Figure 3-4. Click the zoom box a few times and you'll see how zoom remembers the last window size.

Figure 3-4. *Sample 1 window shrunk*

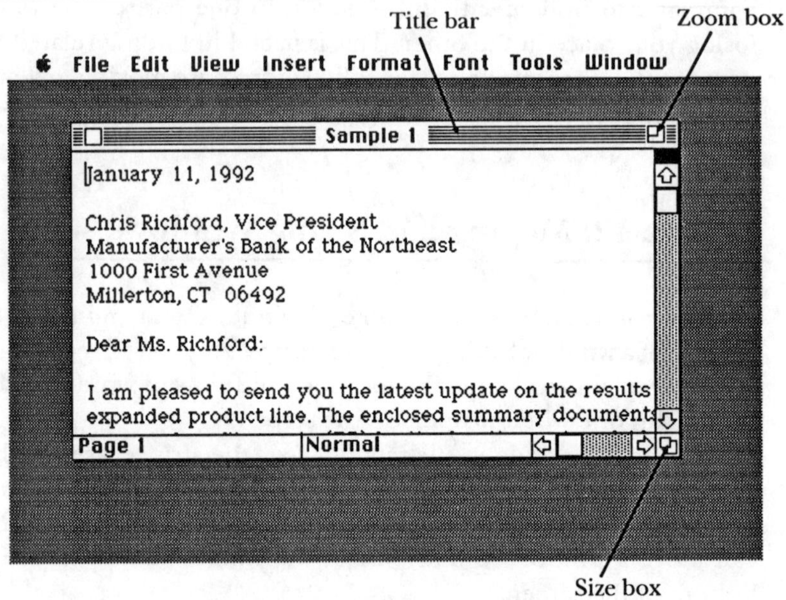

Lesson 13: Using Two Windows in Two Files

You may have already guessed the next step in using windows: using one window to look at one file and a second window to look at a different file. To look at two different files, use the Open command from the File menu to open a window for a new file. You can have many windows open at a time. On Macintoshes with larger screens, you can easily work with four or more windows open at the same time. Word allows you to have over 20 documents open at one time, but it is unlikely that you would want to.

To see how useful multiple windows are, close the Sample 1 window by clicking the close box to clear your experimental modifications out of Word's memory (click No to the prompt of whether you want to save the changes). Give the New command, and enter the short report shown in Figure 3-5. (Use the (TAB) key to line up the figures.) Save this on disk with the name Report 1.

Figure 3-5. *Text of Report 1*

From: Sandra Phillips
To: Thom Mead
Re: Summary of annual figures
Date: January 4, 1992

Here are some preliminary figures on the company; I'll have complete totals early next week.

Total income:	$17,500,000
Total costs:	$14,250,000
Inventory on hand:	$1,250,000

Let me know if you need more detail before then.

Use the Open command to open a window with the Sample 1 file. Word opens a document to the same location and size as you saved it, so the Sample 1 file hides the Report 1 file.

Shrink both windows to about half the size of the screen using their size boxes, and drag the Sample 1 window to the top of the screen and the Report 1 window to the bottom. Your screen should look like Figure 3-6. Note that features are present only in the title bar and scroll bars of the window that is currently active.

You can now look at parts of each file independently. You can scroll each window so that you can see the relevant parts, comparing the text. In Chapter 4, you will see how you can quickly copy and move text from one window to another.

On a small screen, you may not want to have both windows fully showing, since this reduces the amount of text you can see in each window. Instead, you may want both windows large, forcing you to switch from window to window. You can make a window come to the front and be completely visible by clicking anywhere in that window. You can also bring the back window to the front by pressing ⌘-OPTION-W or by choosing the document name in the Window menu.

Figure 3-6. *Both windows visible*

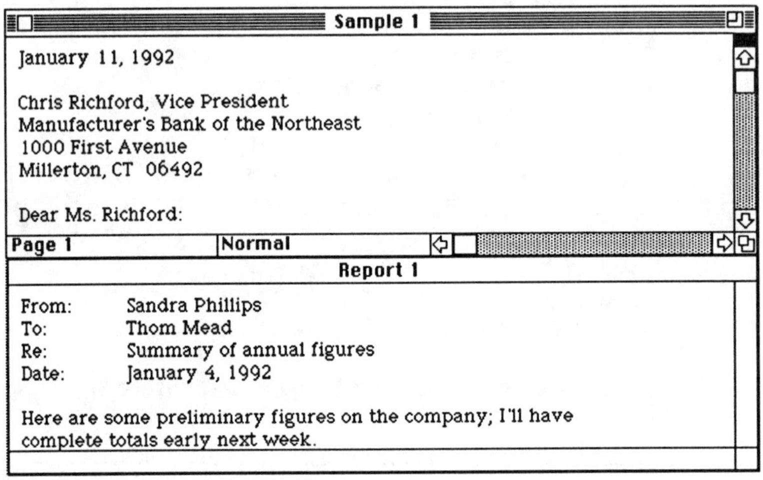

Figure 3-7. *Two windows overlapping*

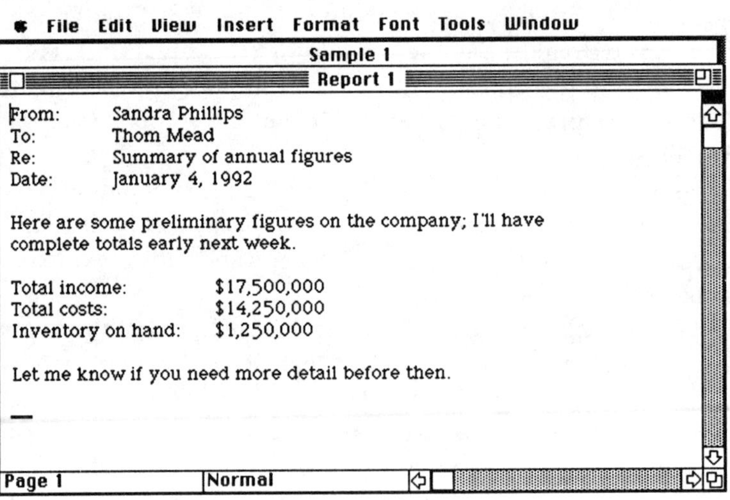

Use the size boxes of the Sample 1 and Report 1 windows to make them almost the full size of the screen, then move them so that they are slightly offset, as in Figure 3-7. Experiment with switching back and forth between windows.

Of course, if you have more than two windows active, you can have that number of files open at the same time. If you have edited the text in a window and want to keep the changes, remember to save it with the Save or Save As command before closing the window. If you don't, Word reminds you that the window has been edited and prompts for whether you want to save the edits.

Review

Open the Magazine practice file that you made in the Chapter 2 review. Split the window in two. Display the beginning and end of that file at the same time.

4

Moving and Copying Text

So far, the editing skills you have learned are how to enter text, how to move the insertion point and selection, and how to delete text from a document. This chapter explains how to use the Cut and Paste commands to move text from one part of a file to another, and how to copy text within a file with the Copy command. You will also learn how to move and copy text between files.

The ability to move sections of text is one of the most useful features of word processing. For example, after writing a report you may decide that you want to change the order of paragraphs or sentences. Since you can rearrange your ideas after seeing them on paper or on the screen, your finished writing will be much better organized. In the next lesson, you will see that moving text is easy to do with Word.

Lesson 14: Using the Clipboard

Word uses the Macintosh *Clipboard* to hold information. You can image the Clipboard as a holder for a single chunk of text or a single picture. Every time you use the Copy or Cut command from the Edit menu in any program, the contents of the Clipboard are replaced with the selected text or picture.

The Clipboard acts like a temporary holder of a single piece of information. It is most useful for moving text: you select the text, move it from its current location into the Clipboard, put the insertion point at the desired location, and copy it there from the Clipboard.

All Macintosh programs interact with the Clipboard using three commands from the Edit menu:

- The Copy command places a copy of the selected text into the Clipboard, replacing its previous contents.
- The Cut command does the same thing as the Copy command, except that it removes the selected text from the document. This is like giving the Copy command followed by pressing the (DELETE) key.
- The Paste command inserts the contents of the Clipboard at the insertion point or replaces the selected text with the contents of the Clipboard. Note that this does not "empty" the Clipboard; instead, the contents remain there until you replace them with another Copy or Cut command.

Word includes a command that is extremely useful. The Show Clipboard command, found in the Window menu opens a window that lets you look at the contents of the Clipboard, but not edit them. This is a handy way to check what you have in the Clipboard.

For example, select the word "latest" in the first paragraph of the Sample 1 letter and copy it to the Clipboard with the Copy command from the Edit menu. Give the Show Clipboard command from the Window menu, and Word displays the Clipboard window:

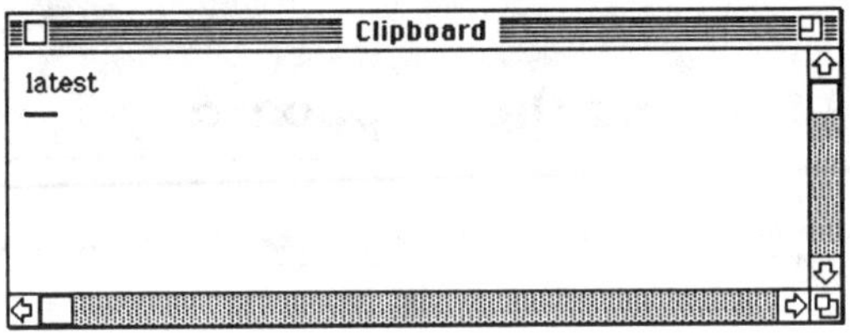

The Clipboard in Word acts just as it does in the Finder and other applications. Thus, if you now select another word from the file and cut it, the Clipboard no longer contains the word "latest"–it contains the word you just selected. If you then give the Undo command from the Edit menu, you will find that the second word is back in text, and if you then give the Show Clipboard command from the Window menu, you'll find "latest" back in the Clipboard.

When the text is no longer in the Clipboard (for example, three edits ago), you cannot use the Undo command to restore it. Notice that deleting characters with the DELETE key does not put the characters into the Clipboard; only the Cut command and the Copy command do. However, you can still use the Undo command to restore text erased with the DELETE key if that erasure is the last edit you made.

This chapter shows you the basic use of the Clipboard. You will also see the Clipboard used in Chapter 7 for importing pictures to your Word documents.

Lesson 15: Moving Text Within a Document

As stated in the previous lesson, the basic method for moving text within a document is as follows:

1. Select the text that is to be moved.
2. Give the Cut command.
3. Set the insertion point at the desired location for the text.
4. Give the Paste command.

For example, try switching the second and third sentences of the second paragraph. To do this, select the third sentence by pointing at a character in the sentence, holding down the ⌘ key, and clicking. Then delete the sentence with the Cut command. Your screen now looks like Figure 4-1.

Now set the insertion point at the beginning of the second sentence and give the Paste command. Press the SPACEBAR to separate the two sentences,

Figure 4-1. *Third sentence cut*

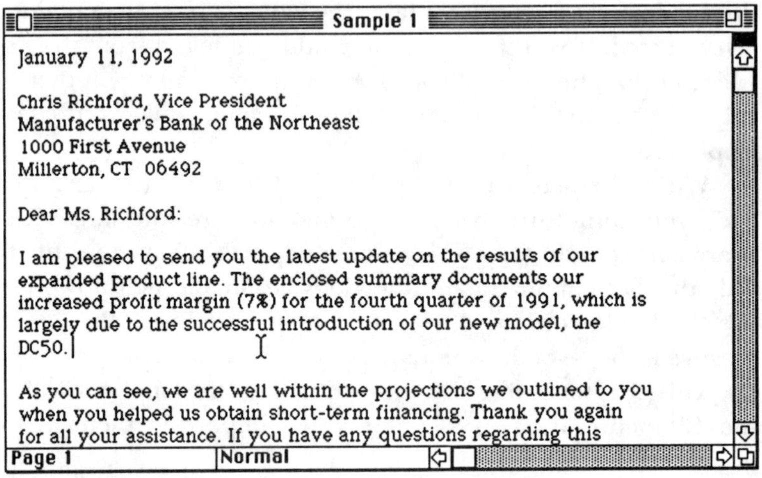

as shown in Figure 4-2. Notice that Word automatically reformats the paragraph for you.

This is the way that you most often use the Clipboard. Since it can hold any amount of information, you can use it to move large portions of your text. This is also a convenient method for moving phrases around in a sentence to see different effects on the sound and meaning. Practice moving text around in your file using the Clipboard and the Cut and Paste commands.

The Copy, Cut, and Paste commands become even more powerful when they are used with split windows, since you can use the Clipboard to move text from one part of the window to the other without losing your place in either part of the file. This lets you instantly see the results of moving text as you perform the commands.

For example, you might want to see the effect of adding "From:" and the sender's name to the top of the letter. You can do this easily while leaving the end of the letter in the bottom part of the window, by showing the beginning of the letter in the top part.

With the window split into two halves, position the text as shown in Figure 4-3. Type **From:** before the salutation on the line above Chris Richford's

Figure 4-2. *Sentence inserted from Clipboard*

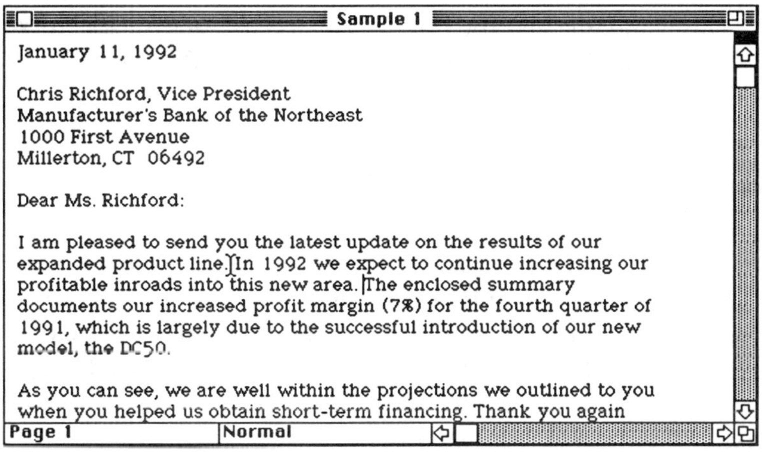

Figure 4-3. *Window split for moving*

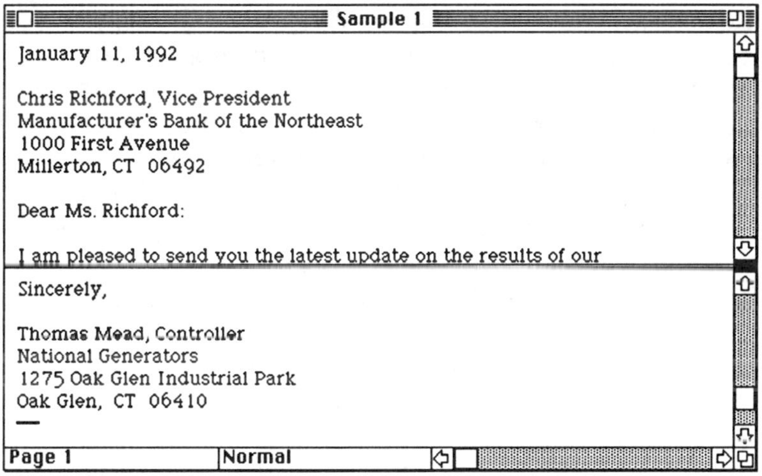

name, press the RETURN key, and move to the lower half. Select the line with Thomas Mead's name, and give the Copy command.

Now move to the top window, click the I-beam on the line beneath "From:" and then use the Paste command to place the line under the "From:". Add another line after the name by pressing RETURN.

Lesson 16: Copying Text

The Clipboard is also useful for making copies of parts of your text. Although copying text is not as common as moving text, you may find that a sentence or a line of text is used over and over in your document. If you copy the text, you do not have to retype it each time it is used. Copying text is also common when you have multiple documents since you may want to repeat part of one document in another.

To copy text, use the Copy command, which puts the contents of the selection in the Clipboard. The original text remains in your document, and a copy of it is placed in the Clipboard. This procedure is the same if you are copying text within a document (such as repeating a quotation in an academic paper) or copying information from one file to another. The contents even remain in the Clipboard when you leave Word and start another application.

In Chapter 3 you learned how to view two files at once (Sample 1 and Report 1). As you are viewing two files, you can also copy or move information between them. (Be sure both Sample 1 and Report 1 are open.)

As you are editing Sample 1, you may need some of the information in Report 1–for example, if you wanted to include the table of numbers. You could see those numbers by scrolling through Report 1, and you could even copy the whole table to Sample 1 with the Copy and Paste commands.

To do this, add text between the paragraphs of Sample 1:

> 1991, which is largely due to the successful introduction of our new model, the DC50.
>
> Our current figures are|
>
> As you can see, we are well within the projections we outlined to you

Now move to the Report 1 window and select the figures, as in Figure 4-4. Use the Copy command to copy these to the Clipboard, switch to the Sample 1 window, and use the Paste command to copy the text from the Clipboard after the new text, as in Figure 4-5.

When using two windows to copy or move information, some people prefer to leave the windows at full size (as in Figure 4-3) while others prefer to make the windows half size so that they can see both windows. As you use Word, experiment with both options.

Lesson 17: Moving Without the Clipboard

The previous lessons showed you how convenient it is to use the Clipboard to move and copy text. However, there are times when you want to move or copy text without using the Clipboard. For example, you may have

Figure 4-4. *Figures selected*

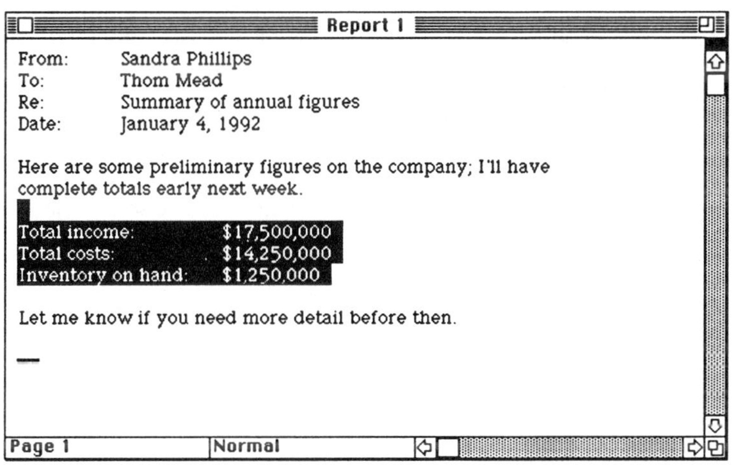

Figure 4-5. *Figures pasted into Sample 1*

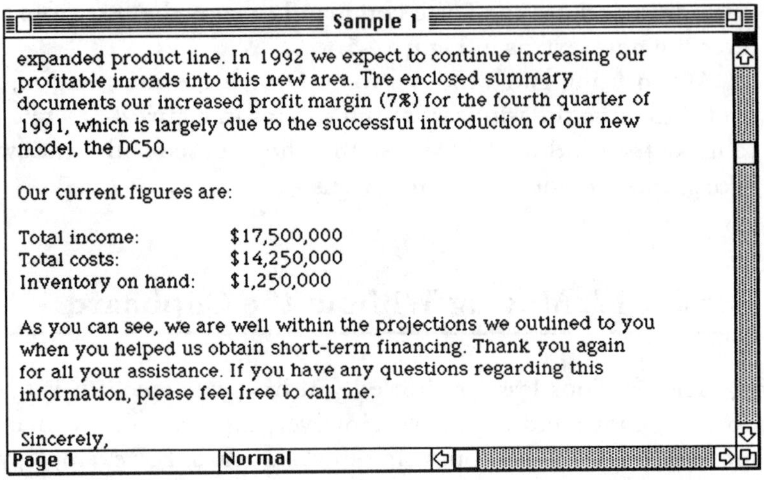
Sample 1

expanded product line. In 1992 we expect to continue increasing our profitable inroads into this new area. The enclosed summary documents our increased profit margin (7%) for the fourth quarter of 1991, which is largely due to the successful introduction of our new model, the DC50.

Our current figures are:

Total income:	$17,500,000
Total costs:	$14,250,000
Inventory on hand:	$1,250,000

As you can see, we are well within the projections we outlined to you when you helped us obtain short-term financing. Thank you again for all your assistance. If you have any questions regarding this information, please feel free to call me.

Sincerely,

Page 1 Normal

something on the Clipboard that you do not want to lose, but do not want to bother to copy to the Macintosh *Scrapbook.* (The Scrapbook is like a more permanent Clipboard that you can store as many graphics or text items in as your disk space permits for as long as you like.)

To move text without using the Clipboard, you use Word's new *drag-and-drop* feature. This allows you to select text and drag it to a new location without cutting and pasting.

To move text with drag-and-drop:

1. Select the text.
2. Point in the selected text and hold down the mouse button. The pointer changes shape to include a gray box at the bottom of the arrow:

3. While still holding down the mouse button, drag to the position where you want the text to move. Notice there is now a dotted insertion point that moves with the pointer.
4. When you release the mouse button, the text moves to the new location.

For example, assume you want to move the second sentence of the last paragraph of the letter to the end of that paragraph. First, select the sentence, including the space in front of it:

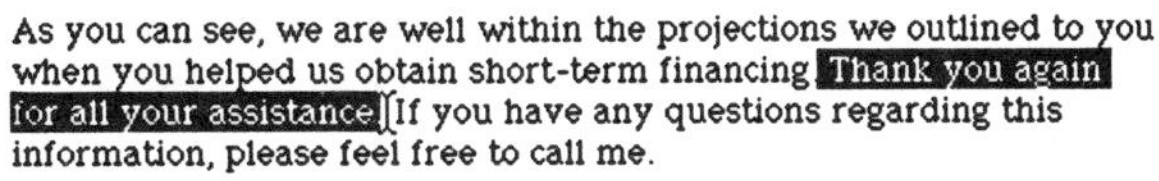
As you can see, we are well within the projections we outlined to you when you helped us obtain short-term financing. Thank you again for all your assistance. If you have any questions regarding this information, please feel free to call me.

Now click in the selected sentence so that the drag-and-drop pointer appears:

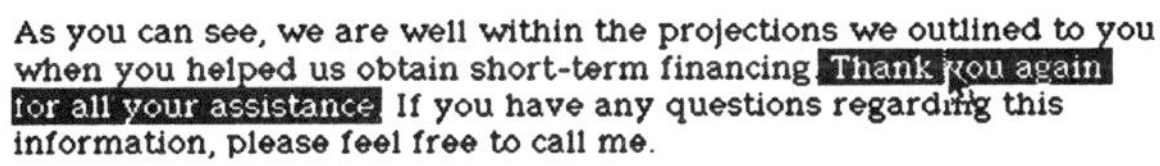
As you can see, we are well within the projections we outlined to you when you helped us obtain short-term financing. Thank you again for all your assistance. If you have any questions regarding this information, please feel free to call me.

Drag the insertion point to just after the period in the third sentence:

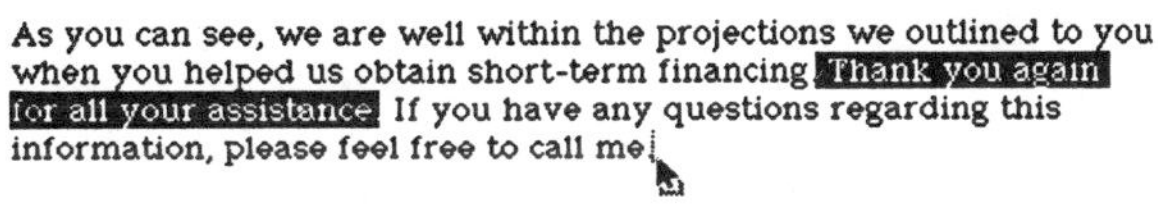
As you can see, we are well within the projections we outlined to you when you helped us obtain short-term financing. Thank you again for all your assistance. If you have any questions regarding this information, please feel free to call me.

Release the mouse button, and the sentence moves:

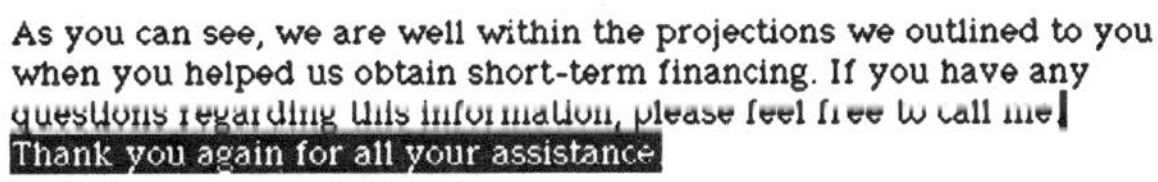
As you can see, we are well within the projections we outlined to you when you helped us obtain short-term financing. If you have any questions regarding this information, please feel free to call me. Thank you again for all your assistance.

If you do not like this feature, you can turn it off in the General options in the Preferences command from the Tools menu.

Review

Open the Magazine and Sample 1 files at the same time. Copy the second sentence of the Sample 1 file (starting with, "The enclosed...") to the beginning of the second paragraph in the Magazine file.

5

Searching and Replacing

As you have seen, you can move the selection around the screen easily and change the selection. If you know where you want to go, for example, about 20 lines down or to the end of the file, you can scroll through your text quickly. However, you often want to select a specific word or phrase in a long document. Instead of searching visually for the phrase, you can move to its exact position with the Find command. The Find command searches for the word or phrase you specify.

Searching with the Find command has many uses other than simply moving to a certain word or phrase. For instance, you can find the first occurrence of a particular word by moving to the beginning of a document and then searching for the word. You can review your text to see whether you defined new terms when they first appeared. Since you can also search for groups of words, you can easily check for phrases that you may have overused.

Replacing text with the Replace command is not as common as searching for text, but still very valuable. For example, you can use the Replace command to look for each occurrence of an overused phrase and replace it with another phrase on a case-by-case basis. You can also use Replace to quickly change every occurrence of something, such as a changed or misspelled name.

Lesson 18: Searching for Text

The Find command quickly moves to the next instance of a word or phrase and selects it. The movement is always relative to your current position in a file; for example, if the insertion point is in the middle of a file and you search for the word "invoice", Word finds the next occurrence of "invoice" that appears in the text. If it does not find the word when it reaches the end of the file, it asks you if you want to search from the beginning. Click Yes and it does.

Move to the beginning of the Sample 1 file and give the Find command from the Edit menu or press ⌘-F. Word brings up the Find dialog box:

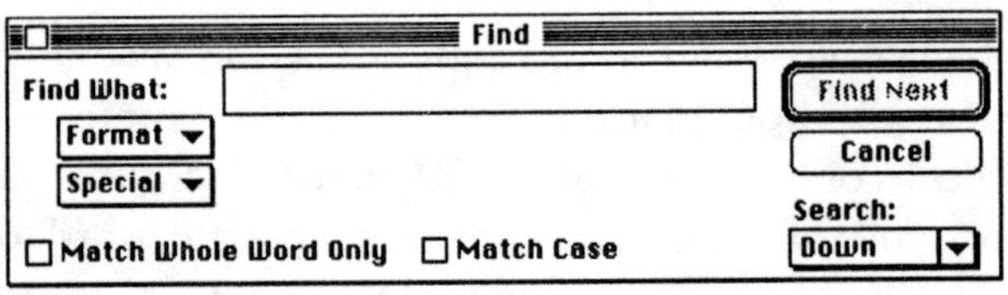

The blinking insertion point in the Find What: box indicates that you should fill in the word or phrase that you want to search for.

Type **please** and click the Find Next button (or press RETURN). The first instance of the word "please" in the letter, which in this case is in the word "pleased", becomes selected, as shown in Figure 5-1.

If you want to search for the same word or phrase again, you do not need to retype it; the dialog box stays open. Simply click the Find Next button or press RETURN, and Word searches again. Note the heavier outline around the Find Next button. This indicates that this button will be activated when you press RETURN.

When you are finished searching, click the close box or the Cancel button in the dialog box. If you close the Find dialog box and want to repeat the search, press ⌘-OPTION-A to repeat the Find command.

Figure 5-1. *"Please" selected*

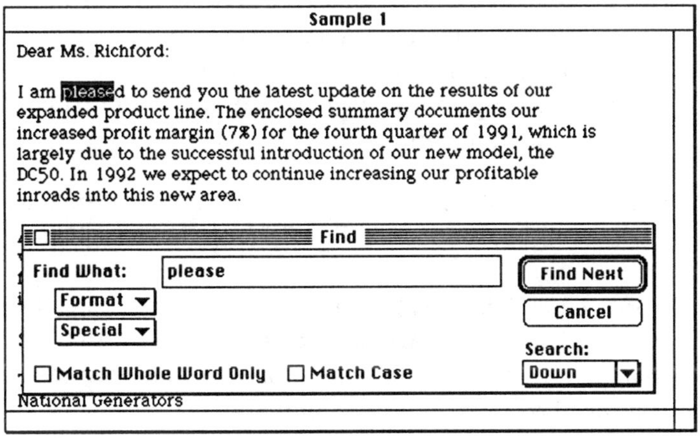

The following are other options for the Find command:

- Choosing Match Whole Word Only indicates that you want Word to restrict your search to whole words and ignore words in which your selection is merely a part. If you choose this option, for example, and the text you are searching for is "the", Word does not stop if it finds "they". If you don't check the box, Word stops, even if the text you are searching for is part of another word, as in Figure 5-1.
- For Match Case, you must decide if Word should pay attention to whether the letters in the text are upper or lowercase. If you do not choose this option, Word ignores case, meaning that Word does not differentiate between upper- and lowercase letters as it searches the text. Clicking the button is more restrictive: the text must be an exact match of the word or phrase you are searching for, including capital letters. Thus, if you click the box to match the case and you are searching for "the", Word does not stop when it finds "The".

- So far, you have only used the Find command to search forward in your document. The Search list lets you choose between Down (that is, forward), Up (backward), All (to automatically start at the beginning of the document regardless of the current position of the insertion point), and Selection (only within the selection). The Selection option is automatically chosen if text is selected when you give the Find command.

You can also search for specific text formatting, such as letters in italics. This is covered in Chapter 9. The Special choice is described later in this chapter.

Word remembers the text in the Find What choice and the setting for each of these choices whenever you use the Find command. For example, if you change the setting of the case choice to check for case, it is still selected the next time you give the Find command.

To see how to use the choices, move the insertion point to the beginning of the first full paragraph of the Sample 1 file and give the Find command. Type **As** (with a capital "A") and click the Match Case button:

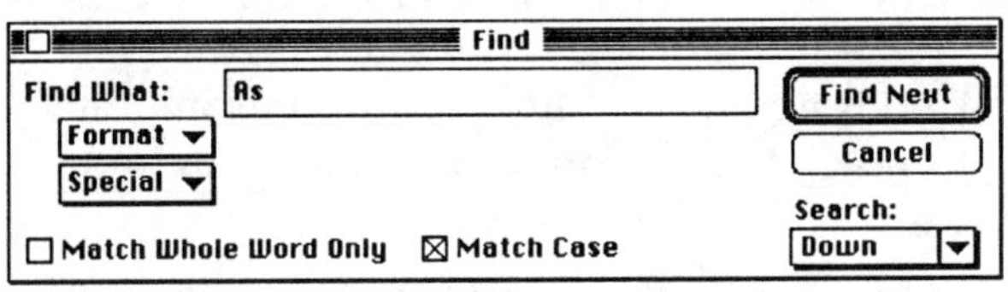

When you execute the command, the word "As" at the beginning of the second paragraph is selected; if you had not chosen to search for the matching case, the lowercase "as" in the word "pleased" in the first paragraph would have been found first. Click the Cancel button to close the dialog box.

To see the effect of the Match Whole Word Only option, move the insertion point to the beginning of the file and give the Find command again. Change Find What to **as**, click the Whole Word button, and click the Match Case button to deselect it. Now, even though the search is not restricted to an uppercase "A", it is restricted to "as" only when it is a separate word. Thus,

Word skips over the "as" in "Northeast" (and in "pleased," "increased," and "increasing"), going directly to the "As" in the second paragraph.

The text that you search for can have as many as 255 characters (you cannot see this much in the Find dialog box, but you can scroll left and right by selecting at the end of the text entry box). If Word finds the text, the entire word or phrase is selected. If the text does not appear in the file, Word displays an alert box with "End of document reached" and does not move the selection or insertion point. If you began the search at any location other than the beginning of the file, Word stops at the end and prompts "Continue search from beginning of document?" Click the No button to stop the search. You can also cancel a search by pressing the ⌘-. key combination.

Lesson 19: Replacing Text

It is common to replace every instance of a particular word or phrase in a document with some other word or phrase. For example, you may want to change "pleased" to "happy" throughout a letter, or you may need to change many, but not all, instances of a person's name to another name. You may also want to replace a wordy or misused phrase with a more concise one throughout a document.

When you give the Replace command from the Edit menu (or press ⌘-H) you automatically change all instances of one word or phrase to another. You can also have Word show you each instance of the phrase you want to change so you can choose whether or not to change it based on its context. You can undo changes with the Undo command.

The choices in the Replace dialog box are similar to those of the Find command. For example, go back to the top of the file, give the Replace command, and enter **pleased** for Find What: and **happy** for Replace With:, as shown in Figure 5-2. Note that the Replace command started with the Find What text from the previous Find command.

The dialog box has buttons labeled Find Next, Replace, Replace All, and Cancel. If you click the Replace All button, Word simply replaces each occurrence of the specified word or phrase throughout your document

Figure 5-2. Replace dialog box

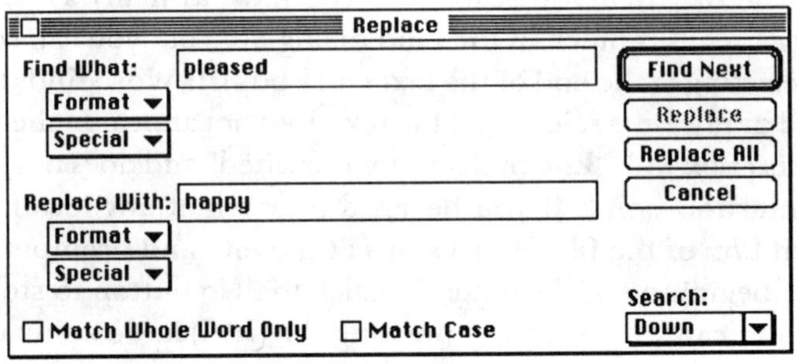

without asking for confirmation. If you click the Find Next button, Word stops at the first word to be replaced. Clicking the Replace button indicates that you want to make the replacement for the current selection, while clicking the Find Next button indicates that you do not. If you are finished replacing words, close the window or click Cancel.

As you might guess, the Replace command can ease the job of changing many items in a long file. For example, if one person is mentioned repeatedly throughout a long memo, and that person changes jobs within the company, you may have to change many instances of the person's name and title. The Replace command allows you to do this with just one command. Should the person's name need to be changed in many, but not all, instances, the confirmation choices let you look through the file easily.

If you do not choose to match the case when replacing text, Word intelligently chooses how to replace the letters. For instance, if you choose to change "airplane" to "boat" with no case requirement and Word finds "Airplane", it replaces it with "Boat", because this is most likely what you would want. The rule is that words with initial- or all-capital letters ("Airplane" or "AIRPLANE") are replaced with corresponding capital letters ("Boat" or "BOAT").

In the Replace command, the Match Whole Word Only option acts like it does in the Find command. When Word searches for the text in the Find What field, it only stops when it finds that text as whole words.

Lesson 20: Using Special Characters in Find and Replace

Word searches for the exact text you specify in the Find and Replace commands. However, there are times when you want Word to search for less specifically defined words. The Find and Replace commands allow you to include a question mark wildcard in order to broaden your search.

If Word sees a question mark in the text you tell it to search for, it assumes that any character can match it. (If you are familiar with "wildcard" characters in filenames on other computers, this is identical to the question mark used there.) For example, if you search for "f?r", Word stops when it finds "far", "for", "fur", and so on. The question mark indicates that any character at all (even numbers and punctuation marks) can be in the position you indicate.

Move to the beginning of the first paragraph and give the Find command. Enter **e?s** for the Find What text, then press the (RETURN) key. Word selects the "eas" in "pleased":

```
I am pleased to send you the latest update on the results of our
expanded product line. The enclosed summary documents our
increased profit margin (7%) for the fourth quarter of 1991, which is
```

Now click the Find Next button and Word selects the "eas" in "increased". Clicking the Find Next button again selects the "ess" in "the successful", and so on.

You may also want to search for characters that are special to Word but that you cannot normally enter in the Find or Replace commands. For instance, you may want to find the word "The" preceded by a (TAB) character. Since you can't normally enter a (TAB) character as text to search for (Word moves to the next choice for the Find command), you need a way to indicate that you want to search for the (TAB) character. You represent many codes with *caret characters*.

Caret characters are special characters that you precede with a caret mark (^). The caret characters are shown in Table 5-1. Note that you use two

Table 5-1. *Caret Characters*

Character	Meaning
^t	(TAB) character
^p	Paragraph marker
^n	Newline character
^d	Section marker or required page break (described in Chapter 12)
^w	White space; this is any number of spaces, tabs, paragraph marks, newline characters, division markers, and page-break characters
^#	Any digit
^*	Any letter
^-	Optional hyphen
^30	Nonbreaking hyphen
^s	Nonbreaking space
^\	The formula character
^1	Picture
^5	Footnote
^^	Caret character (^)
^?	Question mark character (?)
^*number*	Any character, where *number* is its ASCII value

characters, the caret and the character indicated. A caret character is not a control character.

For example, the dialog box to search for the word "me." followed by a paragraph marker and the word "Now" is shown here:

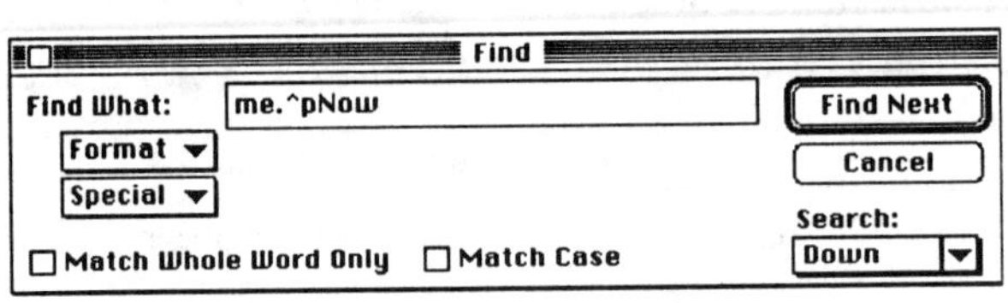

Figure 5-3. *Replacing with the contents of the Clipboard*

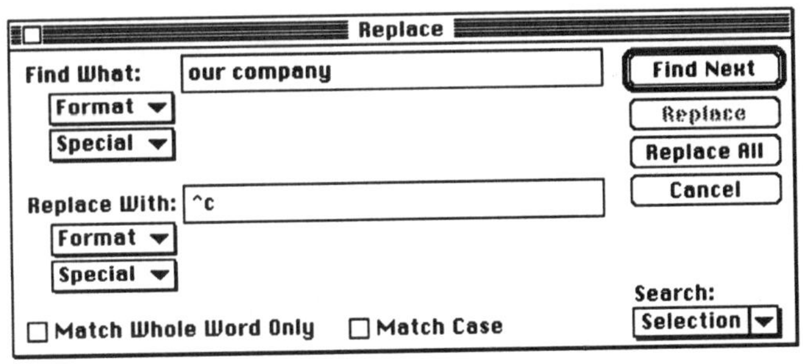

You do not need to remember all these caret characters. In the Find and Replace windows, the Special list shows the names of these characters and inserts them for you. Thus, if you want to search for a TAB character, you would pull down the Special list and select Tab Mark.

In the Replace command, you can enter any of the special characters from the table for the Find What option. In addition, you can also use the same characters in the Replace With field, except the question mark, ^?, and ^w caret characters.

You can also indicate that you want the contents of the Clipboard inserted in place of the text found. To do this, use ^c in the Replace With field. For example, assume that you have copied the name of your company with formatting to the Clipboard. Figure 5-3 shows how you would replace the words "our company" with the contents of the Clipboard using the Replace command.

Review

Use the Magazine file to experiment with the Find and Replace commands and their options. Search for the paragraph marks using the Special drop-down list.

6

Using Glossaries

As you work more with a word processor, you will probably find that particular phrases or blocks of text are used over and over, such as the name of a company or a long product name. Typing this text many times in a report or memo is tedious, and copying it from another file each time can take almost as long as typing it.

Word eliminates this problem by using *glossaries*. A glossary is a set of names that correspond to longer phrases. Instead of repeatedly typing in the longer phrase, you simply type ⌘-DELETE followed by the name. Any phrase or block of text can be abbreviated. The abbreviation can consist of as many as 31 letters or numbers, if necessary, but keeping the names short makes this feature more useful. One glossary is automatically available when you run Word.

For example, in the Sample 1 file, Thomas Mead's name and address could be saved as a name in the glossary for those occasions when he types his address at the bottom of a letter. Chris Richford's name and address and the name "National Generators" could also be saved. Table 6-1 shows the suggested entries for this glossary.

Table 6-1. *Glossary Entries for the Sample 1 File*

Name	Expanded Text
ng	National Generators
thomaddr	Thomas Mead, Controller National Generators 1275 Oak Glen Industrial Park Oak Glen, CT 06410
richford	Chris Richford, Vice President Manufacturer's Bank of the Northeast 1000 First Avenue Millerton, CT 06492

Glossaries can be great time savers since they eliminate the necessity of having to type sections of text that you use often. They also prevent typing mistakes in commonly used terms and names (it could be very embarrassing to misspell a client's company name in a letter). You can also store graphics in the glossary using the same methods you use to store text. You can even add glossary entries to the Work menu, as described in Chapter 16.

The rest of this chapter explains how to set up glossaries and how to use the entries in them. As you read the lessons, remember that glossaries are kept separate from documents, so the glossary entries you save as you create one document can be used anywhere else in your work. Glossaries are usually stored in the same folder as Word.

Lesson 21: Creating a Glossary

You can create a *glossary entry*—a name and its associated text—by giving the Glossary command from the Edit menu. While editing a file, select the phrase or block of text for which you want to use a name. Then give the Glossary command, enter the name, and click the Define button. This creates the entry.

Now use the Sample 1 letter to see how to save entries. To store Chris Richford's name and address under the name "richford", select the text in the letter and give the Glossary command from the Edit menu. The Glossary dialog box appears, as shown in Figure 6-1. Note that New is selected in the list box. In the Name box, type **richford**. Click the Define button. The first few words of the text that you have selected appear in the lower-left corner of the dialog box.

Also notice that the name is now in the list of names. To see what a name stands for, select it from the list. You will notice many items already in the list that you did not create. These are described later in this chapter. Click the Close button to close the dialog box.

When you want to expand a name, set the insertion point at the place where you want the text. You then have three choices:

- Press ⌘-DELETE, type the name as it appears in the page box in the lower-left corner of the window, and press RETURN.
- Give the Glossary command, select the desired name from the list, and click Insert.
- Choose the name from the Work menu (note that this is only available if you add it to the menu as shown in Chapter 16).

To practice expanding names, save the three entries in Table 6-1 to the glossary (you have already saved "richford"). Close the Glossary dialog box

Figure 6-1. *Glossary dialog box*

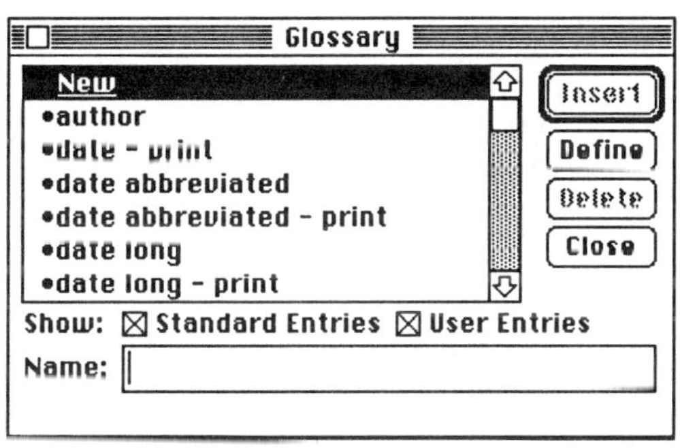

and the Sample 1 window, and give the New command from the File menu to start a new letter. Your finished text will look like Figure 6-2, but you will use the names in the glossary instead of typing the names and addresses or the company name in the body of the text.

Press (⌘)-(DELETE) and type **richford** in the page box in the lower-left corner of the window:

Now press (RETURN). As Figure 6-3 illustrates, the name is expanded into the complete name and address. Continue the letter, using the glossary names when you can. Save this letter as Sample 2.

If you want to remove some of the entries in the glossary, give the Glossary command, select the entries, and click the Delete button. To replace the text of a glossary entry, type the new text that you want for the name in the document and select it. Give the Glossary command, select the name from the list, and click Define.

Figure 6-2. *Sample 2 text*

Chris Richford, Vice President
Manufacturer's Bank of the Northeast
1000 First Avenue
Millerton, CT 06492

Dear Ms. Richford:

This is confirm our conversation earlier today that National Generators will install a new payroll program at the end of this month, and that all of National Generators' payroll checks will be drawn on the new account we set up.

Sincerely,

Thomas Mead, Controller
National Generators
1275 Oak Glen Industrial Park
Oak Glen, CT 06410

Figure 6-3. *Name expanded*

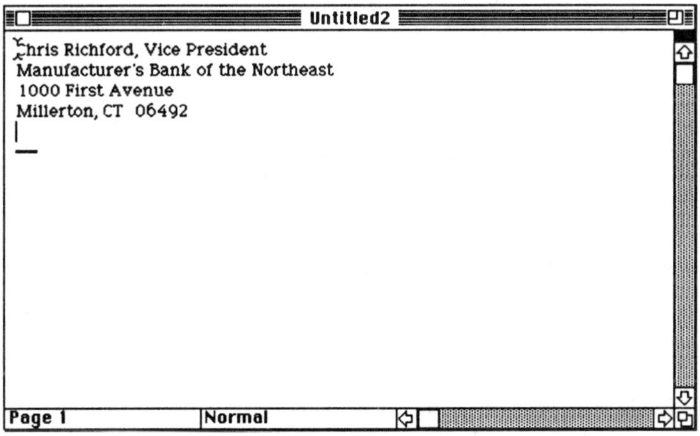

Lesson 22: Storing, Opening, and Printing Glossaries

6

To save the new glossary entries on disk, give the Save As command from the File menu while the Glossary dialog box is open. Word fills in the name of the current glossary in the Save Glossary As dialog box. In this case, click the Save button to save the glossary with the name Standard Glossary, which is the glossary that Word loads automatically when you start it. If you quit Word without saving new glossary entries, Word will ask if you want to save them.

It is rare that you want to keep glossaries other than the standard one. The only reason you would want additional glossaries is if you work in a company and want to use a specialized glossary that someone else created. If you want to use a glossary other than the one Word automatically opens, give the New command and then the Open command from the File menu while you have the Glossary dialog box open. At the prompt, indicate that you want to replace the current entries with the new ones.

To merge the entries from a glossary on disk with the current entries (instead of replacing them as you just now did), open the Glossary dialog box and give the Open command without first giving the New command. If you then save the glossary, it will have both sets of names in it.

As the glossary gets larger, you may forget what is in it. To print out the glossary, give the Glossary command, and, while the Glossary window is open, give the Print command from the File menu.

Lesson 23: Special Glossary Entries

Word has many predefined glossary names whose entries allow you to enter useful information in your documents. There are many other entries that are available if you select the Standard Entries option in the Glossary dialog box. Most of them have names that are descriptive of the contents of the entries.

Table 6-2 lists the predefined entries. Many of the date-based entries have two forms: the date when the entry was used and the date when the document was printed. For instance, the "date long" entry inserts the current date (in its long format) and the "date long-print" entry displays the long format of the date, updated each time you print the document.

Table 6-2. *Special Glossary Entries*

Name	Contents	Example
author	Name from Summary Info dialog box	Thom Mead
date	Date in regular form	January 11, 1992
date abbreviated	Date in short text form	Sat, Jan 11, 1992
date long	Date in long form	Saturday, January 11, 1992
date short	Date in numeric form	1/11/92
day abbreviated	Day name in short form	Sat
day long	Day name in long form	Saturday
day of month	Number of day	11
file name only	Name of the document	Sample 1
file name with path	Name of the document with folder names	Hard drive:National Generators:Sample 1

Table 6-2. Special Glossary Entries (continued)

Name	Contents	Example
keywords	Keywords from Summary Info dialog box	letter, richford
month abbreviated	Month name in short form	Jan
month long	Month name in long form	January
month short	Month in numeric form	1
page number	Current page number	3
print merge	Chevrons for Print Merge command	« »
section	Section number	2
subject	Subject from Summary Info dialog box	Letter to Chris Richford
time	Time	2:17 PM
time with seconds	Time with seconds shown	2:17:03 PM
title	Title from Summary Info dialog box	Funding proposal
version	Version from Summary Info dialog box	2.1
year long	Year number in long form	1992
year short	Year number in short form	92

For example, the entry "date-now-abbreviated" inserts the current date in short form. The entry "date-print-abbreviated" inserts a special marker that becomes the date when it is printed. Thus, it expands to the date when the file is printed, not the date when it was put into the file. There are also many entries for time formats.

Since you rarely need to see these entries, you may want to deselect the Standard Entries choice in the Glossary dialog box. Word remembers this setting and only shows you your own glossary entries when you open the dialog box. When you need to use the standard entries, simply select the choice again.

Lesson 24: Finding Other Uses for Glossaries

Glossaries can reduce typing and increase accuracy in many different applications. The following list should give you some ideas for using glossaries in your daily word processing.

- Complex scientific phrases, such as the names of chemicals, long theory names, process names, and the names of reactions
- Standard legal citations, case names, and legal jargon
- Long, nearly identical names, such as model numbers
- Phrases that are heavily used in a document

Table 6-3 shows examples of some of these uses.

Table 6-3. *Suggested Glossary Entries for Various Uses*

Name	Contents
13cb	anhydrous 1,3-dichlorobenzene, U.S.P.
rsae	Rivest-Shamir-Abel encryption
mcatcom	methyl-selenium catalytic combustion
yrox	Youngblood-Roberts oxidation
fiduc	34 N.E. 2d 68, 70
rw	Roe v. Wade
eqpro	equal protection of the laws
cl12	Colonial 12-422 Model S

Review

Look at some of the writing you are doing (or want to be doing) with Word. Determine which words and phrases would be good candidates for glossary entries. Add a few of them to the glossary. Start a new document and use these entries as you type in some sample text.

7

Pictures in Your Documents

There are times when you might want to include art and graphics in your text. Word allows you to use drawings from graphics programs such as SuperPaint in your text by pasting them from the Clipboard with the Paste command. You can also create graphics from within Word or open graphics files that you have stored on disk.

Lesson 25: Using Art in Your Text

There are two main purposes for including art in your text: to illustrate something that is being written about and to provide decoration. Informational images are useful if you are talking about a product, process, or a location where there are some salient features best described with a picture. Decorative art often makes an otherwise boring report more interesting.

The most common method for including art in your text is to create the art in another program, copy it to the Clipboard in that program, switch to Word, and paste the image into your document using the Paste command. If you are moving many images at the same time, you can use the Macintosh Scrapbook, described in the main Macintosh documentation. As you will see in the next lesson, you can also create images directly in Word and use them in a similar fashion.

For example, suppose that you want to include a product illustration in the Sample 1 file from a Macintosh drawing program you already use. First draw the product illustration in that program and copy it to the Clipboard with the program's Copy command. Quit from the graphics program and run Word. (If you are running MultiFinder or Macintosh System 7, you don't need to quit the drawing program since you can run Word at the same time as the other program.)

Open the Sample 1 file, put the insertion point at the end of the first paragraph, and add a new sentence, **Here is a picture of the DC50.** Now press (RETURN) twice and give the Paste command. Word puts the picture in the letter, as shown in Figure 7-1.

Figure 7-1. *Picture inserted in document*

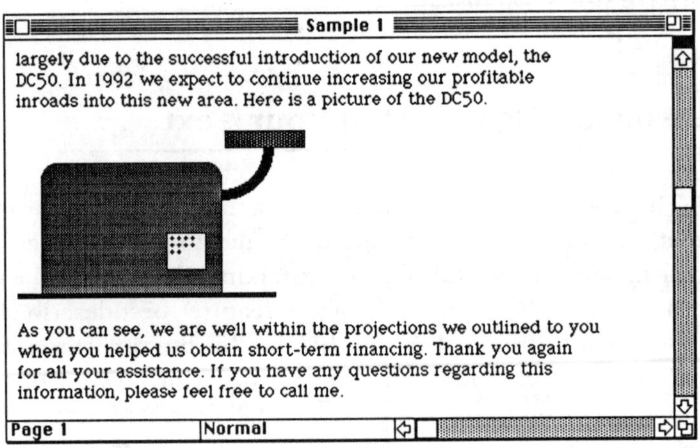

Figure 7-2. *Insert Picture window*

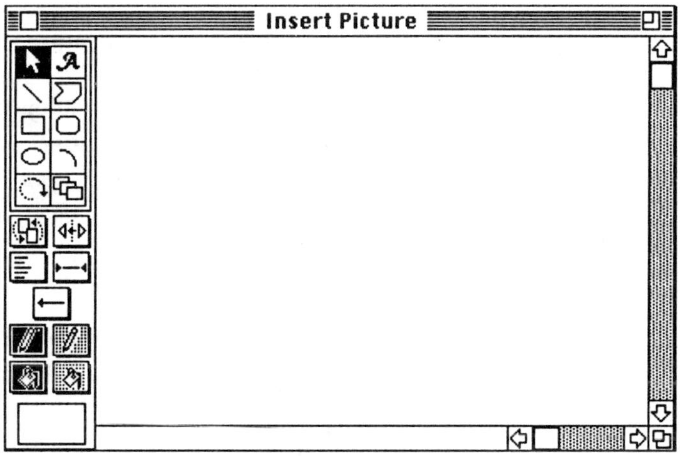

Lesson 26: Creating Graphics in Word

Word comes with a simple drawing program so that you can design graphics for use in Word without using another program. The internal drawing program can create simple drawings but is not a substitute for a real drawing program if you need more advanced pictures.

To create your own graphic in Word, give the Picture command from the Insert menu. In that dialog box, click the New Picture button. This opens the Insert Picture window, shown in Figure 7-2. The major portion in the middle of the window is the *drawing area,* and the area on the left of the window holds the *drawing tools.* Figure 7-3 shows the tool bar and the names of the tools.

If you are familiar with other painting or drawing programs, you will probably be able to create pictures immediately. If not, you may need a bit of practice in order to get good graphics from the Insert Picture window.

Every picture drawn with the Insert Picture window consists of *elements* that make up the entire picture. For example, you might draw a square and put some text in it for a logo. The square is one element, and the text is

7

Figure 7-3. Drawing tools available from the Insert Picture window

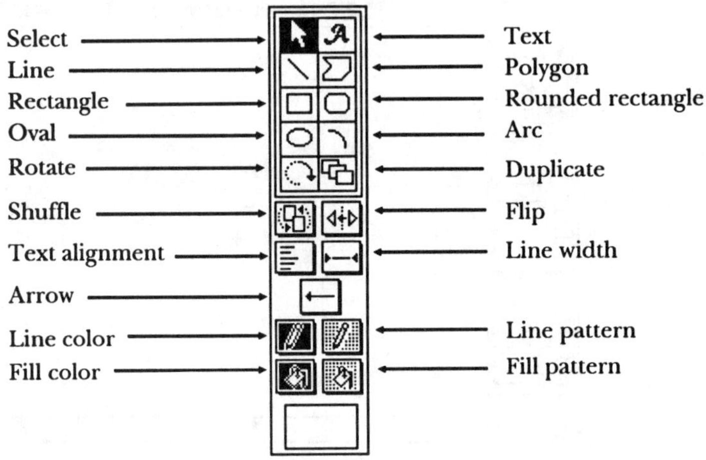

Figure 7-4. Oval drawn

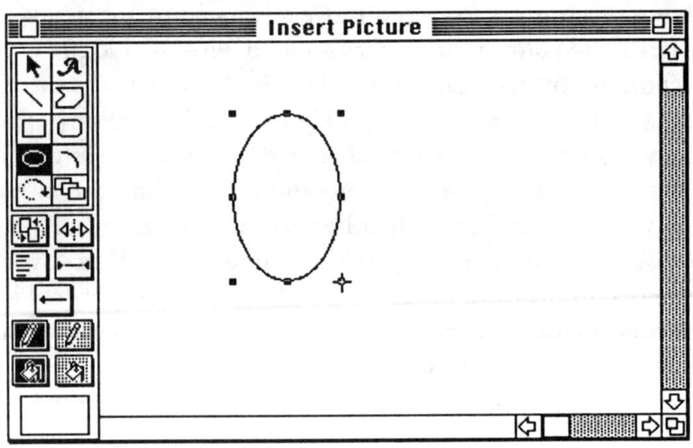

another. You draw and edit elements by selecting drawing tools and using them in the drawing area. You can also Undo your last action.

Some of the tools are for drawing, others are for editing, and others are for specifying parameters for elements. The tools and what they do are summarized in Table 7-1.

You use the line, polygon, rectangle, rounded rectangle, oval, and arc tools to draw elements. With these tools, you click in one corner of the desired element and drag to the diagonally opposite corner. For example, to draw an oval, click the oval tool, click in the drawing area at the upper-left corner of the desired oval, drag to the opposite corner, and release the mouse button. The element is automatically selected. Figure 7-4 shows the result.

With the drawing tools, holding down the SHIFT key while you drag restricts the motion of the tool. Restricting the oval tool causes you to draw

Table 7-1. *Tools in the Insert Picture Window*

Tool	Action
Selection	Selects elements
Text	Inserts text
Line	Draws lines
Polygon	Draws polygons
Rectangle	Draws rectangles
Rounded rectangle	Draws rectangles with rounded corners
Oval	Draws ovals
Arc	Draws arcs
Rotation	Rotates selected element
Duplication	Duplicates selected element
Shuffle	Moves selected element to front or back
Flip	Flips selected element horizontally or vertically
Text alignment	Aligns text within a text element
Line width	Specifies width of lines in elements
Arrow	Adds arrowheads to line elements
Line color	Specifies color of lines in elements
Line pattern	Specifies pattern of lines in elements
Fill color	Specifies color of fills in elements
Fill pattern	Specifies pattern of fills in elements

7

perfect circles, restricting the rectangle tool causes you to draw perfect squares, and so on. Experiment with the drawing tools, with and without the SHIFT key.

The text tool allows you to type text into your drawing. Click the text tool, then click in the drawing window where you want the text to go. Note that the text alignment tool changes the alignment for a text element.

Once you have drawn one or more elements in a drawing, you may want to modify them. To do so, you must first select them with the selection tool. Click the selection tool, then click the element you want to select. You must click directly on a line in the element to select it.

When you select with the selection tool, eight boxes called *handles* appear: one at each corner and one on each side. For example, here is an oval selected:

It is easy to move and resize an element in the Insert Picture window. To move an element, select it and drag its outline to another position. To resize an element, select it and drag any of the handles. Drag a corner handle of an oval, rectangle, or rounded rectangle to change both dimensions; drag a side handle to change its one dimension. If your rectangle (or oval) frame shape is not square when you hold down the SHIFT key and click a corner, a dotted-line image of the frame jumps to square, using the size of the larger side. When you release the button, the frame jumps to that spot. The width and height of the frame are displayed at the bottom.

The duplication tool copies the selected element and puts the copy near the original. This is faster than using the Copy and Paste commands and doesn't involve the Clipboard.

If you want to flip an element vertically or horizontally, select the element and choose one of the options that appear when you click the flip tool. You can combine this with the result of the duplication tool to make interesting mirror images.

The rotation tool lets you change the angle at which the selected element is shown in your document. When you choose the text tool, the cursor turns into a circle with an "X" in it; use this cursor to drag one of the corners of the selected element, rotating it about its center. If, after clicking a corner to rotate, you move the cursor away from the center of the object, while holding the button, you can gain finer control of the increments of rotation. For example, here is a rectangle being rotated with the rotation tool:

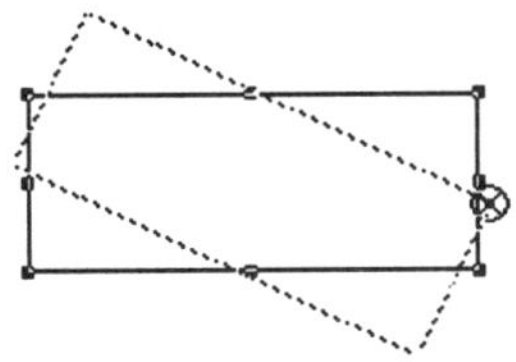

The shuffle tool lets you control how elements appear above and below each other. The choices when you click this tool are to move the selected element to the front or back of the drawing.

The remaining tools affect how parts of elements appear. All elements consist of lines and fills. The *line* is the border of an element while the *fill* is the interior. The line tool specifies how thick the line used in an element is. Create a small rectangle:

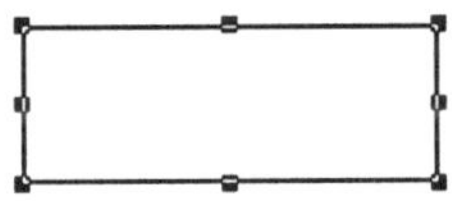

Now click the line tool and select a fatter border from the menu that appears.

Notice that the box at the bottom of the tool menu changes to display the border and fill you have chosen.

You can also specify the color and pattern of the line. For instance, choose one of the gray patterns from the palette that appears when you click the line pattern tool:

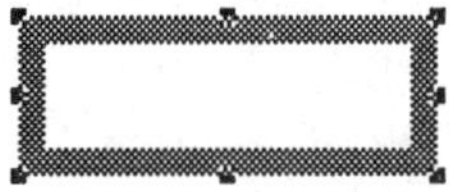

The fill describes how the interior of the element looks. You can choose a color and pattern for the fill. For example, give the rectangle a fancy fill:

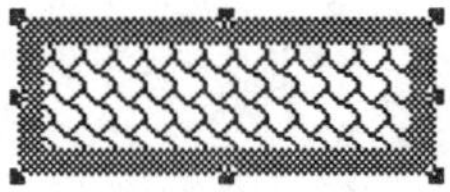

Notice that the fill pattern is different than the line pattern. The tool menu display reflects those changes.

Once you have drawn your picture, give the Select All command from the Edit menu to select all of the elements. Click the close box on the Insert Picture menu and Word inserts the picture at the insertion point in your document.

Note that you can modify your picture (or any picture that you have included in your document) by double-clicking it. This opens the Insert Picture window with the picture in the drawing area. You can use this method to bring in art from other programs and modify them in Word.

Lesson 27: Resizing and Cropping Graphics

Word treats a picture as if it were a character. If you click anywhere in the picture, Word selects the picture and surrounds it in a border with boxes (called *handles*) on the bottom and right edges of the border, as in Figure 7-5. This border does not appear in the printout and disappears when you select any other text. Note that the border may be considerably larger than the graphic in it. This reflects the location of the graphic relative to the upper-left corner of the Insert Picture window. The closer the graphic is to the upper-left corner, the smaller the frame in the main window.

You can resize a picture in the main window by holding down the SHIFT key and dragging on one of the handles. Dragging the handle on the bottom

Figure 7-5. *Picture selected*

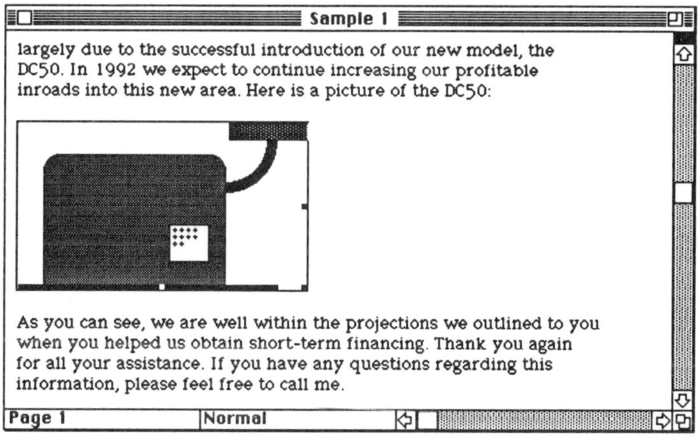

edge while holding down the SHIFT key allows you to stretch or shrink the picture vertically:

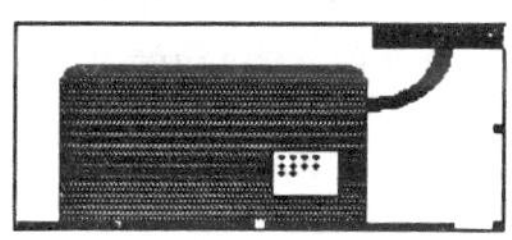

Dragging the handle on the right edge while holding down the SHIFT key allows you to stretch or shrink the picture horizontally:

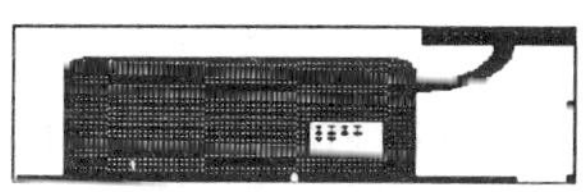

You can resize in both directions keeping the picture proportionally sized by dragging the handle in the lower-right corner while holding down the SHIFT key. This is a good way to keep the vertical and horizontal dimensions the same.

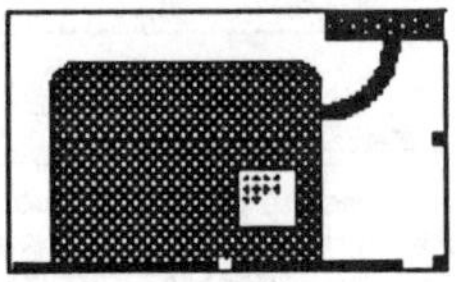

As you resize a picture, the status box shows the percent change if you drag the corner. This is useful if you want to resize by a specific amount, such as 50 percent.

If while in the main window, you don't hold down the SHIFT key, Word *crops* the picture instead of resizing it. Cropping cuts the right side or bottom off the picture if you move the handles inward. If you move the handles outward, Word puts a blank border around the graphic. It is unlikely that you will use Word to crop pictures; resizing them is much more common.

Lesson 28: Opening Graphics Files

Although transferring pictures through the Clipboard from a graphics program is easy, it is not always convenient. For example, if you want to transfer ten pictures into a particular document, you have to switch back and forth between the graphics program and Word. You may find it faster to open that program's graphics files directly in Word. You can also use this method if someone else has created the graphics files for you and you do not have the graphics program on your Macintosh.

To open a picture document, give the Open command from the File menu. In the List Files of Type drop-down list, select Graphics Files. This causes Word to list only graphics files. Select the file that contains the picture you want and open it. Select the picture by clicking it, and give the Copy command to put it in the Clipboard. Click the close box of the picture file's window.

Next, move the insertion point to the position in the file where the picture should go. When you give the Paste command, Word copies the picture from the Clipboard into your document. You can repeat this process for all of the pictures that you have in files.

Word can open many types of Macintosh graphics files, but not all. The types of files it can open are covered in depth in Chapter 22.

Review

Open the Magazine file and choose a spot to insert a graphic. Create that graphic using Word's graphics capabilities (remember, this does not need to be a work of art). Insert the graphic into the text. Select the graphic and make it twice as large.

8

Printing Your Documents

Word has many advanced features that make printing easy. When you edit and format text, for example, you do not need to know what type of printer your text will be printed on. Instead, when you are ready to print, you just give the Print command from the File menu, and it determines what it needs to do in order to use as many of the formats you specify as it can.

This is important because there is no standard method for instructing different printers how to perform certain tasks, such as printing superscripts. Most of the instructions are complex and involve strange character codes. Word does not require you to remember these codes. However, it stores the text formatting with your file, and when you print, it reads a special Macintosh file called a *printer driver* to determine how to use your printer's special features so they correspond to the format.

Different printers, of course, produce output of different quality. They also print at different speeds, have different special features, and range in cost from around $250 to over $10,000.

Although you learned a bit about printing in Chapter 2, this chapter gives you the rest of the information on how to tell Word what type of printer you have and how to use the options of the Print command.

Before you give the Print command, you should tell Word about your printer with the Chooser command from the menu (the menu at the far left of the menu bar). The dialog box for the Chooser looks different for different versions of the Macintosh operating system. Figure 8-1 shows how it looks under System 7. The icons shown each represent a different printer driver. To specify a printer, select the icon of the printer you are going to use and click the close box of the dialog box.

The majority of Word users print on the Apple ImageWriter or Apple LaserWriter printers. The drivers for these printers come with the system software for the Macintosh. Other Word users have printers that act just like the ImageWriter and LaserWriter and thus can use the same printer drivers. Some printers come with their own drivers, which appear in the Chooser dialog box like other printers.

Lesson 29: Using the Page Setup Command

You should give the Page Setup command from the File menu to tell Word the type of paper you are using. The dialog boxes for the ImageWriter

Figure 8-1. *Chooser dialog box*

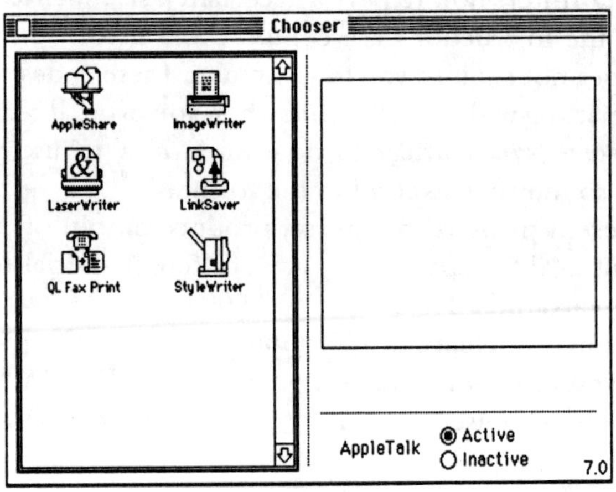

and LaserWriter are shown in Figure 8-2. The default settings are usually correct for most users, and you do not need to give the Page Setup command often.

The Orientation options specify which edge of the paper should be considered the top. The icon on the left indicates that you want to print down the page in the normal fashion; the icon on the right indicates that you want to print lengthwise across the page. These are sometimes known as *portrait* and *landscape*, respectively.

The Document button in the dialog boxes gives you direct access to changing the formatting for the whole document. This is described in Chapter 12.

The Use As Default choice, when selected, causes the settings you have chosen in the dialog box to be the defaults when Word prints.

ImageWriter Options

The Paper options tell Word what type of paper you are using. US Letter corresponds to standard 8 1/2 x 11-inch paper, while US Legal corresponds

Figure 8-2. *Page Setup dialog boxes*

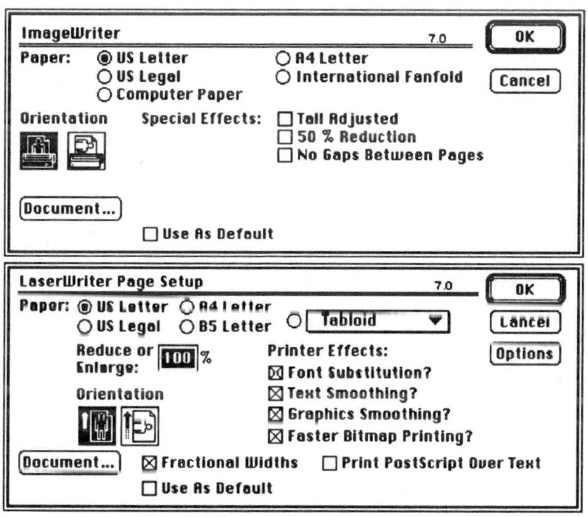

8

to 8 1/2 x 14-inch paper. A4 Letter and International Fanfold are for paper that conforms to international standards. Computer Paper indicates wide-form computer paper (15 x 11 inches).

The other choices on the ImageWriter are Tall Adjusted (makes pictures print in proportion to the page), 50% Reduction (makes everything half as large), and No Gaps Between Pages (does not skip over the perforations on the paper).

LaserWriter Options

The Paper choice tells Word what type of paper you are using. US Letter corresponds to standard 8 1/2 x 11-inch paper, while US Legal corresponds to 8 1/2 x 14-inch paper. A4 Letter and B5 Letter are for paper that conforms to international standards. The other choices in the drop-down menu (if your version of Page Setup provides one) are for rarely used paper sizes.

Other LaserWriter options include the following:

- Reduce or Enlarge lets you specify whether to scale the document before printing. Enter a number that represents a percent of normal size; 100 (unchanged) is the default.
- Font Substitution causes Geneva to be printed as the LaserWriter's internal Helvetica font, New York to be printed as Times, and Monaco to be printed as Courier. Due to the way that the Macintosh prints to the LaserWriter, it is better to use the LaserWriter fonts themselves in your document, rather than Font Substitution.
- Text Smoothing causes non-LaserWriter fonts to be printed without jagged edges.
- Graphics Smoothing causes pictures to have their pixels rounded so that the image looks softer.
- Faster Bitmap Printing prints some documents faster.
- Fractional Widths makes most PostScript fonts print with better spacing between letters.
- Print PostScript Over Text is an advanced option, important only if you add your own PostScript codes in your document.

These options (except Fractional Widths and Print PostScript Over Text) are described in more detail in the LaserWriter manual.

If you click the Options button, a second screen of LaserWriter options appears, showing another list of options and a picture of a page, containing dotted-line margins and an object (a dog or a cow). Click an option to select it, and you can see the corresponding change made on the page icon. Click OK to accept the options for your document, or Cancel to return to the Page Setup screen without changing these options.

Lesson 30: Giving the Print Command

The last set of print options that Word offers is in the Print command from the File menu. You use the Print command when you are ready to print your text (you can use ⌘-P for the command). Figure 8-3 shows the Print dialog boxes for the ImageWriter and LaserWriter.

Figure 8-3. *Print dialog boxes*

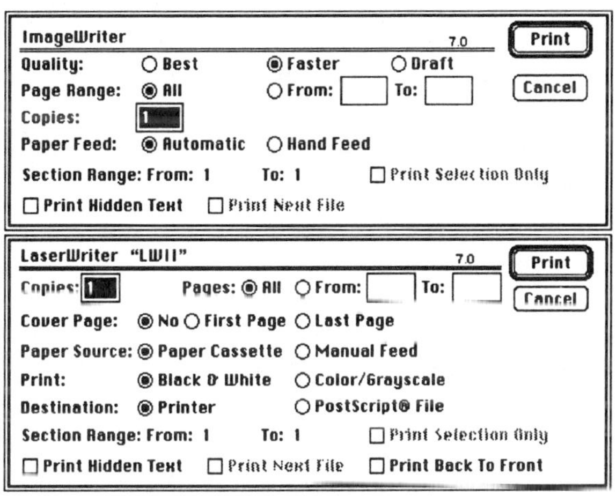

You can choose to print only certain pages from your document by using the Pages or Page Range option. You can instruct Word to print the entire document (All is the normal selection), to print the text on particular pages, or to print just the selection (with the Print Selection Only option). If you click the From button, you can then enter the page numbers. If your document has more than one section (as described in Chapter 12), you can specify the section numbers in the Section Range choices.

If you want to print more than one copy of a file, use the Copies option. This is a convenient way to print many copies of a letter or memo without having to give the Print command over and over.

The Paper Feed or Paper Source option tells Word how your printer handles the paper you are printing on. You can also tell Word to print hidden text (hidden text is described in Chapter 18).

For the ImageWriter, the Quality choices let you decide how your text is printed; this affects both the appearance of the printed output and the speed at which your printer runs. Choose the Faster option if you want normal printing or the Best button if you want Word to use the slower, but better-looking, high-quality printing. Click the Draft button if you want to speed up the printing process; doing this, however, means that you do not see character formats in the printed document.

For the LaserWriter, the Cover Page option tells Word whether or not to print a descriptive cover page for the document. In recent versions of the Macintosh operating system, you can specify whether to print in black-and-white or color (few people have color printers yet). The Destination choice, if your version of the System has it, lets you save your output in a PostScript file, an advanced feature. Print Back to Front prints the last page first.

Review

Experiment with the choices in the Page Setup dialog box by selecting them and printing the Magazine document. If you have more than one type of printer available, try different choices on each type of printer.

II

Using Word to Format

9

Basic Formatting with Word

As part of the editing process, you usually want to alter the way your text looks so your reader will more readily understand your meaning and the information is presented in an interesting form. Word's formatting capabilities let you choose exactly how your text looks when it is printed out.

Adding a formatting characteristic to text is called *direct formatting*. The concept of direct formatting is similar to what you normally do when typing text. For example, when you make changes on a first draft, you might decide to underline a phrase or change the size of the text. In doing this, you are adding characteristics directly to text.

Lesson 31: Introducing Formatting

The basic concept behind formatting with Word is that all text has certain characteristics associated with it. After you have specified the characteristics (such as underlining or indenting), Word automatically displays the text with those attributes. If you move the text to some other place in your document, the characteristics move with it.

You can enter an entire document without worrying about the formatting and then go back over it to add formatting, or if you wish, you can format text as you enter it. Each time you add a characteristic, you see it instantly. Both methods work equally well. You can experiment with different formats, seeing which one best fits the meaning of the text.

Word gives you three units to apply formatting to: characters, paragraphs, and sections. At the level of the smallest unit (character), Word lets you change the format of each character or groups of letters (such as words or phrases). For example, you can underline, boldface, or italicize characters, as well as change type font and size with different formatting commands. Character formatting is most often used to make certain words stand out in your text.

You have already learned to use the (RETURN) key to make paragraphs in Word. Paragraphs are the second formatting unit. The paragraph is important to Word because Word stores formatting information for each paragraph when you press (RETURN). In fact, all of the characteristics of a paragraph are stored in a bit of white space that is placed at the end of the paragraph (this white space is actually a paragraph mark).

For instance, many people like to indent every paragraph five spaces. Some word processors require you to press the (TAB) key at the beginning of each paragraph; Word, however, remembers this format, once you have specified it, and inserts the spaces for you in succeeding paragraphs unless you tell it otherwise. Other paragraph formats that you can specify include the indentation of the entire paragraph, line spacing, and alignment with the margin.

You often want to set different formatting characteristics for a particular paragraph. For example, when you include a long quotation in text, you usually indent the whole quotation a few spaces from the margin.

Since Word stores paragraph formatting characteristics in the paragraph mark, you can use the Copy and Paste commands to copy the formatting characteristics of one paragraph to another paragraph in a different location in your document. You do not need to do this as you type since Word uses the paragraph formatting of the previous paragraph when you start a new paragraph. You can see the paragraph mark by giving the Show ¶ command from the View menu. Copy the paragraph mark that you want to transfer to the Clipboard. Then select the paragraph mark that you want to replace and give the Paste command. All of the formatting characteristics are then applied to the new paragraph.

Word lets you set up different characteristics for each *section,* which is the third formatting unit. These are characteristics such as page headings and margin size that do not change from paragraph to paragraph. You might have many sections in a document if you have many chapters or if you have many different page layouts with one document, such as in a brochure. You can see the section formatting using different views of your Word document.

It is important to remember that each element of text, whether it is a character, a paragraph, or a section, has a set of formatting instructions attached to it. The end result is that formatting documents is easy with Word, since you can copy the specifications from one formatting unit to another.

You may be wondering what all of these characteristics are. They are discussed in the next three chapters. For now, think of a direct formatting characteristic as a description of how the text looks or is positioned on the page.

Lesson 32: Giving Formatting Commands

You can give formatting commands in Word in three ways:

- Give commands from the Format menu.
- Press special key combinations.
- Click icons in the ribbon and ruler.

The formatting commands are much like the editing commands that you have already learned. You apply formatting commands to selected text. If you give a formatting command when the insertion point is in a document (no text selected), the text you type at the insertion point has that formatting applied to it.

You do not need to use the menus to enter every formatting command. There are some character and paragraph formatting commands that can be entered with key combinations such as ⌘-B for boldface characters. These key sequences are described in the next two chapters.

If you have Word display the ribbon and the ruler, you can give character and paragraph formatting commands by clicking icons. These actions are described in the next two chapters.

The most common type of formatting you use is character formatting. For instance, book and magazine publishers commonly use italics for emphasis, foreign words, and book titles. They use underlining and boldface in different kinds of headings. Chapter 10 discusses character formatting, Chapter 11 discusses paragraph formatting, and Chapter 12 discusses section formatting.

Lesson 33: Searching and Replacing Formatting

In Chapter 5, you saw how the Find command looked for text. The Find command normally ignores formatting when looking for text. However, you can specify in the Find dialog box that the command only look for text that has particular formatting with the Format drop-down list, which looks like this:

The Clear option clears any formatting specifications you may have already made. The Character, Paragraph, and Style options bring up dialog boxes similar to those you will learn about in the next three chapters. In those dialog boxes, you choose the type of formatting you want to search for.

If you use the Format choices, you can either search for all text with the specified formatting or only for specific text that has that formatting. To search for the next text that has particular formatting, leave the Find What choice blank, select the formatting choice in the Format drop-down list, and choose the desired format from the dialog box. You can choose many types of simultaneous formatting, such as bold and centered text. When you select formatting from the dialog boxes, the choices are shown to the right of the drop-down list:

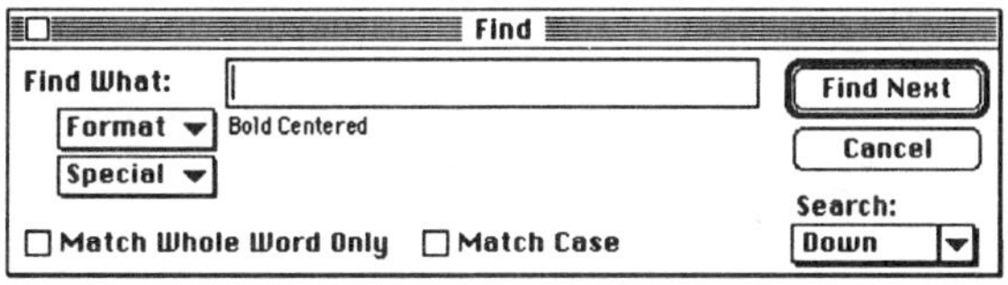

When you click the Find Next button after specifying the formatting, the next text that has that formatting is selected, regardless of the text.

To select specific text with specific formatting, enter that text in the Find What choice. Thus, to find the words "timely fashion" in italics, the dialog box would look like this:

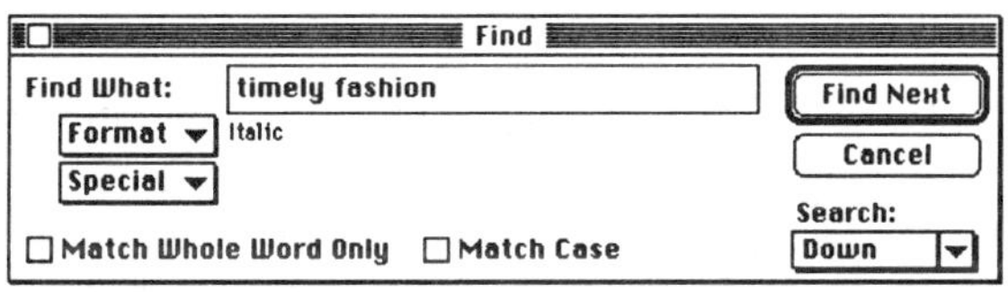

The Replace command works in a similar fashion to the Find command. In addition to finding text with particular formatting, you can also specify the formatting of the replaced text. Normally, Word replaces text with the same formatting as that on the first character that was found. With the Format drop-down list in the Replace command, you can specify the same text with different formatting without having to put the text in the Replace With choice. For example, Figure 9-1 shows how you can quickly replace all instances of "Annual Report" in italics with the same words in bold.

Figure 9-1. *Replacing same text with different formatting*

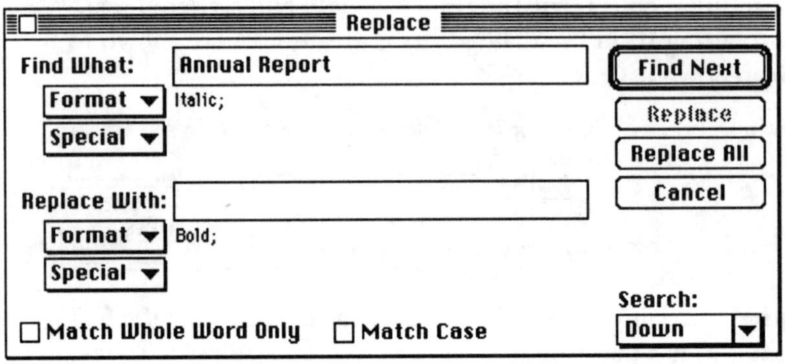

Review

Look in books and magazines that you normally read and pay attention to how character and paragraph formatting is used. Note how much formatting there is on title pages of books and in magazine articles. Think about how you would implement that type of formatting in your work.

10

Formatting Characters

The purpose of character formatting is to make the reader notice a group of characters or words. This is often useful for emphasis, but common publishing practices also require it; for instance, book titles should generally be shown in italics. Examples of some character formats include

bold characters
underlined characters
italicized characters
combinations
characters with different fonts

Lesson 34: Common Character Formatting

Type the text shown in Figure 10-1, which is used to experiment with character formatting. Save this on disk with the name "Character Test." If you want to change the formatting of a group of characters, first select the group, and then give the Character command from the Format menu. The Character dialog box, shown in Figure 10-2, appears.

The standard character formatting, such as for bold, is either on or off. This type of formatting is called a *toggle* because it acts like a toggle switch. Choose it once and it's on; choose it again and it's off. You can change any of the toggles to indicate the formatting you want. In fact, you can choose more than one type of formatting for your text. For example, you might want a title on a report to be both underlined and bold.

You can also set a format toggle from the Format menu by giving the command from the menu. When a toggle is set on, a check mark appears next to it in the Format menu. If you are giving some text more than one format (such as both underlining and italics), you have to choose the options one at a time.

Figure 10-1. *Character Test file*

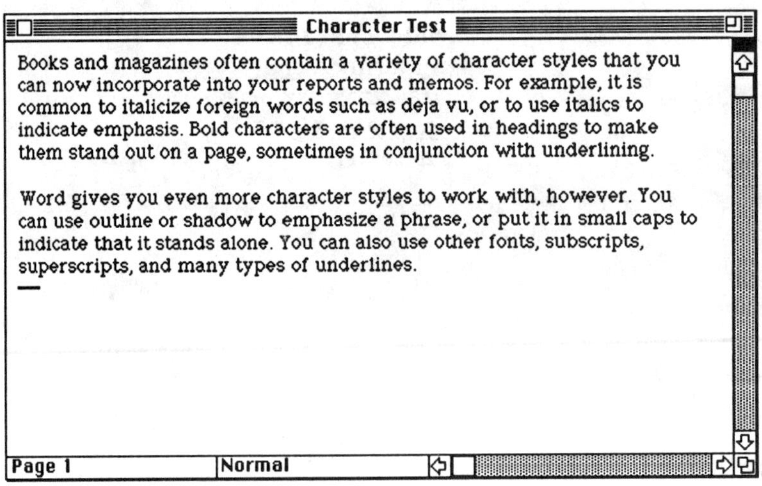

Figure 10-2. *Character dialog box*

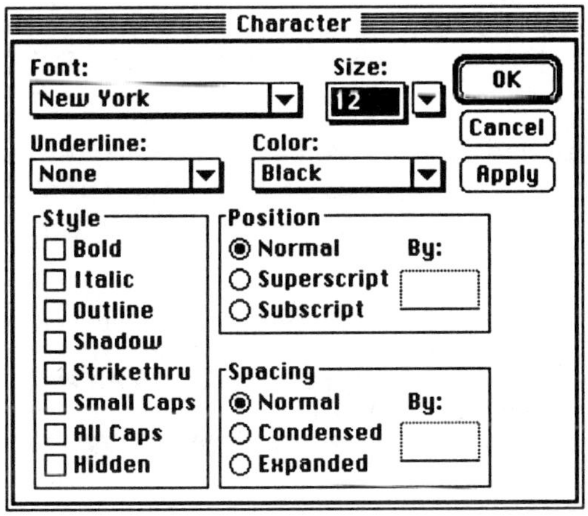

The formats that most people use in their writing are plain (no emphasis), italics, bold, and underlining. Now, as an experiment, select the words "deja vu" in the text and give the Character command from the Format menu. Click the Italic option and then the OK button. When the dialog box disappears, the words "deja vu" become italic:

> Books and magazines often contain a variety of character styles that you can now incorporate into your reports and memos. For example, it is common to italicize foreign words such as *deja vu*, or to use italics to indicate emphasis. Bold characters are often used in headings to make them stand out on a page, sometimes in conjunction with underlining.

Click once in the text to remove the selection so that you can see the italics more clearly.

Choosing bold and underlined is similar to choosing italics. Select the words "stand out" and then make them bold by dragging down the Format menu to the Bold command. Select the word "underlining" and give the Underline command (if you wish, you can also underline the period after the words). The results look like this:

Books and magazines often contain a variety of character styles that you can now incorporate into your reports and memos. For example, it is common to italicize foreign words such as *deja vu*, or to use italics to indicate emphasis. Bold characters are often used in headings to make them **stand out** on a page, sometimes in conjunction with underlining.

As mentioned before, you can apply more than one format to a section of text. To practice this, select "in conjunction" and give the Character command. Now click both Bold and Italic and click the OK button.

Books and magazines often contain a variety of character styles that you can now incorporate into your reports and memos. For example, it is common to italicize foreign words such as *deja vu*, or to use italics to indicate emphasis. Bold characters are often used in headings to make them **stand out** on a page, sometimes ***in conjunction*** with underlining.

You can also use the ribbon to apply simple character formatting. Give the Ribbon command from the View menu or press ⌘-OPTION-R to expose the ribbon.

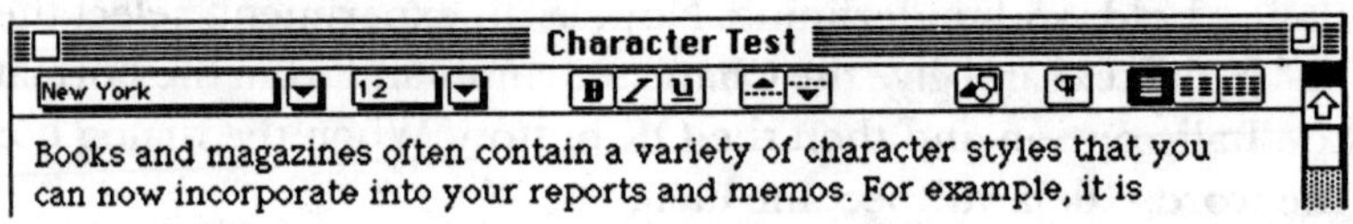

The icons near the middle of the ribbon, marked **B**, *I*, and U are used to make text bold, italic, or underlined. Just select the desired text and click the icon.

Lesson 35: Other Character Formats

Word also lets you specify other types of formatting in the Character dialog box. In the area labeled "Style" (which you should think of as "characteristics"), the other choices are Outline, Shadow, Strikethru, Small Caps, and All Caps (don't worry about Hidden; hidden text will be covered in Chapter 18). You can experiment with these to see what they look like. As you can see from the mixture of formatting in Figure 10-3, it is easy to overuse character formatting. Most book and magazine publishers avoid using too many formats so that the text doesn't end up looking like an old-time circus poster.

In the Underline drop-down list in the Character dialog box, you can choose from one of many types of underlining: single (regular), word, double, and dotted. Here are examples of each:

single underline
word underline
double underline
dotted underline

Subscripts and superscripts are often useful in scientific or technical papers. You choose these from the Position box in the Character command. You define how high or low you want your superscripts and subscripts by entering an amount in the By option.

Figure 10-3. *Text with many formats applied*

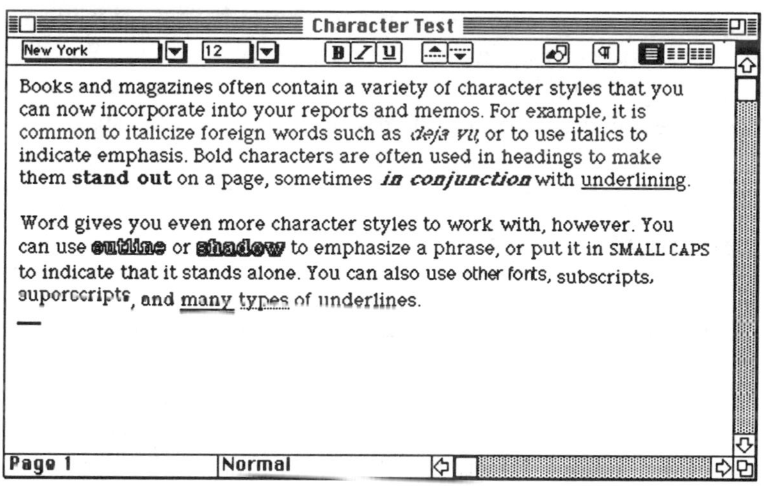

To experiment with superscripts and subscripts, select the word "superscripts" in the Character Test file, give the Character command, and click the Superscript button. Notice that Word fills in "3 pt" (3 points) for the amount in the By option; you can change this to an amount between 0 and 63 points. (Points are described later in this chapter in the discussion of fonts.) Subscripts work the same way as superscripts. Select the word "subscripts", give the Character command, and enter **10** in the By option.

> Word gives you even more character styles to work with, however. You can use outline or shadow to emphasize a phrase, or put it in SMALL CAPS to indicate that it stands alone. You can also use other fonts, subscripts, superscripts, and many types of underlines.

You can also apply superscript and subscript formatting from the ribbon with the icons that are to the right of the bold, italic, and underline icons. Clicking the icon twice returns the text to its normal position.

If you have a color monitor or color printer, you can take advantage of Word's color formatting for characters. Choose a color from the drop-down list. The colors you can choose are black, blue, cyan, green, magenta, red, yellow, and white.

You can assign colors even if you do not have a color monitor or printer. Simply add the formatting to any text in your document. Word remembers the formatting, even if it cannot show it on the screen or printer. This way, if you later have access to a color device, your document will display and print in color.

Lesson 36: Fonts

The Macintosh has many different fonts that you can use in your writing and, unlike other machines, shows them on screen as you've chosen them. A font is a consistent text design. There are many ways to draw the standard alphabet. For instance, you may have very curly letters, very blocky ones, or letters with many intricate details. Each different alphabet set is called a *font*. Actually, a font contains more than just the letters of the alphabet: it contains all the numerals, punctuation marks, and special symbols as well.

If you have not experimented with fonts before, you should find that using different fonts creates different moods for your letters and reports. The following section covers the basics of type and fonts; if you are already familiar with fonts, feel free to skim through it.

Introduction to Fonts

Each font can have variations within it. The two major types of variations are *characteristics* and *size*. You have already seen the different formatting characteristics that Word can produce, such as underline, italics, and bold. You may have noticed that when you applied a format with the Character command from the Format menu, the letters still appeared in much the way they were before. That is because using characteristics causes the letters to retain the basic feeling of a font (such as the character widths).

The *size* of a font is defined as the amount of vertical space the letters take on a line. This amount includes the distance the letter goes above and below the *baseline*, which is where the bottom of most letters line up, as well as the *leading*, which is the space between the very bottom of a letter and the very top of the letter on the next line. Here is an example that shows the elements that make up the size of a font.

Font size is measured in *points*; one point is 1/72 of an inch. For instance, the characters in a 12-point font are 1/6 of an inch high (including the leading). Fortunately, this is easy to translate to the Macintosh, since each dot (properly called a *pixel*) on the screen is also 1/72 of an inch high. (You may have not noticed that the image on your screen is made of dots, but they are easy to see if you look closely.)

Each font has many different design characteristics that help define it. For instance, some fonts have *serifs*, which are little decorative lines used to finish off the stroke of a letter. Fonts without serifs are called *sans serif.* Figure 10-4 illustrates the difference between serif and sans serif.

A font can also have *proportional spacing* or *monospacing.* In a proportional font, the letters have different widths, for example, the “m” is much wider than the “i”. In a monospace font, the letters and punctuation are all given the same amount of horizontal space, regardless of width. It is easy to see the difference:

```
This is a monospaced font.
```

This is a proportional font.

Other design characteristics include whether the type has wide or thin lines, whether the characters are chubby or narrow, what kinds of embellishments are used in the letters, and whether the letters can connect (as in a *cursive,* or script, font).

Each font on the Macintosh has a name (due to Macintosh history, many are named after cities). Figure 10-5 shows some of the fonts available for the Macintosh. You may not have all of these installed. There are thousands of

Figure 10-4. *Serif and sans serif fonts*

Figure 10-5. *Some Macintosh fonts*

Avant Garde	New Century Schlbk
Bookman	Paladin
Courier	Palatino
GaramondCondFLF	Rodchenko
GaramondFLF	Σψμβολ
Helvetica	Times
Kells	*Zapf Chancery*
	ZephyrScript

fonts available for the Macintosh from many sources. See your Macintosh documentation for information on installing additional fonts.

Changing Fonts

When you start entering text, Word uses the font you specified as the default font when you installed Word. You can change the default font Word uses with the Preferences command, as described in Chapter 16.

You can easily change the font of selected text with the Character command. The Character dialog box has two choices that relate to fonts: one for the font name and the other for the font size. For each font, Word lists only the sizes that are installed with the font, but you can enter any size you want between 4 and 16383 points. If you are using System 7, Word lists many sizes for each font.

You can also change the font and size in the ribbon. The drop-down lists in the ribbon act the same as those in the Character dialog box.

For practice, select the first sentence of the text in the Character Test file and give the Character command. Select the Monaco font and a size of 9 points. The selected paragraph now looks like this:

> Books and magazines often contain a variety of character styles that you can now incorporate into your reports and memos. For example, it is common to italicize foreign words such as *deja vu* or to use italics to indicate emphasis. Bold characters are often used in headings to make them **stand out** on a page, sometimes ***in conjunction*** with underlining.

You can enter a font size that is not listed by typing a number for your size choice. However, using font sizes that are not listed often causes the text to look jagged and poorly formed on the screen. Depending on what version of the Macintosh operating system you are using and the type of printer you have, the text may look fine or terrible when printed. Some fonts also look strange on the screen when bold or outlined.

Once you have experimented with all of the available character formatting and some of the fonts, print out the file on your printer to see how it looks. If you are using a version of the Macintosh operating system before System 7 and are using a laser printer, you may see a message while printing that a bitmap of the font is being used. If you see this, you may see that some of the fonts in your printout are not as well-defined as others. See your printer's documentation for more information on how to select fonts that your printer can print at highest resolution.

Lesson 37: Selecting Character Formatting with the (⌘) Key

Using the Character command or the ribbon to change character formatting, fonts, and font sizes can be tedious and slow if you need to give the command over and over. Word allows you to select character formatting and fonts with key combinations to make formatting faster.

Table 10-1 shows the key combinations used to select character formatting, fonts, and font sizes. As before, select the text you want to change, then use the appropriate key combination.

You can change the font by pressing ⌘-SHIFT-E. The page box displays the word "Font":

Type the font name and press RETURN. You don't need to type the whole name, just enough of the name to differentiate it from other fonts in your Macintosh.

Table 10-1. Character Formatting with ⌘-Key Combinations

Format	Key Combination
Normal for style	⌘-SHIFT-SPACEBAR
Italic	⌘-SHIFT-I
Bold	⌘-SHIFT-B
Underline	⌘-SHIFT-U
Word underline	⌘-SHIFT-]
Double underline	⌘-SHIFT-[
Dotted underline	⌘-SHIFT-\
Small caps	⌘-SHIFT-H
All caps	⌘-SHIFT-K
Strikethrough	⌘-SHIFT-/
Shadow	⌘-SHIFT-W
Outline	⌘-SHIFT-D
Subscript	⌘-SHIFT--
Superscript	⌘-SHIFT-+
Change font	⌘-SHIFT-E
Increase font size	⌘-SHIFT->
Decrease font size	⌘-SHIFT-<

For example, select the words "Books and magazines" in the Character Test file; then press ⌘-SHIFT-I to put the words in italics. To add underlining, press ⌘-SHIFT-U. The result looks like this:

> <u>*Books and magazines*</u> often contain a variety of character styles that you can now incorporate into your reports and memos. For example, it is common to italicize foreign words such as *deja vu* or to use italics to indicate emphasis. Bold characters are often used in headings to make them **stand out** on a page, sometimes ***in conjunction*** with <u>underlining</u>.

To make the words normal again, you press either ⌘-SHIFT-SPACEBAR or ⌘-SHIFT-Z. The difference between these two key combinations is that ⌘-SHIFT-SPACEBAR removes all formatting that is different than the standard for the current paragraph style (described in Chapter 13), while ⌘-SHIFT-Z removes characteristics such as bold and italics but not font and font size changes.

Lesson 38: Copying Character Formats

Now that you know how to apply a format to a character, you may be inclined to go back and add character formats to other files that you have created with Word. Giving the commands from the Character menu, the ribbon, or entering ⌘-key sequences can get tedious however, so Word allows you to copy the format of one set of characters to another without having to specify the actual format.

When you want to do this, you begin with one set of characters formatted the way you want. The steps are

1. Select the formatted set of characters.
2. Press ⌘-OPTION-V. The page box in the lower-left corner displays "Format to":

3. Select the characters to which you want to copy the format. Instead of highlighting them normally, Word uses a dotted underline:

> Books and magazines often contain a variety of character styles that you can now incorporate into your reports and memos. For example, it is common to italicize foreign words such as *deja vu*, or to use italics to indicate emphasis. Bold characters are often used in headings to make them **stand out** on a page, sometimes ***in conjunction*** with underlining.

4. Press (RETURN). The characters you selected have the formatting copied to them.

These steps are best explained by example. Suppose that you want to change the first word in each sentence in the Character Test file to Monaco 9-point, underlined (this is admittedly strange, but it is a good exercise). Notice that the word "Books" already has this formatting; select it. Press (⌘)-(OPTION)-(V) and select the word "For" in the second sentence:

> Books and magazines often contain a variety of character styles that you can now incorporate into your reports and memos. For example, it is common to italicize foreign words such as *deja vu*, or to use italics to indicate emphasis. Bold characters are often used in headings to make them **stand out** on a page, sometimes ***in conjunction*** with underlining.

Press (RETURN), and the word "For" is changed to the new formatting:

> Books and magazines often contain a variety of character styles that you can now incorporate into your reports and memos. For example, it is common to italicize foreign words such as *deja vu*, or to use italics to indicate emphasis. Bold characters are often used in headings to make them **stand out** on a page, sometimes ***in conjunction*** with underlining.

Now press (⌘)-(OPTION)-(V) again and select the word "Bold" in the third sentence. Press the (RETURN) key again.

> Books and magazines often contain a variety of character styles that you can now incorporate into your reports and memos. For example, it is common to italicize foreign words such as *deja vu*, or to use italics to indicate emphasis. Bold characters are often used in headings to make them **stand out** on a page, sometimes ***in conjunction*** with underlining.

You can continue to do this for any number of words or phrases.

Lesson 39: Formatting Graphics

Word treats graphics just like characters. Thus, you can use the character formatting you learned in this chapter such as outlines with graphics that you put in your documents. There are two things you are most likely to do with graphics formatting: put a border around a graphic and move it up and down on its line.

To format a graphic, select it as you learned in Chapter 7. Next, give the Character command from the Format menu and choose the character formatting you want. The only interesting format is Outline, which can be modified with the bold and shadow formats.

Word lets you put a border around a graphic using outline formatting. To see this, use the graphic that you created in Chapter 7:

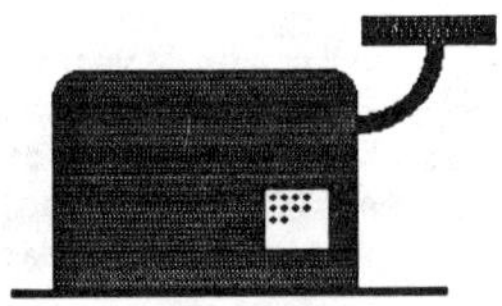

Select the graphic, give the Character command, and select Outline:

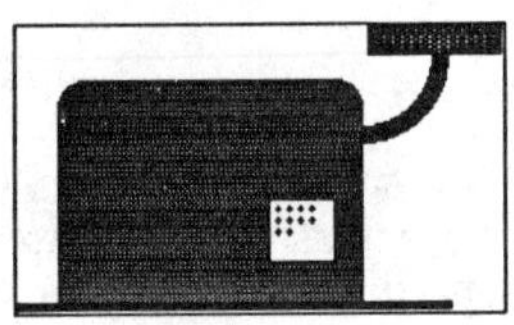

Once you have an outline around your graphic, you can add shadow and bold formatting. For instance, you can add a shadow to the outline to give a nice effect:

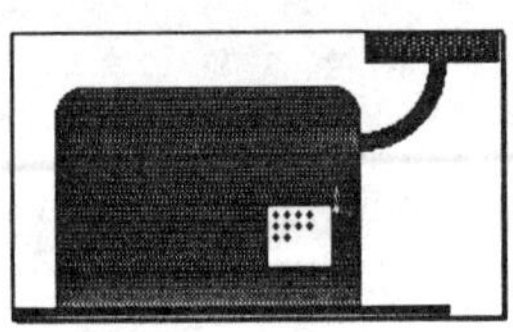

You can also use superscripts and subscripts to position the graphic on the line. Select the graphic and use the superscript and subscript formatting as you would for regular characters. This allows you to position graphics exactly where you want them.

Review

Open the Magazine file and add character formatting to various words and phrases. Add more than one type of formatting to some words and notice how the formats combine.

Look at the Font menu in Word. Create a new document that is a list of all the font names, where each name is formatted with that font. Save and print this list for future reference.

11

Formatting Paragraphs

One of the best ways to make letters and reports look professional is to use consistent formatting throughout the document. For example, if you indent your paragraphs, all paragraphs should be indented the same amount.

All headings should also be formatted consistently so that the reader can quickly determine what you are saying. In a report, it is often important to see section headings and topics quickly. If your document is organized around an outline, consistently formatting each level of information helps the reader to understand the meaning of the whole document.

Formatting paragraphs in Word is quite easy because Word associates a format with each paragraph. You can specify paragraph formatting when you enter the paragraph, and you can change the formatting later if you change your mind (just as you can with character formatting, described in Chapter 10). Word automatically uses the same format for each paragraph until you tell it otherwise. As a result, all of your text paragraphs will look the same until you give different formatting commands.

Tab stops are a format characteristic that you can set for a paragraph. Word's tab stops work just like those on a normal typewriter, but with one additional feature: if your writing includes figures and columns, you can use one set of tab stops for one set of columns and a different set for another set of columns.

There are many other interesting paragraph formatting features. For example, you can tell Word that you want a border (such as a solid line) around a paragraph to make headings stand out. You can also specify when you want two paragraphs to appear side by side.

Lesson 40: Basic Formatting for Paragraphs

Word stores a paragraph's format in the mark at the end of the paragraph. You may have noticed that an extra blank character is inserted at the end of each paragraph after the period; this is the paragraph mark that is inserted when you press the (RETURN) key. You can see the paragraph mark by giving the Show ¶ command from the View menu.

You can choose from a variety of paragraph formatting options. To see a list of them, select any text in the paragraph or place the insertion point anywhere in the paragraph and give the Paragraph command from the Format menu. For example, load the Sample 1 file into Word and put the insertion point in the first text paragraph. Now give the Paragraph command. Notice that Word automatically shows the ruler and that the Paragraph dialog box is displayed in the middle of the screen, as in Figure 11-1. Remember from Chapter 2 that you can show the ruler at any time by giving the Ruler command from the View menu or pressing (⌘)-(R).

The ruler sets and shows where your paragraph indentations are and where each tab stop is in the selected paragraph. The numbers on the ruler are incremented by inches. When you enter the settings for paragraph indentations, you normally give the position in inches, but you can change this with the Preferences command described in Chapter 16. You also use the ruler in this command to set tab stops, alignment, line spacing, and space around the paragraph. The following illustration shows the parts of the ruler.

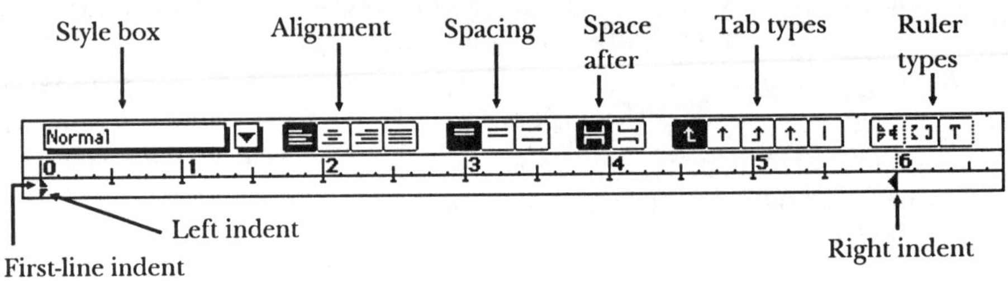

Figure 11-1. *Paragraph command displays the ruler and Paragraph dialog box*

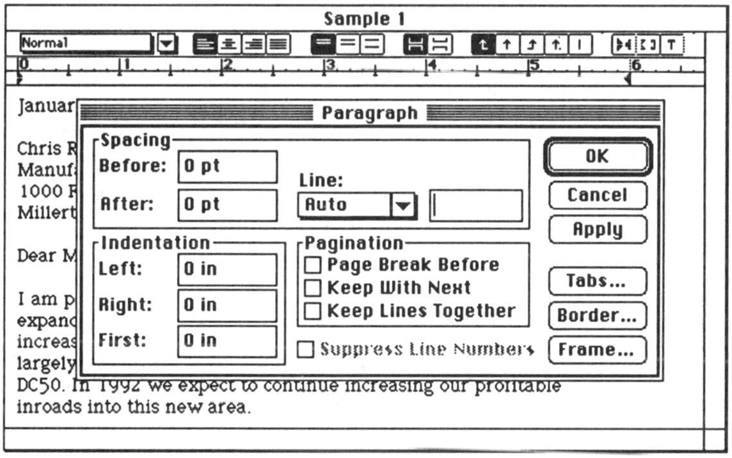

In the Paragraph dialog box, as in other Word dialog boxes, you simply choose the characteristics that you want the selected text to have. Since paragraph formatting applies to whole paragraphs, if you have only part of a paragraph selected or the insertion point placed in it, Word applies the formatting to that entire paragraph. The choices in the Paragraph command are described in the following lessons. Many of the paragraph formatting commands can be executed with (⌘)-key sequences (like those used in character formatting) instead of from the menu.

Remember that you can change the formatting of a paragraph at any time. Word has default settings for all of the paragraph formatting choices (sometimes called the *normal* choices), but it is likely that these might not be the best choices at all times. For example, you may enter some text in a memo with normal paragraph formatting and then decide later to indent the paragraph from both margins to make it stand out on the page. You can change the margins, see how the paragraph looks, and decide whether to keep the new format. You can, of course, change it back at any time as well.

Lesson 41: Indenting Paragraphs

The most common changes that you make to paragraph formats are to the indentation of the whole paragraph and of the first line. These can be changed with the markers for the left indent, first line, and right indent on the ruler. Throughout this section, remember that paragraph indentation is always relative to page indentation, which is covered in Chapter 12.

To drag the left-indent marker without moving the first-line indicator, hold down the SHIFT key as you drag the indicator. Note that you can change measurements on the ruler whether or not the Paragraph dialog box is open, if you have the ruler showing.

In common business letters and memos, the first line of each paragraph is indented from the margin by five spaces, or about half an inch. To do this, drag the first line indicator on the ruler (the top triangle on the left) over to 1/2 inch:

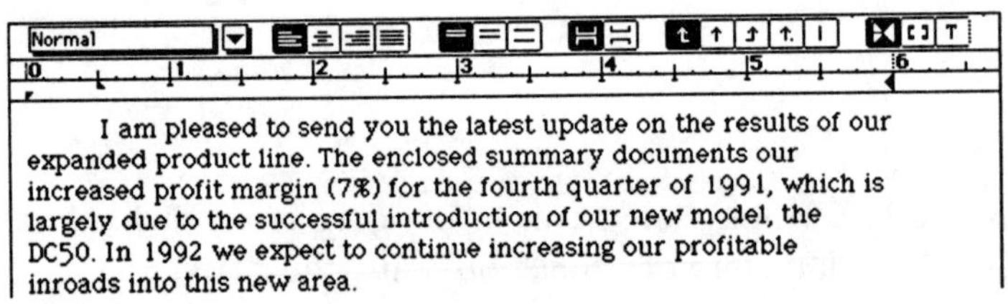

As you drag, Word displays the measurement in the page box in the lower-left corner of the window. This is a fast way of formatting paragraphs as you work; simply keep the ruler showing and make your changes there. Although the ruler only lets you specify some paragraph formatting, it is the most common formatting that you will change. When you change the indentation from the ruler, the text is automatically wrapped around, just like it is when you enter text by typing.

Instead of dragging the indicators on the ruler, type the value for the placement in the boxes labeled "Left," "Right," and "First" in the Paragraph dialog box. Using the Paragraph dialog box lets you specify values that are more exact than dragging the indicators on the ruler.

Figure 11-2. *Date indented three inches*

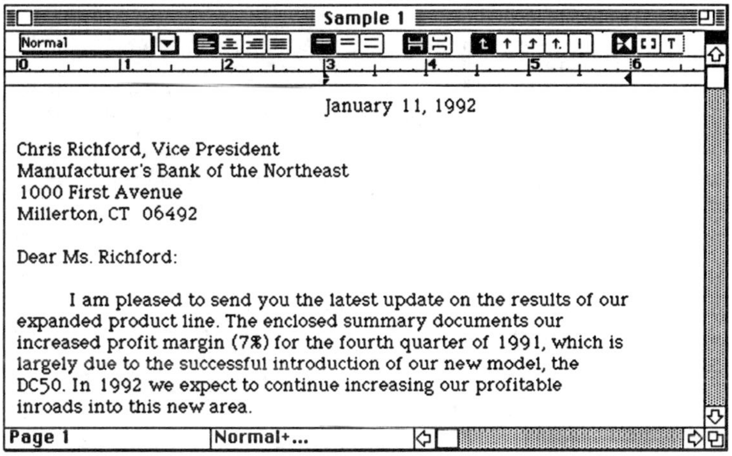

Sometimes you may want to indent an entire paragraph from the left and right margins. This is common for direct quotations in reports. Indenting is also used a great deal in letters, especially for the date and closing (remember that these are considered paragraphs in Word). On a normal typewriter, you use the (TAB) key or (SPACEBAR) to move to the place you want. In Word, you indicate the indentation from the left margin, and every new line (unless you've selected a different first-line indent) starts there.

To see how this is done, select the date at the beginning of the Sample 1 letter and drag the left indent indicator on the ruler to 3 inches. If you want to use the Paragraph dialog box, enter **3 in** (or just select the 0 and type **3**) in the Left option. Figure 11-2 shows the new position of the date. If you move the date, you will probably also indent the closing and the name and address.

The measurement indicated by the first line indicator is relative to that in the left indent indicator. For example, if you want to indent the entire first paragraph 1 inch (from the page margin), and indent the first line 1/2 inch

Figure 11-3. *New first-line indentation 1/2 inch beyond left indent*

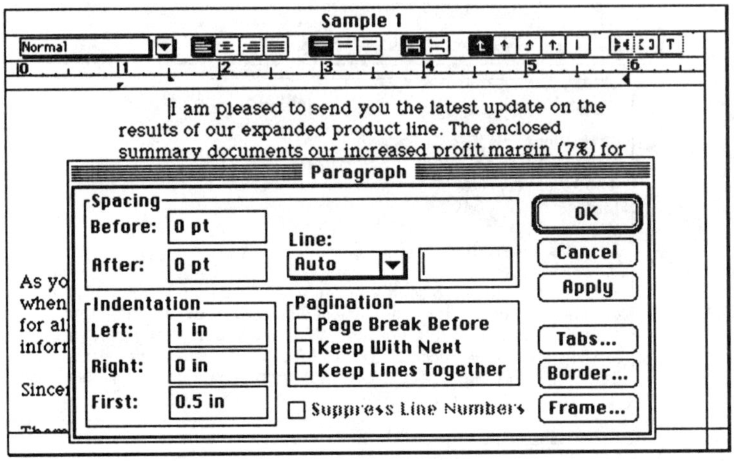

beyond that, drag the left indent to 1 inch and the first line to 1/2 inch past that. Note the result on the ruler and dialog box in Figure 11-3. If you do not want to indent the first line but want to move the entire paragraph 1 inch from the margin, you would set the left indent to 1 inch and the first line to 0 inches.

This brings up an interesting situation–what if you want the first line to start to the left of the rest of the paragraph? This format is called a *hanging indent* or an *outdent.* To see how this is formatted, select any part of the first full paragraph, give the Paragraph command, and set the Left option to 1 inch and the First option to –0.5 (negative 1/2) inch. You can also do this on the ruler. The result is shown here:

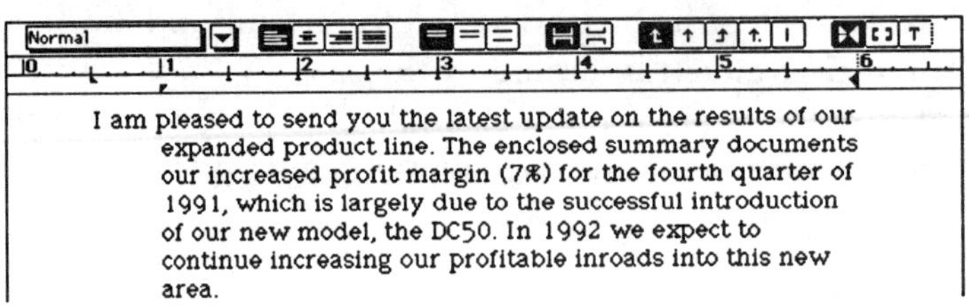

It is unlikely that you will change a paragraph's right margin unless you are also changing the left margin. Experiment by changing the right indent on the first full paragraph to 1 inch:

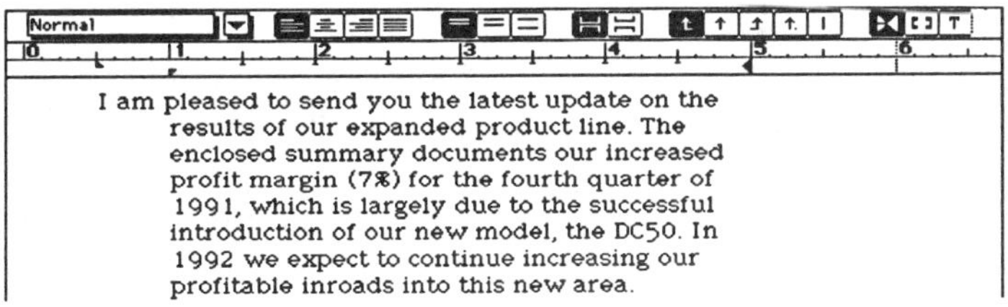

As always, the Undo command removes the effects of the last changes.

These indentation choices illustrate the reason that you want to treat related text (like an address) as one paragraph by using newline instead of (RETURN). Remember that you use newline ((SHIFT)-(RETURN)) to go to a new line without starting a new paragraph. When you change the margin with the Paragraph command, all the lines are formatted together since they are in one paragraph.

For example, assume that you want to move the lines with Thomas Mead's name, company, and address 3 inches from the left margin. If each line ends in a newline character, you can give just one command for the set of four lines, instead of having to format each line. To see how this works, change the paragraph's breaks to newline characters (if you did not use newline originally) by selecting the blank character at the end of each line:

January 11, 1992

Chris Richford, Vice President
Manufacturer's Bank of the Northeast
1000 First Avenue
Millerton, CT 06492

Replace the paragraph mark with the newline character ((SHIFT)-(RETURN)). Notice that the screen looks the same. Do this for all lines in the address except for the last. Then select or leave the insertion point in any part of this paragraph, give the Paragraph command, and set the left indent to 3 inches. All of the lines move.

Lesson 42: Line Spacing for Paragraphs

In Word you can modify the number of lines above, below, and inside a paragraph. In the examples that you have typed up to this point, you have inserted blank lines between paragraphs as if you were doing so on a typewriter–by pressing the RETURN key an extra time. Now you will see how to have Word do this automatically with the Paragraph command.

Although this method is not much easier than pressing the RETURN key a particular number of times after each paragraph, it allows you to enter text more consistently. Remember that one of the goals of using Word's formatting features is to make your documents look as consistent as possible. Instead of having to remember how many lines you want after each paragraph and pressing the RETURN key that many times, Word remembers to do this for you in the paragraph format.

To see the utility of using automatic spacing in your document, first eliminate all of the extra blank lines. You can do this by selecting the blank paragraph marks and deleting them. An easier method, however, is to move the insertion point to the beginning of the document, give the Replace command from the Edit menu, enter **^p^p** in the Find What option (to indicate two consecutive paragraph marks), and enter **^p** in the Replace With option (to indicate a single paragraph mark). This is shown in Figure 11-4.

Figure 11-4. *Replacing doubled paragraph marks with single ones to eliminate blank lines*

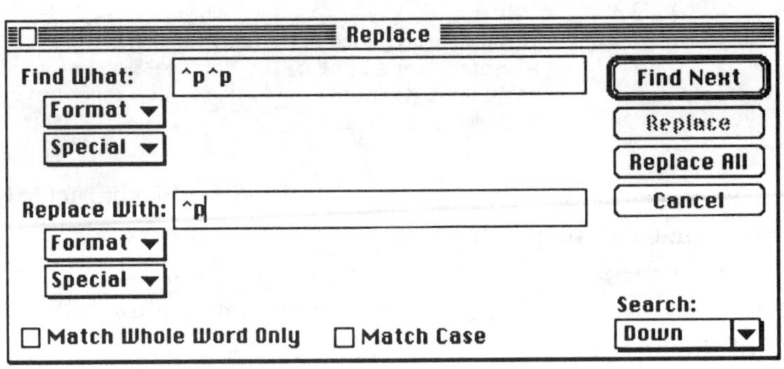

11

Figure 11-5. *Blank paragraphs removed*

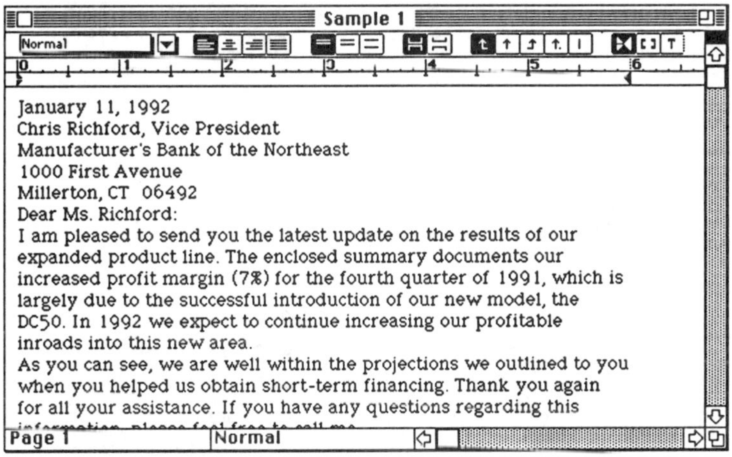

Click the Replace All button to change all the instances of the double paragraph mark. Your document now looks like Figure 11-5.

If you want to insert blank lines between paragraphs, it is usually better to specify them as space before the paragraph, not after. Thus, you should change the Before option in the Paragraph command to 12 points (the current font size) for the first text paragraph in Sample 1. The exception to this general rule is that you usually change the amount of space after headings.

You can enter the Before or After measurements in many ways. The simplest is to enter the number of points, since you usually want the space to be related to the size of the characters in the paragraph. For example, to keep a blank line before a paragraph that is in 12-point font, you would enter **12 pt** or just **12** for the Before option. You can also give the measurement in inches or lines. In this case, type **1 li** into the box. When you return to the screen, the effect is the same as 12 points. If you then look back in the After box, it shows "12 pt".

Reformat each paragraph in the letter by selecting the entire document, giving the Paragraph command, and specifying 12 points before. The result

Figure 11-6. *Double-spaced paragraph*

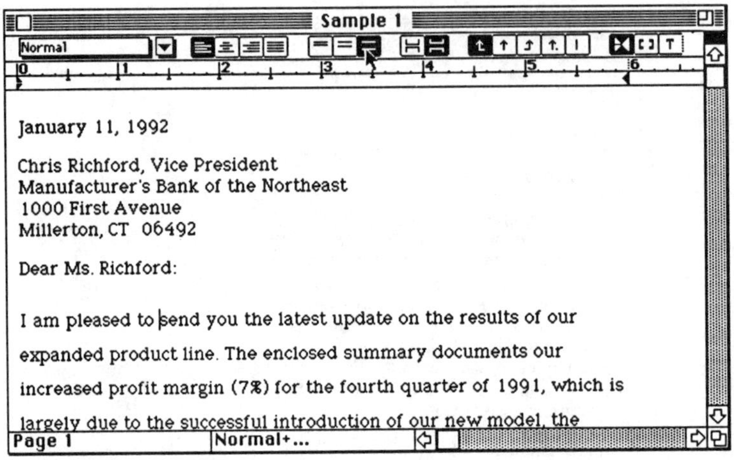

looks just like the letter with the extra blank paragraphs. However, the lines between the closing and Thomas Mead's name should be specified as two lines before the name.

The Line option in the Paragraph command allows you to specify that a particular paragraph is double- or triple-spaced. For example, to double-space a paragraph, select any part of it and type **2 li** for "Line".

You can also double-space by clicking the double-spacing icon in the ruler (the third spacing icon from the left). The result is shown in Figure 11-6. You can also click the double-space indicator on the ruler for the same result.

Word normally starts with the Line choice set to Auto. This setting lets Word adjust the line height for you if you change font sizes and gives your text a generally open look. The drop-down list under the Line option lets you change this. The two other choices are "At least", which indicates that Word should give at least the amount you specify if the font sizes change or you have superscripts and subscripts within the paragraph, and "Exactly", which means that the amount you specify is used regardless of font size and placement.

Table 11-1. *Paragraph Formatting with ⌘-Key Combinations*

Format	Key Combination
Normal	⌘-SHIFT-P
Indent first line 1/2 in.	⌘-SHIFT-F
Decrease left indent 1/2 in.	⌘-SHIFT-M
Increase left indent 1/2 in.	⌘-SHIFT-N
1/2 in. hanging indent	⌘-SHIFT-T
1 line before	⌘-SHIFT-O
Left-aligned	⌘-SHIFT-L
Justified	⌘-SHIFT-J
Centered	⌘-SHIFT-C
Right-aligned	⌘-SHIFT-R
Double-spaced	⌘-SHIFT-Y

Lesson 43: Selecting Paragraph Formatting with the ⌘ Key

With direct formatting, you can choose many of the paragraph formats with ⌘-key combinations, just as you did in Chapter 10 with character formatting. Table 11-1 shows the formats available.

As you can see, some of these key combinations, such as ⌘-SHIFT-M and ⌘-SHIFT-N, do not set an absolute format. Instead, they change the current settings of the paragraph by a small relative amount. You can use these key combinations repeatedly to move the margins.

For example, select or move the insertion point into any part of the first text paragraph of the letter; then press ⌘-SHIFT-N. Notice that the paragraph moves one-half inch:

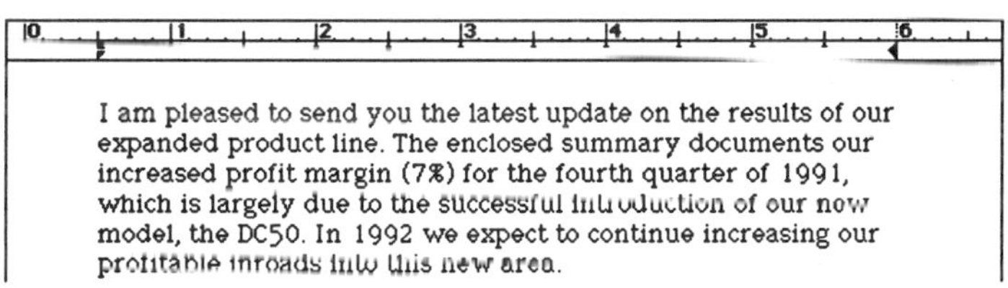

I am pleased to send you the latest update on the results of our expanded product line. The enclosed summary documents our increased profit margin (7%) for the fourth quarter of 1991, which is largely due to the successful introduction of our new model, the DC50. In 1992 we expect to continue increasing our profitable inroads into this new area.

If you press (⌘)-(SHIFT)-(N) again, the paragraph moves farther to the right:

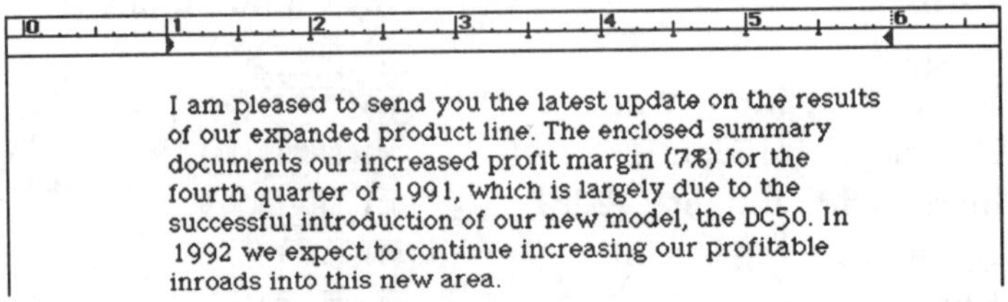

To move it back, you can use (⌘)-(SHIFT)-(M).

Lesson 44: Aligning Paragraphs and Using Keeps

All of the paragraphs you have typed in so far have been *left-aligned*. This means that each line begins all the way at the left margin (unless you have indented the paragraph) and is formatted with wordwrap, but the right margin is *ragged*, which means that if a word falls a little short of the right margin, it stays there. Books and magazines often use *justified* margins, which means that, in addition to beginning at the left margin, the lines are filled with spaces so that each one ends on the right margin (for example, this book uses justified margins). Justified text is not only easy to read, it gives a professional look to your reports.

Almost all of your writing will be either left-aligned or justified; however, Word also lets you center each line of text in a paragraph, which is often useful for headings or for text that needs to stand out on a page, such as warnings. For a trendy look, you can even format right-aligned text, which makes the left margin ragged and aligns the right margin. The four types of paragraphs (left-aligned, justified, centered, and right-aligned) are illustrated in Figure 11-7.

Clear the Sample 1 file from your screen and enter the text for each example paragraph. Then use the ruler to set the alignment by selecting part of the paragraph and clicking the desired alignment icon at the top. For example, to center-align a paragraph, you would click the second icon:

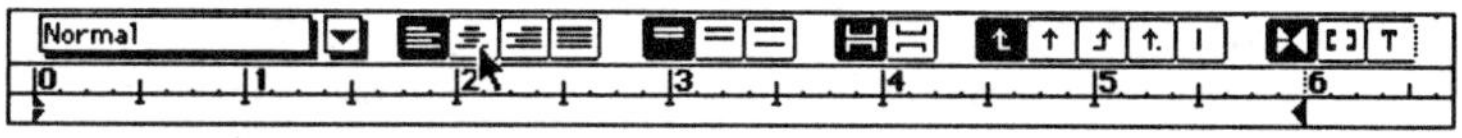

Experiment by adding text to the centered and right-aligned paragraphs to see how Word shuffles the characters as you type them.

Remember that you can use the newline character to start a new line without starting a new paragraph. You can use newline together with the centered format to make text stand out on a page. For example, enter the following text as a single paragraph with newline characters:

WARNING!
Do not use this product
without first consulting your physician.

Now center the paragraph from the ruler or by pressing ⌘-SHIFT-C. The result should look like this:

WARNING!
Do not use this product
without first consulting your physician.

Figure 11-7. *Examples of alignment*

This is a normal paragraph that is left-aligned. This means that the right margin will be ragged, but that each line begins on the left margin.

This paragraph is justified. When you finish typing each line, Word puts extra spaces on the line to make it line up with the right margin.

A centered paragraph has white space on each line equal
distance from the two margins. This is usually only used for
headings or special text.

This paragraph is right-aligned. As you can see, each line is
lined up against the right margin, but the left margin is ragged.
This is an interesting, but rarely used, format.

When you write memos and reports that are longer than one page, you may find that Word breaks the last paragraph on the page in an inappropriate place. Word automatically prevents *widows* (only the last line of a paragraph on the top of a page) and *orphans* (only the first line of a paragraph on the bottom of a page) by moving lines to or from a page as necessary. Word never leaves one line of a paragraph stranded on a page unless you deselect the Widow Control option in the Document command from the Format menu.

There are times when you want to keep the whole paragraph together—in tables or figures for instance, where blank space at the bottom of a page is preferable to splitting up the information. To keep a paragraph together, choose the Keep Lines Together option in the Pagination part of the Paragraph dialog box.

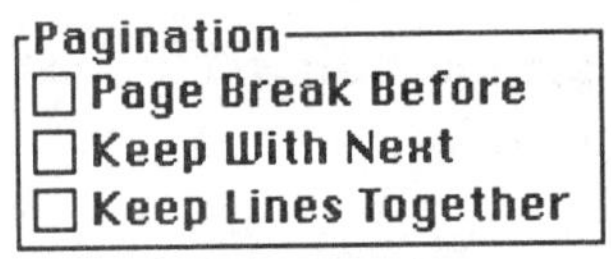

If you want to keep the selected paragraph with the paragraph that follows it, select Keep With Next in the Paragraph dialog box. This tells Word that the two paragraphs must stay on the same page, which can be useful for keeping a heading with the text that follows it or a caption under a quotation.

Lesson 45: Using Tabs

Setting up aligned columns in your text is often one of the hardest chores in word processing. Even if the tabs are set just right, your data often does not fit on the page. Adding a column of text can be nearly impossible. However, if you set the tabs correctly with Word, you will find that making columnar text is very easy. You can set your tab positions either before or after you enter your tabbed text.

There are two methods for creating tables in Word. You can set up tables with tab stops, similar to the way you might on a typewriter, or you can use the table feature. For a short columnar table, using tab stops is quick and easy. However, there are disadvantages to tabs that the table feature overcomes. For example, if you use tab stops, only the rightmost column can have text automatically wrap in the column. Also, changing the width of a column is more difficult with tab stops. This chapter shows you how to use tab stops to align columns, since they are easier to learn than the table feature. Tables are covered in Chapter 15.

You set and move tabs with the ruler. In your text, you skip to the tab stop the same way you do on a typewriter—by pressing the (TAB) key.

Word comes with a set of tabs defined as the default. These are set to every half inch. This is useful when you are typing letters and memos that don't require any special tab stops. You can change the setting for the default tab distance in the Document command from the Format menu. When you enter a new tab stop, Word automatically erases all the default tabs to the left of that new tab.

Word has four different types of tabs: *left*, *center*, *right*, and *decimal*. The type of tab indicates where the text lines up against it. A left tab is like a tab stop on a typewriter: the text begins at the tab stop and continues to the right. A right tab is the opposite of a left tab: the text starts to the left of the tab stop and ends at the tab stop.

The following example should clear up any confusion between these two types of tabs.

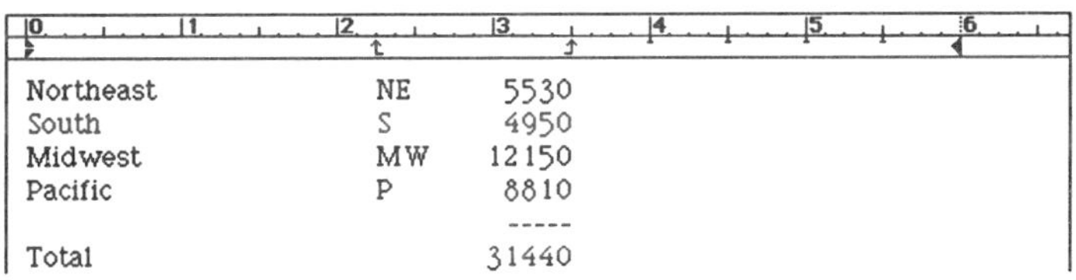

Northeast	NE	5530
South	S	4950
Midwest	MW	12150
Pacific	P	8810

Total		31440

The first tab (at 2 1/4 inches) is a left (normal) tab stop and the second (at 3 1/2 inches) is a right tab stop. Notice that the numbers in the third column (that is, after the second (TAB) character) all end at the tab. In general, left tabs are used for text and right tabs are used for numbers. Right tabs are especially useful if you include a sum for the group of numbers, because numbers of different lengths then line up correctly.

A center tab causes the text to be centered around the tab stop, much like a centered paragraph; this tab is useful for headings of columns. A decimal tab causes numbers with decimal points to line up with the decimal point on the tab.

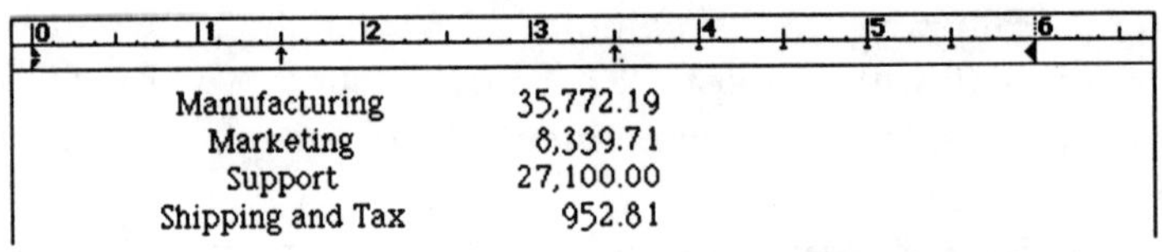

Here, the tab stop at 1.5 inches is a center tab and the tab stop at 3.5 inches is a decimal tab. These two types of tabs are used much less frequently than left and right tabs.

Word has another type of tab you should know about. The *vertical bar* is not really a tab because it does not affect the way you use tab characters, but you place it on the tab line in the ruler. Setting the vertical bar causes Word to draw a vertical line through the paragraph at that position. This is useful for drawing forms. Here is an example of using a vertical bar tab:

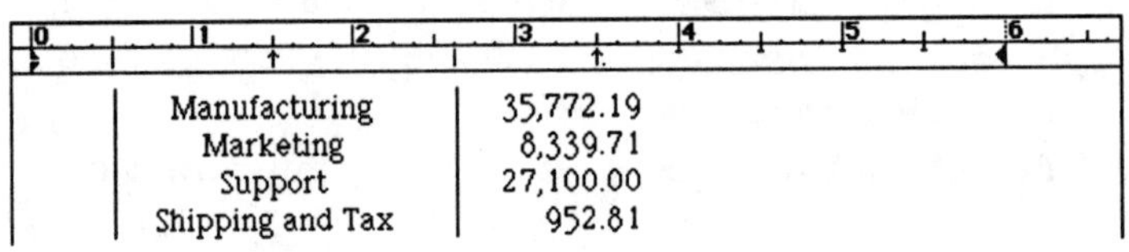

Lesson 46: Setting Tabs

Setting tabs on the ruler is fairly easy. You select the type of tab you want from the icons on the ruler:

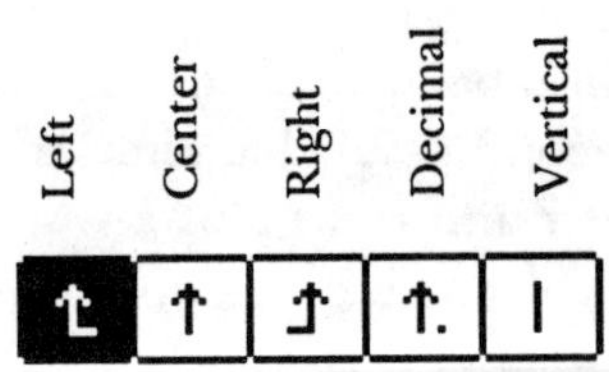

Then you point to the upper part of the ruler and click where you want the tab to be set. You can repeat this for as many tabs as you want. You can also drag the icons down to the ruler.

For example, to set a left tab at 2 1/4 inches, click the icon for the right tab stop in the ruler and drag down to the space between 2 and 2 1/2 inches in the ruler:

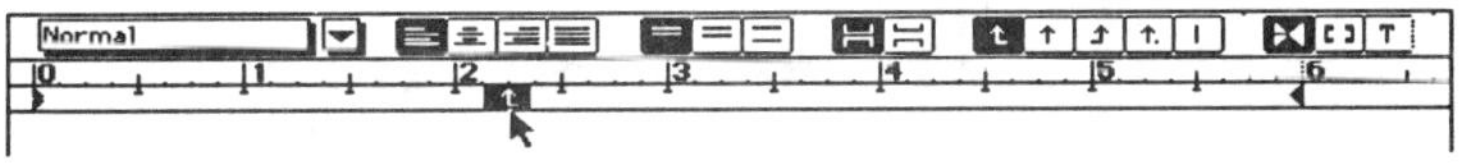

You can move a tab setting on the ruler line by dragging it around. For example, drag the tab you just set to 2 1/2 inches. To delete a tab stop, drag it down off the ruler. Set up the columns shown here for practice.

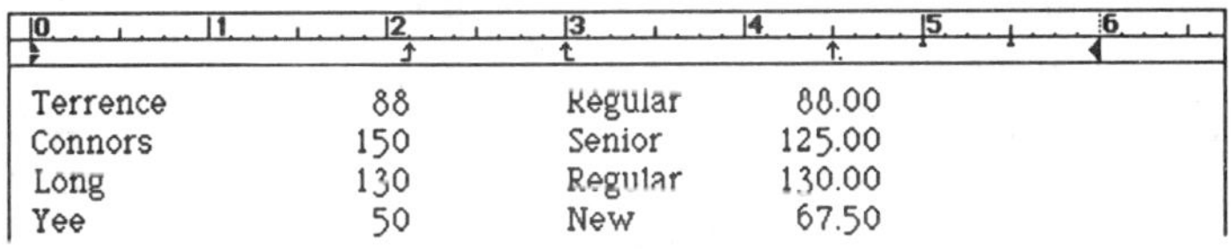

The second column is right-aligned, the third column is left-aligned, and the fourth column is decimal-aligned. (If you need help setting this up, the three tab stops are a right-aligned tab at 2 1/8 inches, a left-aligned tab at 3 inches, and a decimal-aligned tab at 4 1/2 inches.)

You can also specify a tab by clicking the Tabs button in the Paragraph dialog box. Double-clicking a tab stop in the ruler also brings up this dialog box. The Tabs dialog box looks like this:

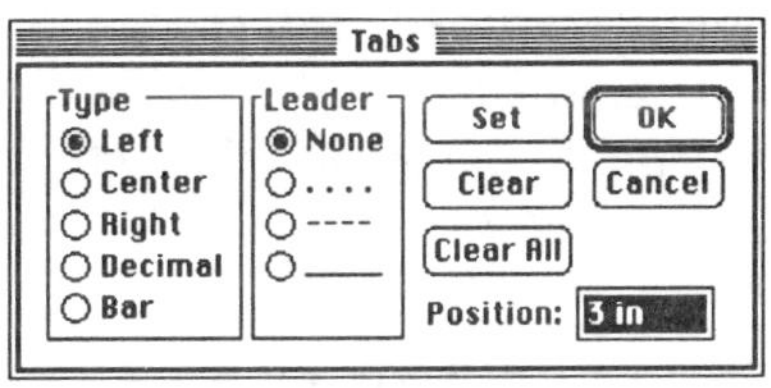

In that dialog box, select a type of tab, then enter the desired location in the Position choice. You can use this choice to fine-tune the position of a tab. For example, if you have a tab set at 1 inch and you want it at 1 1/8 inches, select the tab stop on the ruler, type **1.125** in the Position choice.

To change the type of a tab, select it on the ruler and click a different button in the Type choices. If you wish, you can clear all the tabs you have set for this paragraph by clicking the Clear All button. Be sure to select all the paragraphs that you want to work on before changing the tabs.

Lesson 47: Using Leader Characters

You may have noticed the Leader choice in the Tabs dialog box. Many columnar lists, such as financial summaries and tables of contents, often use characters to connect the columns of information across the page. These characters, usually dots, are called *leader characters* because they lead to the text at the next tab stop. Unless you specify otherwise, Word does not use a leader character.

For practice, change the first tab stop in the previous example to include a dot leader character. With the Tabs dialog box open, click the tab stop on the ruler, then choose "...." from the Leader section. The columns then look like this:

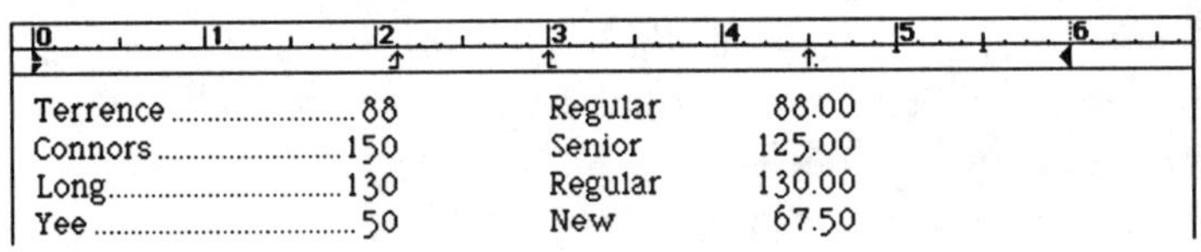

This is a great deal easier than typing all the periods yourself. It is also easy to change to another type of leader character in a column since you don't have to erase the old characters and type the new characters for each entry. For example, try changing the leader character to dashes or underscores.

Lesson 48: Working with Columns of Tabs

If you are editing a columnar list, you may want to move or delete a column of information. For example, you may want to switch two columns or add a column in the middle of your list. To make such a move you need a way of selecting a single column.

There are other times when you would want to manipulate columns of text. If you want to add a column in the middle of some other columns, you need to add a new column of tab characters.

The procedure for selecting a column of text is

1. Put the insertion point at one corner of the column. Usually, you should select a character in the upper-left corner.

Terrence	88	Regular	88.00
Connors	150	Senior	125.00
Long	130	Regular	130.00
Yee	50	New	67.50

2. Press the (OPTION) key to activate the column selection feature.
3. Extend your selection by holding down the mouse button and dragging to the other corner of the column. If you are editing a column made with tabs, be sure to include the tab characters that are before or after the column in your selection.

Terrence	88	Regular	88.00
Connors	150	Senior	125.00
Long	130	Regular	130.00
Yee	50	New	67.50

You can select more than one column at a time with this method. Word simply treats everything that you select as a single column. Note that you can select any text, not just text that is arranged in columns, in this method.

Once you have selected a column of text, you can treat it as you would any other text. You can cut it, copy it to the Clipboard, delete it, add character formatting to it, and so on.

To switch the position of two columns, select the desired column, give the Cut command, point to the first character of the column you want to paste in front of, and give the Paste command. If you want to move one column of several over to the far right, you must first make sure that in each line, the right column has a (TAB) pressed before the (RETURN) or newline. In Show ¶, this looks like a thick right arrow. Then (having already cut the column you want to move) move the insertion point in front of the top ¶ or newline and give the Paste command.

Lesson 49: Positioned Paragraphs

In a normal Word document, each paragraph appears on the page after the one that is before it. However, there are many times when you want a paragraph to appear in a particular spot on the page and for other paragraphs to flow around this. That is, you want to specify the position for the paragraph (such as "in the middle of the page, 3 inches from the left margin and 4 inches from the top margin" or "at the bottom of this column"). To do this in Word, use the Frame command from the Format menu. This is called *framing* because you move the frame of the paragraph to a position on the page.

Positioned paragraphs are often used to add interesting layout elements, such as pictures or excerpts from your text. Figure 11-8 shows how a picture in a two-column document can make the page look more interesting. You can also use positioned paragraphs for highlighting information or important quotations.

Any paragraph in Word can be positioned. If you are positioning a picture, that picture should be the only character in the paragraph. Select the paragraph and give the Frame command from the Format menu. The Frame dialog box is shown here:

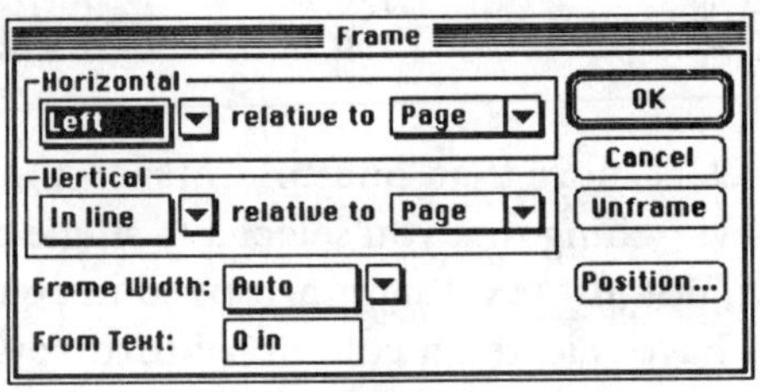

When you set the position of a paragraph, you do not see the result on the screen unless you are in page layout mode, as described in Chapter 12. For now, use the Frame command to set the paragraph and then click the Position button in that dialog box to see the result. The different views of the screen are explained more fully in Chapter 12.

When you define a paragraph's position, you specify both the horizontal and vertical positions. These measurements can be relative to the margin or to the edge of the page; the horizontal position can also be relative to the column (columns are described in Chapter 12). For example, to center a

Figure 11-8. *Picture in the middle of a two-column document*

I. Introduction

National Generators has the opportunity over the next five years to take a commanding lead in our established markets and to penetrate a new market, the construction industry, where our products will be particularly attractive. This report is intended to provide an overview of the company's business development strategies along with a description of those areas for which we require funding.

National Generators can become the premier producer of electrical generation equipment for the entertainment and exposition industries. Our portable yet sturdy generators have acquired a solid reputation in these fields. As the number of outdoor concerts, large conventions, and other events that use portable generators continues to increase each year, we will be better able than our competitors to satisfy the demand for reliable equipment.

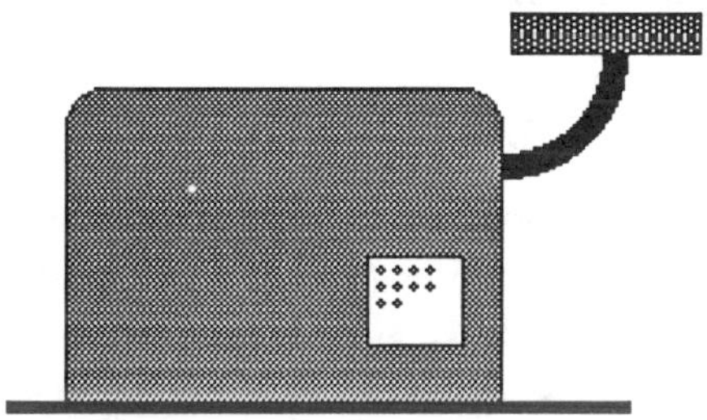

While accelerating efforts aimed at our existing base of industrial users, we propose to enter the construction industry. We have already begun developing a small, quiet generator for this market. Research is also underway to design a larger, more efficient generator for heavy construction projects that can replace several smaller ones.

II. Market Analysis

National Generators currently has a 42% share of the markets we now serve. Our nearest competitor, Regional Outdoor Electricity, has 34%, with the rest divided among other manufacturers. We believe that our superior products will insure that we will increase our share of the entertainment and exposition industries' needs for portable generators. Some of our smaller competitors will be unable to match our new technology, and we will pick up their business.

Over the next five years we anticipate gaining 15% of the market for generators in the construction industry.[1] Two important trends favor our planned new products over any now available or known to be coming on the market. Anti-noise pollution legislation restricts the level of noise at urban construction sites, while OSHA legislation protects workers from damage to their hearing caused by equipment.

III. Expansion Costs

In order to carry out the entrance into the construction industry and to keep ahead of growth in the entertainment and exposition industries, we will require $4MM to be allocated in three areas:

picture in the bottom of the text area, you could specify a horizontal position of "centered" relative to the margins and a vertical position of "bottom" relative to the margin. You can also specify a measurement for the position, such as "3.25 inches from the left margin" or "2 inches from the top margin."

To experiment with positioning graphics, create a small logo for National Generators like this:

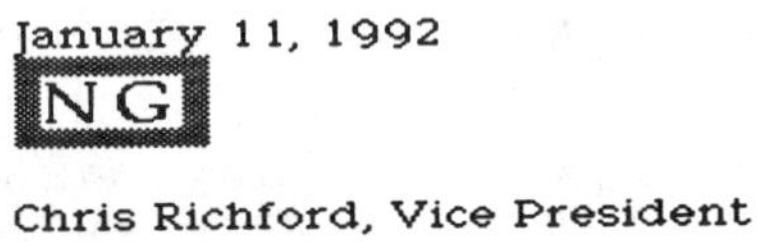

You can do this by creating a blank paragraph near the beginning of the document and giving the Picture command from the Insert menu, as described in Chapter 7. Select the picture and give the Frame command from the Format menu.

The choices for horizontal position are Left, Center, Right, Inside, and Outside. Inside and Outside refer to even- and odd-numbered pages, described in the next chapter. If you choose Left, Right, Inside, or Outside and set the Relative To choice to Page, Word can position the object outside of the margins. The choices for vertical position are In Line (that is, at the position that it would appear after the preceding paragraph), Top, Center, and Bottom. For both choices, you can also type a measurement.

For instance, select the logo, give the Frame command, and specify that the paragraph should be centered horizontally and 2 inches from the top, as shown here:

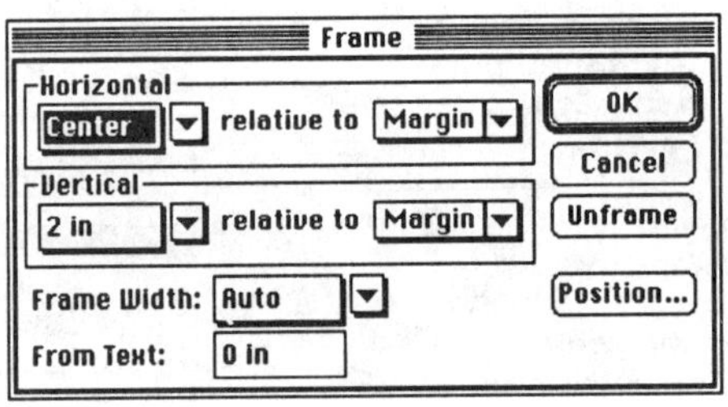

The result when printed would look like Figure 11-9.

The From Text choice specifies how far the edge of the paragraph is from the text that surrounds it. Giving a larger number specifies more white space around the graphic.

Figure 11-9. *Logo placed in a document*

January 11, 1992

Chris Richford, Vice President
Manufacturer's Bank of the Northeast
1000 First Avenue
Millerton, CT 06492

Dear Ms. Richford:

I am pleased to send you the latest update on the results of our expanded product line. The enclosed summary documents our increased profit margin (7%) for the fourth quarter of 1991, which is largely due to the successful introduction of our new model, the DC50. In 1992 we expect to continue increasing our profitable inroads into this new area.

As you can see, we are well within the projections we outlined to you when you helped us obtain short-term financing. Thank you again for all your assistance. If you have any questions regarding this information, please feel free to call me.

Sincerely,

Thomas Mead, Controller
National Generators
1275 Oak Glen Industrial Park
Oak Glen, CT 06410

The Frame Width choice sets the width of the positioned paragraph; this affects how text flows around the paragraph. You can set the paragraph width either with the indents in the Paragraph command or here, in the Frame dialog box. For a graphic, the width should be Auto. For text, you may want to change the width depending on how much text you have.

So far, you have only seen how to position graphics. You may also want to position paragraphs of text, such as quotations. You use the same methods for text paragraphs as you do for graphics.

Figure 11-10 shows a page with a text paragraph positioned. Here is the Frame dialog box for that paragraph:

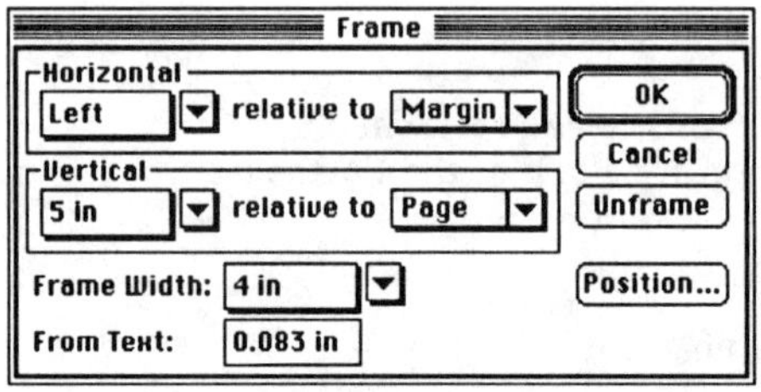

The paragraph has a border, described later in this chapter.

Lesson 50: Copying Paragraph Formats

In Chapter 10 you learned how to copy character formats from one set of characters to other sets; here you will learn the similar process for copying paragraph formats. Remember that character formats are copied by selecting the text with the format that you want to apply, pressing ⌘-OPTION-V and pressing RETURN. Paragraph formats are copied in much the same way, except that you select the paragraph you want to copy the format from instead of selecting just the characters.

Lesson 51: Highlighting Paragraphs with Borders

Word lets you emphasize a paragraph by surrounding it with a border or by placing a bar above it, below it, or next to it. You have a wide selection of borders and bars. To add a border to a paragraph, select any part of the paragraph and give the Borders command from the Format menu. Word displays the dialog box shown in Figure 11-11, which lets you place lines and select the distance from text, line type, and shading.

You can add lines to the top, bottom, left, and right of a paragraph; if you select all four, you put the paragraph in a box. To select a line to add, click

Figure 11-10. *Paragraph with border in the middle of a two-column document*

Excerpts from a Proposal for Bank Funding

I. Introduction

National Generators has the opportunity over the next five years to take a commanding lead in our established markets and to penetrate a new market, the construction industry, where our products will be particularly attractive. This report is intended to provide an overview of the company's business development strategies along with a description of those areas for which we require funding.

National Generators can become the premier producer of electrical generation equipment for heavy construction projects that can replace several smaller ones.

II. Market Analysis

National Generators currently has a 42% share of the markets we now serve. Our nearest competitor, Regional Outdoor Electricity, has 34%, with the rest divided among other manufacturers. We believe that our superior products will insure that we will increase our share of the entertainment and exposition industries' needs for portable generators. Some of our smaller competitors will be unable to match our new technology, and we will pick up their business.

We believe that our superior products will insure that we will increase our share of the entertainment and exposition industries' needs for portable generators.

the entertainment and exposition industries. Our portable yet sturdy generators have acquired a solid reputation in these fields. As the number of outdoor concerts, large conventions, and other events that use portable generators continues to increase each year, we will be better able than our competitors to satisfy the demand for reliable equipment.

While accelerating efforts aimed at our existing base of industrial users, we propose to enter the construction industry. We have already begun developing a small, quiet generator for this market. Research is also underway to design a larger, more efficient generator for

Over the next five years we anticipate gaining 15% of the market for generators in the construction industry.[1] Two important trends favor our planned new products over any now available or known to be coming on the market. Anti-noise pollution legislation restricts the level of noise at urban construction sites, while OSHA legislation protects workers from damage to their hearing caused by equipment.

III. Expansion Costs

In order to carry out the entrance into the construction industry and to keep ahead of growth in the entertainment and exposition industries, we will require $4MM to be allocated in three areas:

1. Research and development of new products

Figure 11-11. *Borders dialog box*

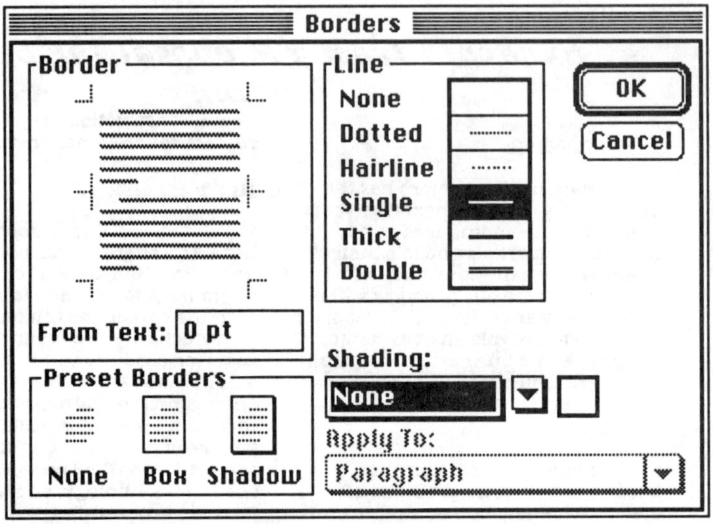

between the guides in the dialog box. To deselect a line, click None in the Preset Borders box. You can also choose from the three preset border types (none, simple box, or shadowed box) from the lower-left hand corner of the dialog box.

You can also add lines between paragraphs. If you select two paragraphs and double-click outside the guides, Word puts both paragraphs in a single box. However, if you want a line between the boxes, click between the center guides, as shown in Figure 11-12.

Each line can have a line style, selected from the choices at the right side of the dialog box. A hairline appears as a single line, but prints as a thinner line on laser printers such as the LaserWriter.

The From Text choice lets you specify how far outside the paragraph the lines should be drawn. Normally, Word puts lines 2 points outside the paragraph. If you put a measurement in the Spacing box, Word adds that measurement to the normal 2 points and draws the line out that far. If you want to change the setting, select None in Preset Borders and start over.

Figure 11-12. *Specifying a line between paragraphs*

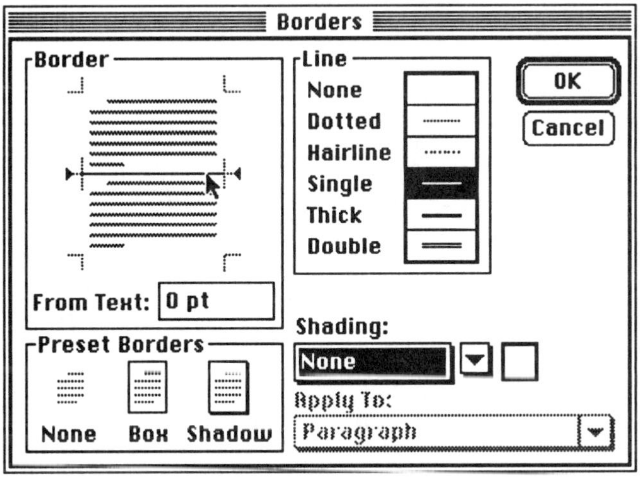

The Shading drop-down list lets you select an amount of shading to put behind the paragraph. This is rarely used since almost any level of shading makes it hard to read the text. Due to the way that most laser printers are designed, any choice other than 10 or 12.5 percent comes out much too dark.

Review

Add paragraph formatting to your Magazine file. Experiment with combinations of first line and left indentations.

Add a numbered list of steps you perform in a task in your job to the bottom of the Magazine file. Type **1.**, press (TAB), then type the first step. Press (RETURN), type **2.**, press (TAB), and so on. Make sure at least one step takes more than one line. Select the steps and give them hanging indent formatting so that the numbers appear to the left of the steps and all lines in the steps line up vertically.

12

Formatting Sections and Documents

This chapter describes the two remaining types of formatting: section and document formatting. *Section* formatting lets you specify such things as newspaper column headers and footers, while *document* formatting specifies things like page margins and footnote placement.

Lesson 52: Using Word's View Modes

Section and document formatting characteristics do not show up in Word's normal mode. Word has many viewing modes. Section and page formatting are only visible in some of the modes. Except for the section marker, none of the section formats appear in normal mode. For example, if you specify the placement of the page number at the bottom of each page, you won't see the number on the screen, only on the printed page.

There are three main view modes:

- *Normal* mode is the view you have seen so far. You can edit in this mode, but you do not see section and document formatting. This is sometimes called *galley mode*.
- *Page layout* mode also lets you edit your document, and you can also see section and document formatting.
- *Print preview* mode lets you see how your pages will look with all their formatting when printed, but you cannot edit in this mode.

(There is another mode, *outline* mode, described in Chapter 17.)

The page layout and print preview modes let you see exactly how your document will look when it is printed. Even though what you see on the screen in normal mode is generally what your document looks like when printed, it is not exact. For instance, you cannot see where the margins are positioned or how absolutely positioned paragraphs will appear when viewing in normal mode.

Using the page layout and print preview modes is faster than printing out your documents, and it doesn't waste paper. You can use these modes at any time. The difference between the two modes is that page layout mode lets you edit your document, while print preview mode only lets you look at it and change the margins.

Page Layout Mode

If you need to see how your page will look as you edit, page layout mode is very useful, although it reduces Word's performance. This is because Word has to make many more calculations about placement of text as you edit or scroll. On fast Macintoshes, this is not very noticeable, but page layout mode is often difficult to use on slower Macs.

To switch from normal mode to page layout mode, give the Page Layout command from the View menu. This page layout window is similar to the normal mode window. However, the few differences help you navigate easily around the pages in your document.

In page layout mode, you can edit your text as well as other parts of the page that you cannot see in normal mode. For example, you can edit the headers and page numbers, which are described later in this chapter. In addition, you can see where positioned paragraphs will appear when printed. This helps you place these paragraphs exactly where you want them.

One major difference in page layout mode is the addition of two arrows with dots in them along the bottom of the window:

The arrows with dots let you quickly scroll up and down a full page.

You can also add boundary lines around text items by choosing the View option in the Preferences command from the Tools menu. Boundaries surround such parts of text as headers, tables, positioned paragraphs, and so on.

If you have a larger screen, you may find it useful to split the window into two panes—one in normal mode and the other in page layout mode. Splitting the window is covered in detail in Chapter 3. This can help you enter text quickly in normal mode but still see the exact results in page layout mode. To do this, drag the split bar down the window, select some text in one part of the window, and give the Page Layout command.

In page layout mode, you can use the keys on the keypad to move quickly around the screen. Table 12-1 shows the keys that move around the text areas

Table 12-1. *Keys for Page Layout Mode*

Key	Moves to
⌘-OPTION-keypad-4	Text area left
⌘-OPTION-keypad-6	Text area right
⌘-OPTION-keypad-8	Text area above
⌘-OPTION-keypad-2	Text area below
⌘-OPTION-keypad-9	Preceding text area
⌘-OPTION-keypad-3	Next text area
⌘-OPTION-keypad-7	First text area
⌘-OPTION-keypad-1	Last text area

on the screen. If you have only one text area (that is, no positioned paragraphs or headings), they have no effect.

Print Preview Mode

The print preview mode has a much more limited use than the page layout mode. You enter print preview mode by giving the Print Preview command from the File menu. Generally, you only use it if you want to check the positioning on one or a few pages. When you give the Print Preview command, Word opens a new window, as shown in Figure 12-1. To close the Print Preview window, click either the Page Layout or Close button to go to page layout or normal modes, respectively.

To scroll through the pages of your document while in print preview mode, click the scroll bar on the right of this window. You can also drag the scroll box to go to a specific page. As you drag the scroll box, the page indicator at the top of the window tells you the page or pages that will appear when you let go of the mouse button.

Figure 12-1. *Print Preview window*

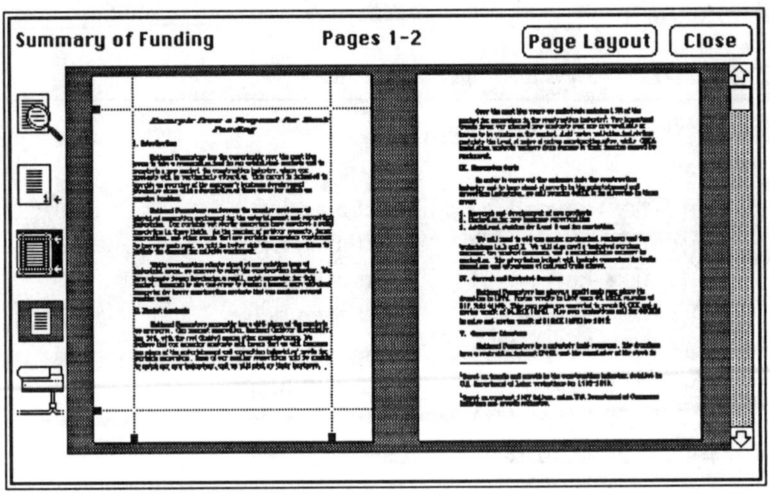

The five icons on the left of the window (from the top) are:

- Magnify icon
- Page number icon
- Margins icon
- Single-to-double page layout icon
- Print icon

The magnify icon lets you see an enlargement of a specific part of a page that you are viewing. Click the icon, and then click the part of the page you want to see enlarged. You can go back to the less magnified view by clicking the icon again or double-clicking in the middle of the page.

The page number and margins icons are used to change the location of the page numbers and the margins. These topics are discussed later in this chapter. You can change the margins by clicking the margins icon, and dragging the squares at the end of the margin lines. To see the effect of your changes, double-click the page after dragging the margin line.

If the paper you are using is larger than 8 1/2 x 11 inches, or if you are using a large-screen Macintosh, you may want to use the single-page display mode instead of the double-page display that is the default. This lets you see the text on the page more clearly. To switch, click the single-to-double page layout icon.

The print icon lets you print directly from the Print Preview window. Clicking this icon brings up the standard Print command dialog box, as described in Chapter 8.

Lesson 53: Introduction to Sections

So far you have learned how to format characters and paragraphs to improve their appearance. The third unit of formatting is the *section*, which allows you to specify the page formatting of your text when it is printed out. Page formatting, often called *page layout*, generally consists of setting the page margins and the position of the headers and footers (the text at the top and bottom of each page, such as the chapter name and the page number).

Most often you will use the same page layout throughout a document. Sometimes, however, you may use a few different page layouts in one document. For example, the preface of a report may have different page number formatting than the main text. Word lets you change the page layout for each section (which generally can be considered a "chapter").

If you want your document to be one long section, you do not need to do anything special. To split a document into two sections, put the insertion point where you want the section break and give the Section Break command from the Insert menu or press ⌘-ENTER. If you are in normal mode (but not if you're in page layout mode), Word displays a double dotted line:

You can get rid of the section mark with Undo, if you've just done it, or you can put the insertion point in front of the first text that follows the double dotted line and BACKSPACE over it.

Use the Section command from the Format menu to change the format for a section. The formatting characteristics of each section are kept in the section marker at the end of the section, just as paragraph characteristics are stored in the markers at the end of a paragraph. You can also bring up the Section command by double-clicking the section mark. A section mark holds the section formatting for the section preceding the mark.

When you give the Section command, you see the Section dialog box shown in Figure 12-2. The Start option, which specifies where to start the beginning of the section, lets you choose whether you want the section to continue on the same page as the previous section or to start on a different page. These choices are defined in Table 12-2.

Table 12-2. *Choices for Beginning a New Section*

Choice	Result
No Break	Continues from previous section without break
New Column	Starts section in the next column (multicolumn text)
New Page	Starts section on the next page
Even Page	Starts section on the next even page
Odd Page	Starts section on the next odd page

Figure 12-2. *Section dialog box*

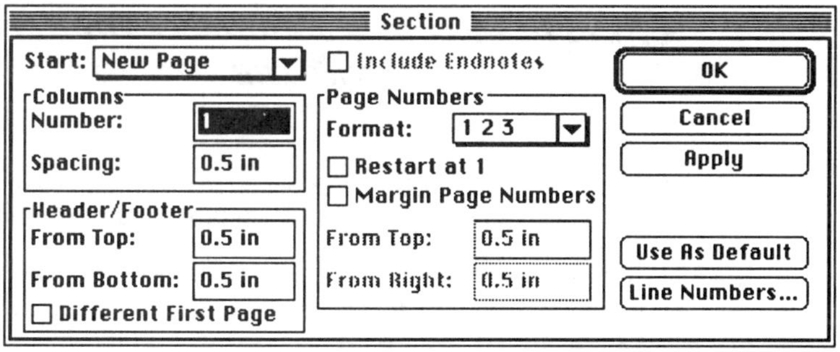

Figure 12-3 is the beginning of a summary for a funding proposal. It is used to illustrate formatting throughout this chapter and the next one. You do not need to type the report into Word; however, you may want to type in sections when trying out the examples.

Lesson 54: Page Numbering

If you want the page number to appear on each page in your document, you have two choices:

- Page numbers in the margin
- Page numbers in headers and footers

The main difference between these two is that margin page numbers are easier to insert in your document, but page numbers in headers and footers are much more flexible.

You should use margin page numbers when you want page numbers with no elaboration at the edge of your pages. It is quick and easy to specify margin page numbers. However, it is likely that you will use page numbers in headers and footers much more often because you can modify the page number there easily, for example, adding the word "Page" before the number.

Figure 12-3. *Funding proposal summary*

Excerpts from a Proposal for Bank Funding

I. Introduction

National Generators has the opportunity over the next five years to take a commanding lead in our established markets and to penetrate a new market, the construction industry, where our products will be particularly attractive. This report is intended to provide an overview of the company's business development strategies along with a description of those areas for which we require funding.

National Generators can become the premier producer of electrical generation equipment for the entertainment and exposition industries. Our portable yet sturdy generators have acquired a solid reputation in these fields. As the number of outdoor concerts, large conventions, and other events that use portable generators continues to increase each year, we will be better able than our competitors to satisfy the demand for reliable equipment.

While accelerating efforts aimed at our existing base of industrial users, we propose to enter the construction industry. We have already begun developing a small, quiet generator for this market. Research is also underway to design a larger, more efficient generator for heavy construction projects that can replace several smaller ones.

II. Market Analysis

National Generators currently has a 42% share of the markets we now serve. Our nearest competitor, Regional Outdoor Electricity, has 34%, with the rest divided among other manufacturers. We believe that our superior products will insure that we will increase our share of the entertainment and exposition industries' needs for portable generators. Some of our smaller competitors will be unable

Both page numbering methods use the Page Numbers choices in the Section dialog box:

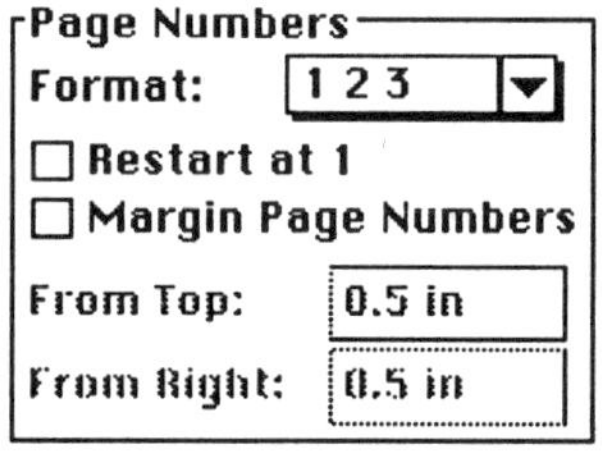

The Format and Restart at 1 options apply to both types of page numbers.

Page numbering can start at 1 in each section or at the number after the last page of the previous section. If you do not choose the Restart at 1 option, Word continues numbering from the previous section in the file; if this is the first section, it starts at 1.

You can also choose a format for page numbers. This is extremely useful when you submit articles and reports for publication, because many publishers have guidelines about the format of page numbers. Table 12-3 shows the formats for the page numbers that are available on Word.

Margin Page Numbers

To specify margin page numbers, select the Margin Page Numbers choice in this dialog box and specify a position in the From Top and From Right choices.

If you want margin page numbers, you have to decide where you want them in the From Top and From Right choices. The measurements here are from the edge of the page. If you want just the page number in the report,

Table 12-3. *Page Number Formats*

Format	Choice
Numeric	1 2 3
Roman (upper)	I II III
Roman (lower)	i ii iii
Alphabetic (upper)	A B C
Alphabetic (lower)	a b c

you can, for example, place it in the lower-right corner of each page, about 8 inches down and 1/4 inch to the right from the edge of the page.

If you wish, you can create and position a margin page number in print preview mode. To do this, give the Print Preview command, and then click the page number icon. You can now click it any place on the page to position it. Word automatically updates the placement of margin page numbers in the Section command. You can also select the page number in page preview mode and drag it around. This method lets you experiment easily with different placements.

Page Numbers in Headers and Footers

For page numbers in headers and footers, do not select Margin Page Numbers. Instead, use the Open Header and Open Footer commands described in the next lesson.

Lesson 55: Using Headers and Footers

Word allows you to put headers and footers at both the top and bottom of the page and to change their text as often as you want. Your headers and footers can be more than one paragraph, or they can be just a page number on the page.

The concept of odd and even pages is basic to many choices in section and document formatting, particularly in headers and footers. If you examine books and magazines, you find that they always begin on the right page (for example, look at the beginning of this book). This means that all right-hand pages have odd numbers (1, 3, 5, and so on) and all left-hand pages have even numbers (2, 4, 6, and so on).

Knowing whether a page is odd or even often helps in formatting your pages, as you will see in this chapter. You only need to specify a difference between even and odd pages if your document will eventually be printed *back-to-back* or *double-sided*, meaning on both sides of a piece of paper. If your document will only be on one side of the paper, you can ignore the difference between even and odd pages. If you use margin page numbers, you cannot differentiate between odd and even pages for the page number placement.

To tell Word to differentiate between odd and even pages, you must select the Even/Odd Headers option in the Document command of the Format menu. This is shown in Figure 12-4.

A header or footer can appear on odd or even pages. You can also specify that the first page of a section will also have a unique header and footer. Depending on your requirements, you can have up to six different headers and footers in a document. Often, however, you will have similar or identical text at the top or bottom of even or odd pages or no text at all.

Using page numbers in headers and footers is more flexible than margin page numbers. This allows you to quickly change the positioning by changing the format of just the header or footer instead of having to change the entire section format. Using headers and footers also makes it possible to include text around the page number, as in "Page 5" or "-5-".

Creating headers and footers is fairly easy. First, decide what information you want to present; then decide which part of that information should be at the top or bottom of the page. If you are in normal mode, you can enter the text in the window opened by the Header and Footer commands in the View menu. If you are in page layout mode, you can type the text directly in your document.

Within the paragraphs that are headers and footers, you can use any character or paragraph formatting you want. For instance, you might have a

Figure 12-4. *Document dialog box (note the Even/Odd Headers option)*

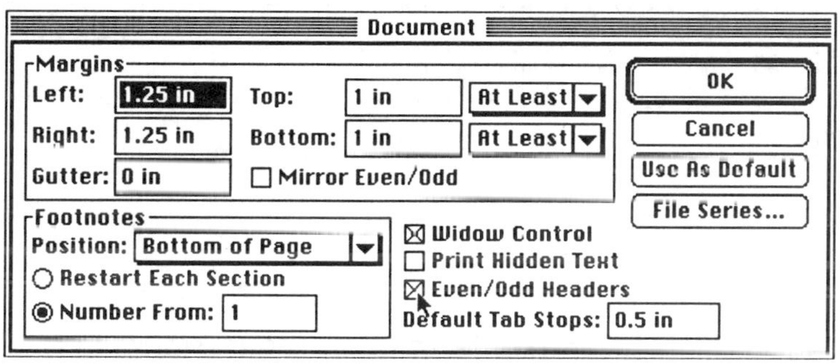

chapter name in bold and the page number in italics. You can use paragraph formatting to line up the parts of the header or footer with the margins or to center them between the margins. Tab stops, described in Chapter 11, are especially helpful here.

The Header and Footer windows look like other text windows. Figure 12-5 shows a typical footer window. The three icons at the left of the top of the window let you enter the page number, date of printing, and time of printing, respectively, in your header without having to use glossary entries. For instance, to have a footer that says "Page" and the page number, type **Page**, a space, and click the page number icon. Alternatively, you could use the "page number" entry from the glossary.

Header and Footer windows also include a Same As Previous button. This is one of the most confusing features in Word, since it is sometimes not available. You use the Same As Previous button if you want the header or footer that you are editing to be the same as the one in the previous section. When you create a new section in a document, Word automatically copies all the headers and footers to that new section, so this button does not normally need to be used. If the header you are viewing is already the same as that in the previous section, the button is dimmed, indicating that you cannot click it.

For example, if you want to show just the page number and chapter name on a page, you may want the chapter name centered at the top and the page number centered at the bottom. Figure 12-6 shows this format for the second page of the report.

Figure 12-5. *Footer window*

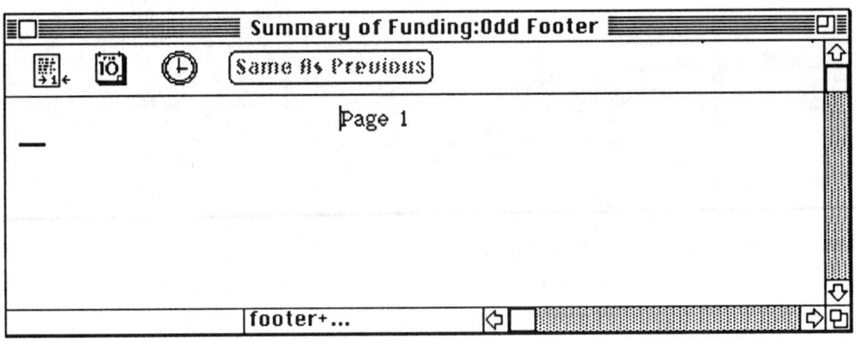

Figure 12-6. *Header and footer on page*

Market Analysis

legislation protects workers from damage to their hearing caused by equipment.

III. Expansion Costs

In order to carry out the entrance into the construction industry and to keep ahead of growth in the entertainment and exposition industries, we will require $4MM to be allocated in three areas:

1. Research and development of new products
2. Marketing for new business opportunities
3. Additional staffing for R and D and for marketing.

We will need to add one senior mechanical engineer and two technicians in R and D. We will also need a technical services manager, two product managers, and a merchandising manager in marketing. The advertising budget will include campaigns in trade magazines and attendance at national trade shows.

IV. Current and Projected Earnings

National Generators has shown a profit each year since its founding in 1974. Pretax profits in 1987 were $3.25MM on sales of $17.5MM (20%). This year sales are expected to reach $19MM and a pretax profit of $4.2MM (22%). Five year projections call for $50MM in sales and pretax profit of $12MM (25%) by 1993.[2]

V. Company Directors

National Generators is a privately held company. The founders have a controlling interest (70%), and the remainder of the stock is held by the Joffee Group and Japanese-American Enterprises. The members of the board of directors are:

Samuel Ross, President (founder)
Albert Normandy, V.P., research and development (founder)
Irene Yashimoto, V.P., operations
Philip Bushnell, V.P., marketing
Hon. Louise B. Dart, The Joffee Group
Yuji Ko, Japanese-American Enterprises

---

[1] Based on trends and growth in the construction industry, detailed in U.S. Department of Labor projections for 1985-1990.

Page 2

You next specify the header and footer positions. You can specify the position in the Section command, or you can modify them visually in print preview mode. In the Section command, the Header/Footer choices look like this:

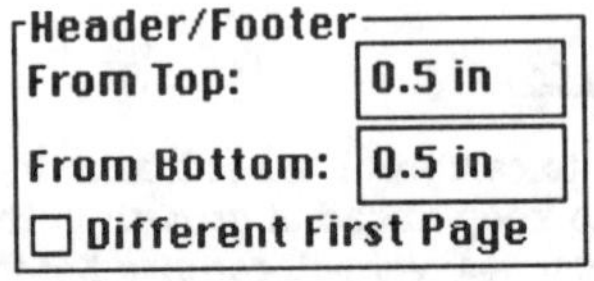

Enter values for From Top and From Bottom to place the header and footer.

In the Print Preview window, you change the header and footer positions by dragging the header and footer text area around. Give the Print Preview command, click the margins icon, select the header or footer text area as shown in Figure 12-7, drag it up or down to the new position you want, and double-click the page to reformat the document.

Next, decide if there should be a distinction between even and odd pages. If you will have different headers on even and odd pages, you should put the

Figure 12-7. *Header selected in print preview mode*

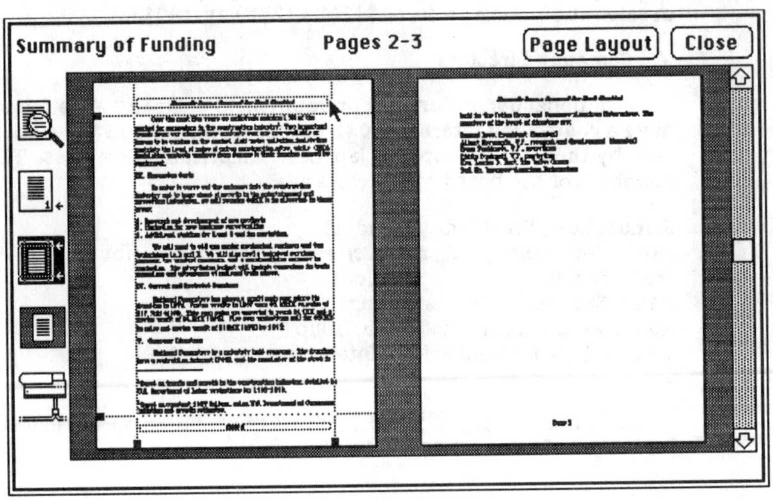

headers and footers on the right side of odd-numbered pages and the left side of even-numbered pages so that the information appears on the outside edge of the printed document. Again, look at a few books to see how this is done.

Finally, decide whether you want headers and footers on the first page of the section. You usually do not want a header, since a header distracts the reader from the chapter title. If you want different headers and footers on the first page of a section, select Different First Page in the Section command.

Now you can actually create the header. Here are the steps for creating the header, "Funding Proposal, page ", and the page number on the right side of the page (for odd pages):

1. Be sure the Even/Odd Headers option of the Document command is selected. If it is, you see four commands near the bottom of the View menu, as shown here:

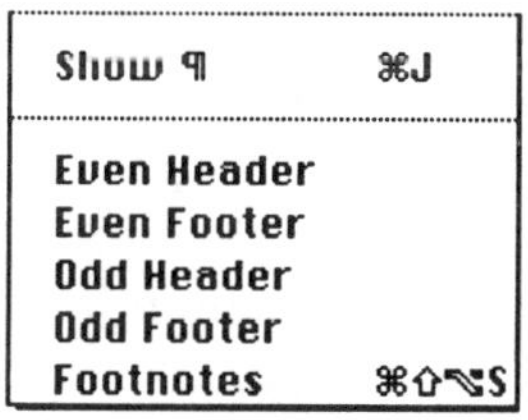

   If you have the Different First Page option selected in the Section dialog box for this section, you see two more commands on the menu: First Header and First Footer. Note that if you are in page layout mode, you only see the Header and Footer commands.

2. Give the Odd Header command to open the window shown in Figure 12-8. Note that the title of the window tells you which header or footer you are editing.
3. Add the text **Funding Proposal, page** followed by a space.
4. Click the page number icon at the left near the top of the Odd Header window. Word inserts the page number in the heading. Don't worry that it shows an actual page number; the real page number will appear when you print.
5. Click the close box of the Header window.

Figure 12-8. *Odd Header window*

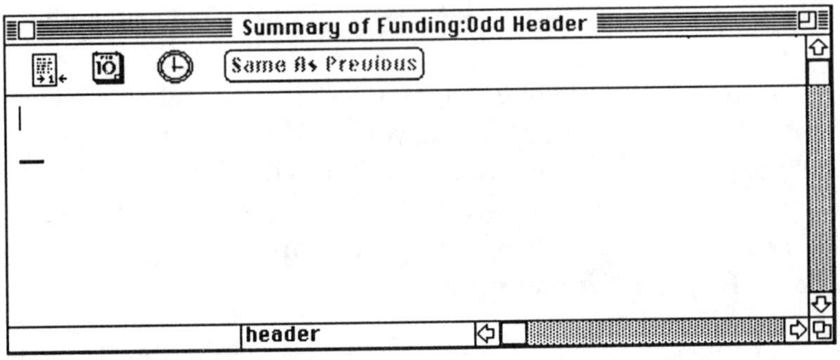

6. Give the Section command and specify the location you want the header to appear on the page, such as **1 in**.

Enter other headers and footers in the same way.

You can change the text of the headers and footers in page layout mode simply by editing the text. Remember that headers and footers are the same throughout a section, so changing the text of a header or footer on one page in page layout mode changes that text for the rest of the section as well.

Lesson 56: Creating Text with Newspaper Columns

You can use Word to print out newsletters and other material formatted with two or more columns on a page. These columns are called *newspaper* columns, since they snake on the page as in newspapers. When you use more than one column, Word adjusts whatever formatting commands you have given so that they work within the columns.

It is usually convenient to edit in page layout mode if you are editing a document that has two or more columns and many headings. Using this mode lets you see if a heading is falling near the bottom of a column and how the columns balance out.

The Section command has two choices for producing multicolumn text:

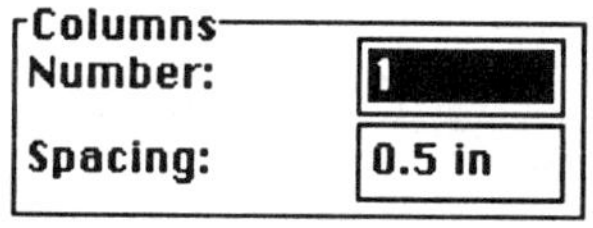

Number is the number of columns you want in this section and Spacing is the amount of white space between two columns in the columns box.

For example, to make a three-column document with 1/4 inch between columns, set the characteristics as

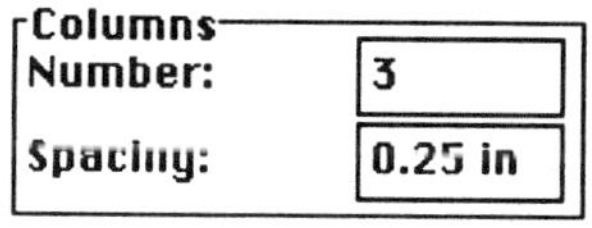

Word will calculate the column widths. Remember that you will not see the multiple columns on the screen in normal mode, only in page layout or print preview modes. Figure 12-9 shows the result of these settings.

Splitting a page into columns greatly reduces the number of words per line, so you may want to format the paragraphs as left-aligned, rather than as justified, unless you are using a small font. Justifying narrow columns usually results in a great deal of white space between words. For example, compare the columns in Figure 12-10.

You will also want to use as many nonrequired hyphens as possible in order to make the lines more even. Automated hyphenation is described in Chapter 19.

Even though multicolumn text is not often used in business documents, you may find that it enhances the appearance of some reports.

Lesson 57: Numbering Lines in Your Document

The legal profession often requires that line numbers be printed on documents such as pleadings and depositions. One method is to use forms with line numbers already printed on them. However, this limits the kind of text you can include, and it is difficult to line up the text and the paper in

Figure 12-9. *Three-column document*

Excerpts from a Proposal for Bank Funding

<u>I. Introduction</u>

National Generators has the opportunity over the next five years to take a commanding lead in our established markets and to penetrate a new market, the construction industry, where our products will be particularly attractive. This report is intended to provide an overview of the company's business development strategies along with a description of those areas for which we require funding.

National Generators can become the premier producer of electrical generation equipment for the entertainment and exposition industries. Our portable yet sturdy generators have acquired a solid reputation in these fields. As the number of outdoor concerts, large conventions, and other events that use portable generators continues to increase each year, we will be better able than our competitors to satisfy the demand for reliable equipment.

While accelerating efforts aimed at our existing base of industrial users, we propose to enter the construction industry. We have already begun developing a small, quiet generator for this market. Research is also underway to design a larger, more efficient generator for heavy construction projects that can replace several smaller ones.

<u>II. Market Analysis</u>

National Generators currently has a 42% share of the markets we now serve. Our nearest competitor, Regional Outdoor Electricity, has 34%, with the rest divided among other manufacturers. We believe that our superior products will insure that we will increase our share of the entertainment and exposition industries' needs for portable generators. Some of our smaller competitors will be unable to match our new technology, and we will pick up their business.

Over the next five years we anticipate gaining 15% of the market for generators in the construction industry.[1] Two important trends favor our planned new products over

---

[1]Based on trends and growth in the construction industry, detailed in U.S. Department of Labor projections for 1985-1990.

Figure 12-10. *Justification in a narrow column compared to left-aligned text*

National
Generators has
the opportunity
over the next
five years to
take a
commanding
lead in our
established
markets and to
penetrate a new
market, the
construction
industry, where
our products will
be particularly
attractive.

National
Generators has
the opportunity
over the next
five years to
take a
commanding
lead in our
established
markets and to
penetrate a new
market, the
construction
industry, where
our products will
be particularly
attractive.

many printers. For example, footnotes (which are common in pleadings) do not line up with the numbers on preprinted forms.

Word's line numbering capability enables lawyers (and anyone else who requires numbered lines) to edit and print documents easily. Line numbers only appear on the printed document and in page preview mode (not in normal or page layout mode).

To turn on line numbering, simply click the Line Numbers button in the Section command. This brings up the following dialog box:

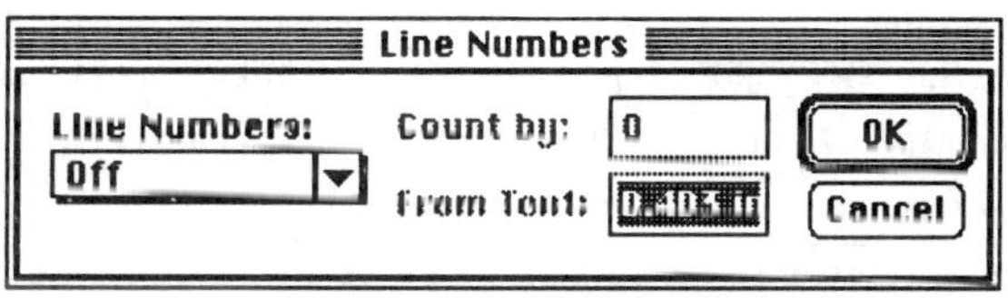

The choices for the Line Numbers drop-down list are Off, By Page, By Section, and Continuous. Generally, you want the numbering on each page to begin with 1, so you should select By Page. If, instead, you want the lines of your document numbered from beginning to end, choose By Section (for numbering in each section) or Continuous (for the whole document).

You also can specify whether to show every line number or only a few. For example, if you enter **5** for Count By, Word only prints every fifth line number. You can also specify how close the line numbers appear to the text by using the From Text option.

Usually, you want to number the lines in all the paragraphs in your document. If you want to exclude some paragraphs from line numbering, select them, give the Paragraph command, and then select the Suppress Line Numbering option. This prevents the line numbers from appearing and removes those lines from the counting sequence.

Lesson 58: Document Formatting and Setting Margins

Use the Document command from the Format menu to specify the page margins and other document-wide formatting considerations. Figure 12-11 shows the Document dialog box.

The choices in the Document command let you specify

- The left, right, top, and bottom margins and the gutter measurement
- Where to place the footnotes in the document and how to number the footnotes (footnotes are described in Chapter 15)

Figure 12-11. *Document dialog box*

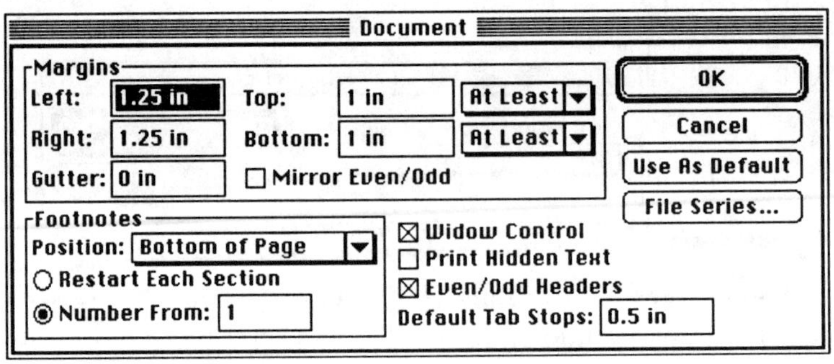

- Whether to use widow and orphan control
- Whether to print hidden text (described in Chapter 18)
- Whether or not odd and even pages are treated differently
- The default tab stops for the paragraphs for which you don't set tab stops
- The name of the next file and options for keeping the page numbering consistent in multifile documents

Some users get confused between margins and indents. Page margins are measured from the edge of the paper; paragraph indents are measured from the left and right page margins. Page margins are set in the Document command for the entire document, while paragraph indents are set by the Paragraph command for each paragraph.

If you are going to bind the document, you may want to set a gutter width after selecting Even/Odd Headers. The *gutter* is the center space between two pages of a book that is not used in printing; in this case it is the amount of space that is used in binding the document. Since binding a document or punching holes takes up a certain amount of space from the left side of odd-numbered pages and the right side of even-numbered pages, Word allows you to stretch the margins, alternating between left and right pages. Set the gutter width to the amount that would be lost in binding. When your pages are printed and bound, the text does not run into the gutter and will thus be easier to read. Note that the margins on this book are wider on the inside of each page, since the binding steals a bit of paper width.

If the difference between inside and outside margins and gutters is confusing, click the Mirror Even/Odd button. The choices in the Margins area now change to

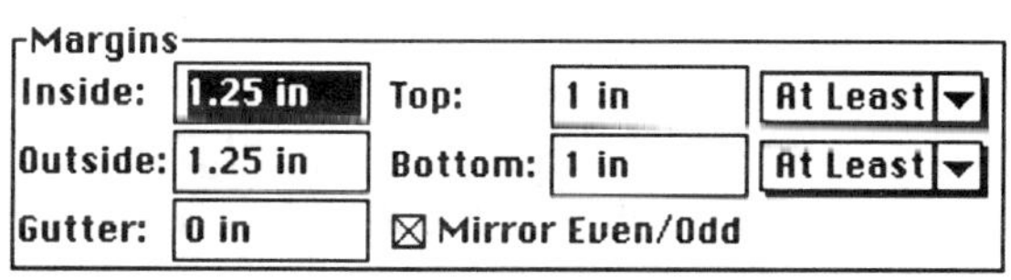

Note that you can now directly specify just the inside and outside margins without worrying about even and odd pages.

Word determines the line length of a page in this way:

line length = page width – (left margin + right margin + gutter)

The top and bottom margins are set by default to 1 inch, and the left and right margins are set to 1.25 inches. These four values are the ones you are most likely to reset. Word gives you wide margins so that your headers and footers do not appear too near the edge of the page. You may, however, need different settings. For example, many publishers insist on a 1.5-inch border around text submitted for publication.

If you click the Use As Default button, Word makes the current choices the default for the Document command in other documents. For example, if you always use the Even/Odd Headers option, you can make that the default. This only affects new documents, not ones you have already created.

Lesson 59: Repaginating and Page Breaks

Word keeps track of where each page break is in your document in normal mode by default. This makes the program run a little slower than if it didn't do this, but it is usually not noticeable. To turn off automatic repagination, use the Preferences command in the Tools menu. In page layout mode, Word always repaginates your document as you edit.

If you don't have Word automatically repaginate, and you want to cause Word to update all the pagination and show where the page breaks fall, use the Repaginate Now command from the Tools menu. Word puts a line of widely spaced dots across the page at the places where page breaks occur:

To force Word to start a new page, set the insertion point at the desired location and give the Page Break command from the Insert menu or press SHIFT-ENTER. Word prints a line of tightly spaced dots across the screen to indicate the forced page break:

If you want to get rid of a page break, go past it and (BACKSPACE) over it.

If you want to be sure that a particular paragraph appears at the top of a page, you can format the paragraph to cause a page break instead of inserting a forced page break. To do this, select the paragraph, give the Paragraph command, and select Page Break Before in the Pagination choices.

If you want to move from page to page, you can use the Go To command from the Edit menu. You can also open the Go To dialog box by double-clicking the page box in the lower-left corner of the document window. The dialog looks like this:

Enter a page number, and Word moves the selection indicator to the beginning of that page. If your document has more than one section, you can also use the Go To command to go to a particular page in a particular section. For example, to go to page 7 of the third section, type **P7S3** in the Go To dialog.

Review

Add a header and footer to the Magazine file. Put the page number in the right corner of the header and a description of the article in the right corner of the footer.

Make the file two columns and view the results in normal and page view modes. In page view mode, change the page number in the header to the middle of the page.

Change the margins to be narrower by .5 inch in each direction. Note how that changes the document in normal and page view mode.

13

Using Styles to Simplify Formatting

Up to this point you have had to specify the formatting characteristics for each paragraph in your text. Microsoft Word also allows you to define a set of *styles* for your documents that is automatically used when you format. When you use styles instead of formatting each paragraph, you specify the style for each type of paragraph (such as a normal paragraph or a section heading), and Word formats the paragraph by finding the corresponding style in the document's set of style characteristics in the document's *style sheet*—the collection of styles.

Word is one of the few word processors offering formatting styles, so even if you are familiar with many other word processing packages, this concept may be unfamiliar to you. In recent years, advanced desktop publishing packages have adopted styles as the preferred method for formatting.

A style sheet can be thought of as a formatting guide that contains a list of types of paragraphs and the formats associated with them. For example, to format a normal paragraph in your text, your instructions might be "justified text, indent the first line 1/2 inch, and skip a line before the paragraph." Instead of having to format each paragraph this way when you enter or edit the text, you simply tell Word that you are entering a normal paragraph. Word looks up the formatting for your normal paragraph in the style sheet.

Using styles in Word consists of two steps. First, you must create the style sheet by defining the types of styles you want. To do this, you use the Style command from the Format menu. You can also use the many predefined styles that come with Word. After you design the styles, you format your document by labeling its elements with styles. As you will see, there are many ways to specify the styles used in your documents. Word lets you copy style sheets from document to document easily.

One of the excellent features of formatting with styles is that you can have many different style sheets in different documents that use the same style elements but format them differently. Thus, a normal paragraph in one style sheet might be double-spaced and ragged right, but in another it might be single-spaced and justified. You might use the first style sheet to print rough drafts so you can correct mistakes easily, and then use the second style sheet to print your final document.

Word lets you specify the types of styles you want and allows you to modify and add styles easily; you do not need to stick to predefined styles. You might have styles for normal paragraphs, long quotations, running heads, section headings, and so on.

Using styles does not prevent you from using direct formatting; however, you will probably find that using styles almost exclusively will make writing and printing easier. If you have used only styles and want to change the format of one type of paragraph in all of your different documents, you do not need to change any of them individually–simply change your style sheets. Your new formatting is automatically used. Of course, you cannot do this with direct formatting. While you can use style sheets for most of your text, you can also use some direct formatting when it is faster or when you are sure you will not want to change the format.

Another big advantage of styles is that you can easily change a format without having to change anything in your documents. For example, you may have a style called Chapter Heading that corresponds to boldface centered text at 24 points. If you later want all the chapter headings to be underlined and left-aligned, you only need to change the style; not search through all of your files for the chapter headings.

If you want to begin using styles but do not yet want to create your own styles, you can use the predefined styles supplied by Microsoft. These appear in the Styles command along with your own styles. Of course, you can modify the attributes of these predefined styles if you wish.

If you convert a directly formatted document to styles, you should first unformat the entire document. To unformat a document, select the entire document by pressing ⌘-A, press ⌘-SHIFT-P to make all paragraphs normal, and then press ⌘-SHIFT-SPACEBAR to remove all character formatting.

The next lesson shows you how to create two styles from scratch and how to specify your own style elements. The lesson after that shows how to save your style sheet in your document. You will then learn how to specify styles in your documents.

Lesson 60: Creating a Style Sheet

Now that you understand the concept behind style sheets, the next step is to add a style to a document's style sheet with which you can experiment. In addition, you will modify some of the predefined styles.

The rest of this chapter uses the report shown in Chapter 12 for its examples. You may want to enter the first section heading and the first few paragraphs of the report so you can try out examples as they are presented. When you enter the text, be sure not to use any direct formatting commands. The top of the text is shown in Figure 13-1.

To start making styles, give the Style command from the Format menu. This is shown in Figure 13-2. Click the All Styles button to show the predefined styles, which are shown with a *bullet* (•) before the names.

You will create one style for this sample sheet for the report title. You will also modify two other styles: the "heading 1" style used for the section headings and the Normal style that is used for all regular text paragraphs.

There are two ways to define a style:

- Give a paragraph the formatting you want, then give the Style command, enter the name of the style, and click OK.

Figure 13-1. *Top of report with formats removed*

Excerpts from a Proposal for Bank Funding
I. Introduction
National Generators has the opportunity over the next five years to take a commanding lead in our established markets and to penetrate a new market, the construction industry, where our products will be particularly attractive. This report is intended to provide an overview of the company's business development strategies along with a description of those areas for which we require funding.
National Generators can become the premier producer of electrical generation equipment for the entertainment and exposition industries. Our portable yet sturdy generators have acquired a solid reputation in these fields. As the number of outdoor concerts, large conventions, and other events that use portable generators continues to increase each year, we will be better able than our competitors to satisfy the demand for reliable equipment.
While accelerating efforts aimed at our existing base of industrial users, we propose to enter the construction industry. We have already begun developing a small, quiet generator for this market. Research is also underway to design a larger, more efficient generator for heavy construction projects that can replace several smaller ones.

Figure 13-2. *Style dialog box*

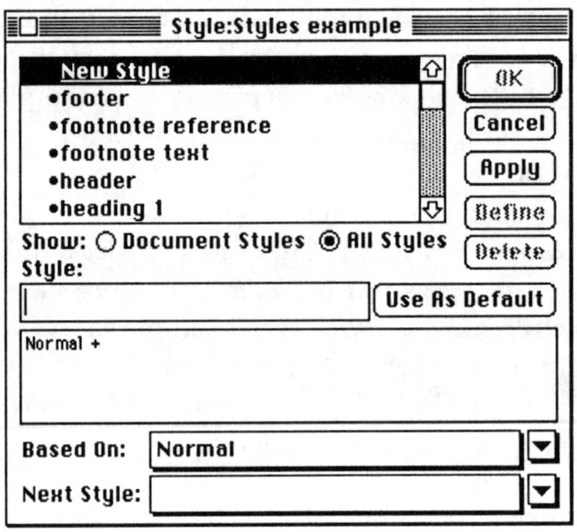

- Start with an unformatted paragraph, give the Style command, give the formatting commands that define the style while the Style dialog box is shown, and click Apply.

To begin, select the title paragraph. This is currently in Normal style (as is everything in a file before you start giving style commands). You can see what style is used on any paragraph by looking in the style box next to the page number at the bottom of the window:

Add some direct formatting to this paragraph so you can see how Word learns formatting from text. Make the characters 18 point, bold, italic, and centered, with 12 points after. The top of your document now looks like this:

Now give the Style command. Make sure that New Style is selected in the list of styles, and enter the new style's name in the box labeled Style. For this example, type **Title**. Note the character and paragraph formatting for this paragraph are shown in the box two-thirds of the way down the dialog box:

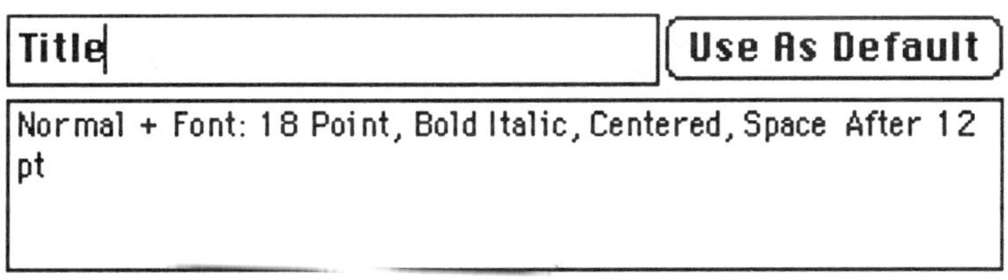

Click the Define button, and the new style is defined.

Next, you want to modify the predefined style called "heading 1" so that you can use it on the headings in the report. Be sure the All Styles button is selected. Click the "heading 1" name in the list at the top of the dialog box; it now looks like Figure 13-3.

In the case of the headings, you want them to be New York font, bold, underlined, 14 point, and kept with the next paragraph. Note that this predefined style already comes with some formatting, namely "underline," "keep with next," and the Helvetica font.

To change the formatting to what you want, you can use the Character and Paragraph commands in the Format menu, just as if you were using direct formatting. You can also choose the font name and size from the Font menu. You can use these commands, even though the Styles dialog box is still shown on the screen (this may seem strange to experienced Macintosh users). If you wish, you can also use the icons on the ruler or ribbon to set the styles or use the other formatting commands in the Format menu.

When you are finished changing the formats for this style, click the Define button. Don't click the OK button, which has a very different meaning here.

Figure 13-3. *Style dialog box with heading 1 selected*

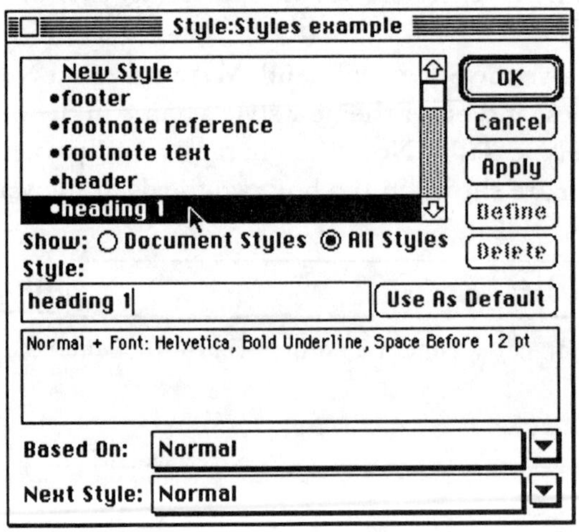

Next, change the style for normal paragraphs. Select Normal from the list of styles, give the Paragraph command, and specify 12 points before and justified. Again, click the Define button.

You have now added a new style and changed the formatting in two predefined styles. Click Cancel, not OK, to close the Style dialog box. Don't worry, this is one place where clicking Cancel does not lose the work you have done in the dialog box. Clicking OK would apply the last style you edited to the current selection, which is *not* what you want to do right now.

Lesson 61: Using Styles in Your Documents

Now that you have a style sheet, you can start applying styles to your documents. When you use Word, you can either set up a style sheet and enter the styles as you type new text or you can convert a directly formatted document to styles.

You are now ready to start applying styles. You can give text a style by selecting the text, pressing ⌘-SHIFT-S, and typing the name of the style you want to apply. The page box in the lower-left part of the window shows the word "Style":

As you type, your style name appears there. If you change your mind, press ⌘-. to cancel the command.

For example, select any part of the first section heading, "I. Introduction". Now press ⌘-SHIFT-S and type **heading 1** to indicate that this is a section heading and press RETURN. The result is shown in Figure 13-4. Notice that the paragraph is now formatted properly and that "heading 1" now appears in the style box, next to the page box.

You can also assign styles from the style box in the ruler. This box is a drop-down list of all the styles created for your document. Simply select part of whatever paragraph you want in the style and select that style from the list.

Figure 13-4. *Section heading with formatting*

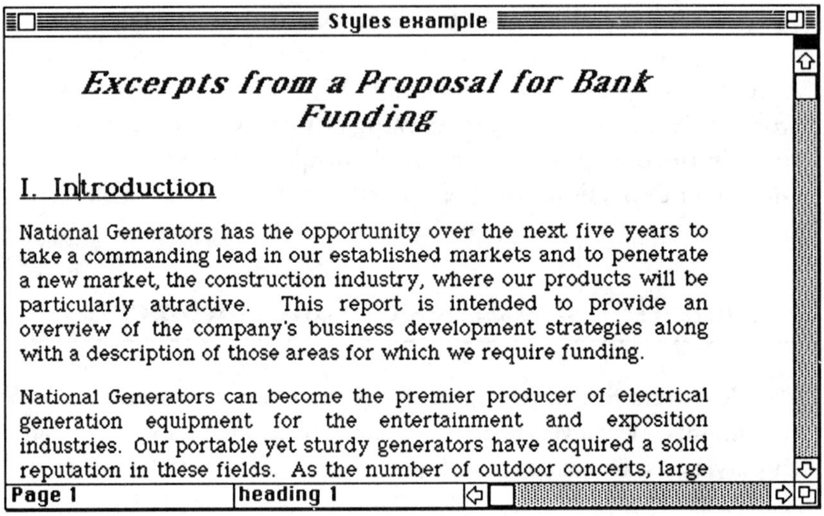

For example, select any part of the document title, pull down the style list, and choose the Title style.

To see the power of style sheets, suppose that you decide not to justify the normal paragraphs and want to change them to left-aligned formatting. Give the Style command, select Normal from the list, change the formatting to left-aligned, click Define, and click Cancel. As soon as you return to editing, all your normal paragraphs have changed to the new style, as shown in Figure 13-5.

Lesson 62: Working with Style Sheets

Although a style sheet is saved as part of a document, you may want to create your own *master* style sheet. A master style sheet would hold all the style definitions that you normally use. You can create a file, perhaps called

Figure 13-5. *New style applied to normal paragraphs*

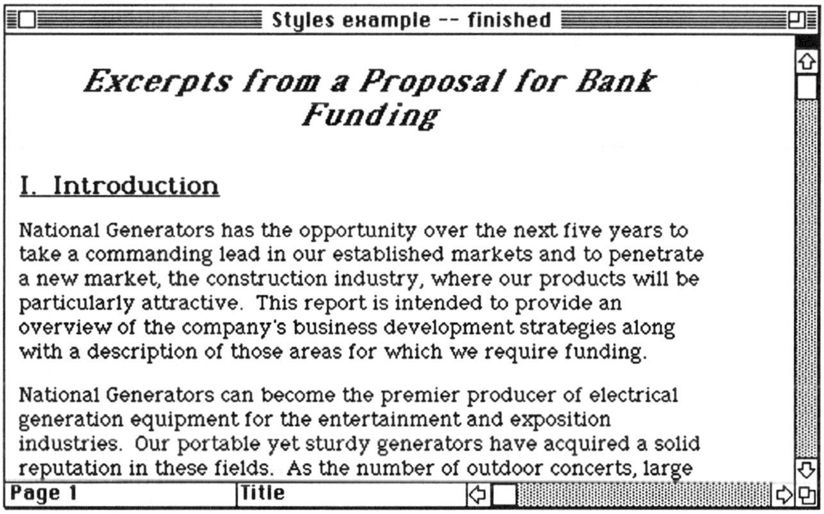

Master Style Sheet, and read the styles from that master into your document when you want to be sure that the definitions in the document match the master.

The process of merging styles is fairly easy. Give the Style command; then, while the Style dialog box is open, give the Open command from the File menu. Select the document that has your master style sheet, click Open, and the styles from the master are merged in your current document. In the merging process, Word takes three actions:

- If the same style name exists in the master and the target documents, the document's formatting for that style name is changed to the master's format.
- If the master has a style that does not exist in the document, that style is added.
- Any styles in the document not in the master are left as they are.

This method for keeping style sheets opens up new areas for using styles. For example, it is usually most convenient to edit text on the screen when it is single-spaced (so that more lines fit on the screen) but more convenient to edit it on paper when it is double-spaced (so that you can write additions or corrections between the lines). You can keep a master document that has its Normal paragraph formatted for double-space. When you merge this master file's style sheet into a single-spaced document, it causes all the Normal paragraphs to be double-spaced. You can then print the document and close it without saving the changes (in this case, the double spacing).

You can use Word's stationery feature to assure that new documents use the master styles. Put the styles you want new documents to have (such as the styles from your master style sheet) in the stationery document you use to open new documents, and new documents will use them automatically.

Lesson 63: Basing Styles on Other Styles

You may have noticed that the formatting box in the Styles dialog box starts out with "Normal +" for each predefined style. This, plus the Based On choice near the bottom of the dialog box, are part of an advanced style feature that lets one style be affected by another. By default, all predefined styles are based on the Normal style.

To see this, assume that a style called A is based on a style called B. The formatting for A is "B + Bold", and the formatting for B is "Normal + Centered". This means that A is like Normal, but bold and centered. If you now change the formatting for B to be "Normal + Justified", A automatically changes to justified alignment as well. This is because A is still "B + Bold", so A changes to whatever B does, plus adds bold.

The power of this feature is that since everything is based on Normal, you can change one formatting feature of the Normal and have that change be reflected in all other formats as well. For instance, assume that you use the New York font throughout a document and you decide that you want to use Palatino instead. You need only change the font for the Normal style, and all styles that are based on Normal also change to Palatino.

A formatting characteristic in a style based on another style does not change if the changed style has the same characteristic. For example, if your headings are based on Normal but they use the Courier font, and you change the font for the Normal style to Palatino, the fonts in the heading styles stay in Courier. This means you can safely change the formatting of your "base" styles without having to respecify all the formatting for styles based on them.

To specify which style you want to base another style on, first select the style you are changing, then choose the style it is based on in the Based On drop-down box. The formatting shown changes to reflect the differences between the style and the style it is based on, instead of the differences between it and the Normal style.

Lesson 64: Getting the Most from Style Sheets

Style sheets can make formatting all your documents, from letters to entire books, a much easier task. Even for large reports it is unlikely that your style sheet will contain more than 15 styles, and only 5 or so will probably be used with any frequency. If you want, you can remove styles in a style sheet by using the Cut command when the Styles dialog box is open.

You will find that style sheets have many advantages over direct formatting, and in the few places where styles are not appropriate, you can still format directly. Once you start thinking in terms of style elements ("this is a heading," "this is a normal paragraph," and so on), you will find that your printed documents are much clearer, since they are presented in a more organized manner.

Copying styles from one piece of text to another is identical to copying other paragraph formats. You can convert files that use direct formatting to style-sheet formatting by applying a style to one paragraph and then copying that style to all other paragraphs to which it applies. Select the paragraph with the style that you want to apply, press (⌘)-(OPTION)-(V), and press (RETURN). You can also search for styles with the Find command.

If you edit with the ruler showing, you can use the style box at the left side of the ruler for more than just choosing styles. If you have selected a paragraph that already has formatting on it and select a style from the list, Word lets you redefine the formatting for that style to be the formatting in the paragraph.

To print your style sheet, give the Style command and, while the dialog box is open, give the Print command. Word prints each style and its elements.

Review

Look in books and magazines and think about how they might use styles for the various types of paragraphs such as headings, subheads, and normal paragraphs.

III

Other Word Features

14

Creating Form Letters

When Word first appeared in 1984, only a few word processing programs included features that let you create form letters from a file of names and addresses. This feature is sometimes referred to as *mail merge*. Today, many programs give you this capability in a limited fashion. The merge feature in Word is more sophisticated than in other word processing programs and produces letters that look much more personalized.

The basic concept behind the merge feature is fairly simple. Your *main document* contains the letter you want to send to many people, with special place holders (*fields*) for the parts that change from letter to letter (like the recipient's name and address). Your *datafile* contains the names of the fields and the information that Word puts into the fields in the main document. All the information for each letter is in one paragraph or one row of cells (called a *record*) of the datafile. The main document contains the text that is the same in each letter, while the datafile contains the text that is different from letter to letter. Both files are regular Word documents that you can edit and format using the methods you have learned so far.

Instructions in your main document tell Word which file is to be the datafile. You create the main document with Word and create the datafile with Word, a database management system like FileMaker Pro, or with a spreadsheet program like Excel. The format of the datafile is very straightforward, so it is not difficult at all to set up datafiles to go with your main documents.

When you print your file with the Print Merge command from the File menu, Word reads the first record from the datafile, substitutes the field information for the field names into your main document, formats your letter, prints it, reads the next record from the datafile, and so on.

You can include fields in the middle of a paragraph, and Word formats the paragraph with the new information in it (few other programs format the paragraph after putting in the new information). Thus, if you have a field called "amount," and that field in one record of your datafile is equal to 1533, Word properly reformats a paragraph that contains the sentence "You still owe us $1533, which we would like you to send immediately."

You assign a name to each field consisting of up to 253 letters or spaces, such as "amount" or "last payment." You use the field name in both the main document and the datafile, and the names must match. However, the order in which the field names are used in the main document does not need to match the order in which the field names appear in the datafile. In fact, you can use the data assigned to a field many times in your main document.

Lesson 65: Creating the Main Document and Datafile

You enter the body of your main document just as you normally enter text with Word. For now, don't enter any field names, since Word helps you with that after you create the datafile. Instead, just type **XX** where the fields would go.

Type the example in Figure 14-1, which is a main document that could be used to inform customers of balances due. Note the "XX" where the field names from the data document will be put later. Save this file as Balance 1.

You can create the datafile manually, but it is much easier to use the Print Merge Helper feature. The Print Merge Helper command, given from the View menu, creates a new file that has a table in the exact format needed by the Print Merge command. Tables are discussed in Chapter 15, but you can use them here without knowing much about them.

Figure 14-1. *Balance 1 text*

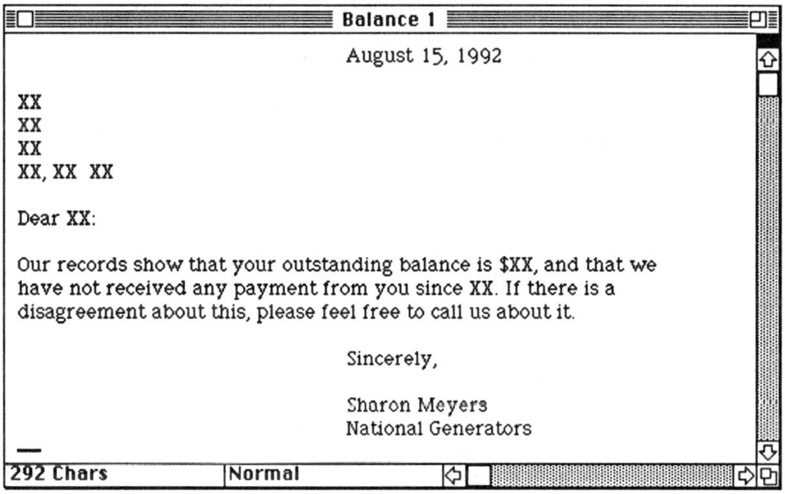

Before giving the Print Merge Helper command, be certain that the Balance 1 file is open and that the insertion point is at the beginning of the main document. This is important because the Print Merge Helper has to put information about your datafile there.

For this example, you need fields to match the Balance 1 letter. These are

- company
- name
- address
- city
- state
- zip
- amount
- last payment

It doesn't matter whether you use upper- or lowercase letters.

Figure 14-2. *Prompt for datafile*

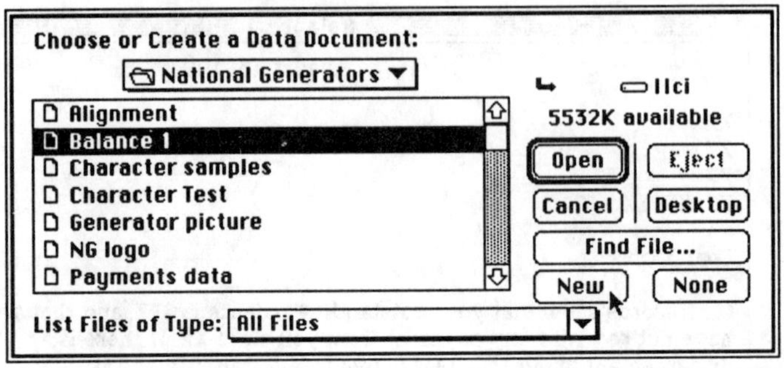

When you give the Print Merge Helper command from the View menu, you see the dialog box shown in Figure 14-2. Click the New button, since you want to create a new datafile. You then see the Data Document Builder window, shown in Figure 14-3.

Enter the name of the first field in the Field Name box and click the Add button (or press (RETURN)). Remember that the order of the fields in the datafile does not matter. In this case, type the name **company** and click Add; type

Figure 14-3. *Data Document Builder window*

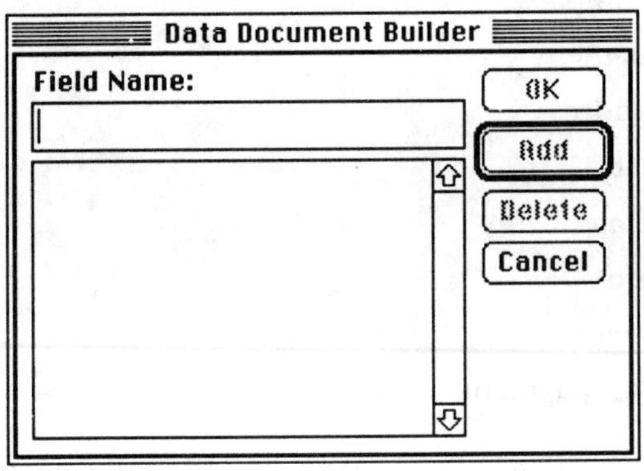

Figure 14-4. *All fields entered*

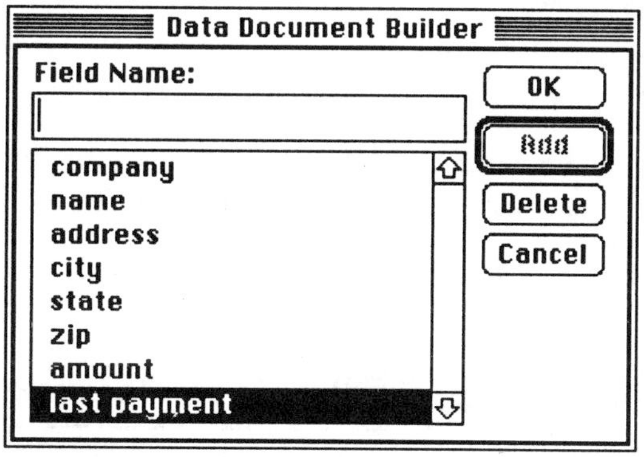

name, click Add; and so on for all the field names. When you have finished, the window looks like Figure 14-4. Click OK to close the window.

Word now displays a standard Save As dialog box. This allows you to save the datafile that you have just specified on disk. Enter the name **Payments data** in the Save Current Document As box and click Save. When Word displays the Summary Info window, just click OK to disregard it. Word now does two things:

- It starts the datafile in a second regular document window, the top of which looks like this:

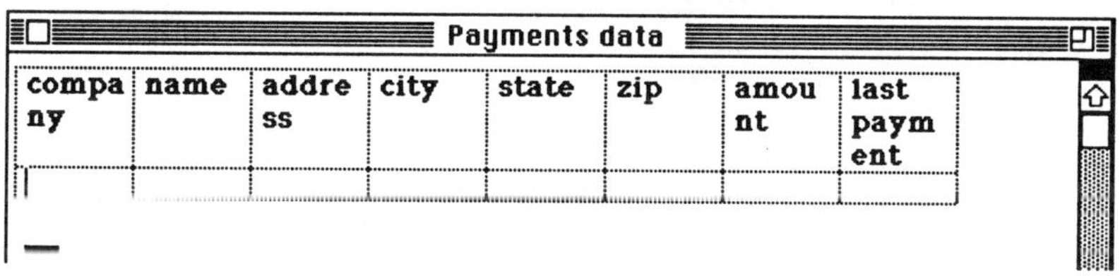

- It inserts the name of the datafile at the beginning of your main document using special *merge characters* and opens the Print Merge Helper bar at the top of the window:

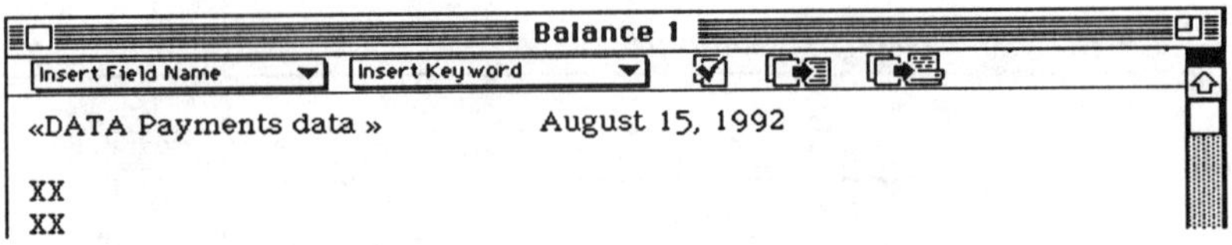

Don't be concerned if this displaces your first line a bit (the date, in this case) or if it shows the name of the folder that you have saved it in.

Lesson 66: Finishing the Main Document and Datafile

Switch to the datafile by clicking on its window, if it is visible, or using the Window menu if, for example, the Balance 1 window takes up the full screen and is covering the Payments data window.

The dotted lines in the table in the datafile are the cell borders. Notice that the cells are narrower than some of the names you entered; that is perfectly acceptable. The way that the data looks in the table does not affect how it looks in your printed form letters. Word wraps text in the cells of a table just like it does in paragraphs.

You now want to start entering the data. To enter data into a table, you simply type what you want and press the (TAB) key to move to the next cell. To start a new row in a table, put the insertion point in the last cell in the last row and press (TAB) again. This is described in more detail in Chapter 15.

For now, start typing the information for the form letters. The first company name is Industrial Mining Co., so type that in the first cell in the blank row:

company	name	address	city	state	zip	amount	last payment
Industrial Mining Co							

Press (TAB) and type the name, **Michael Townsend**, like this:

company	name	address	city	state	zip	amount	last payment
Industrial Mining Co.	Michael Townsend						

Enter all the information for the first record in the same way:

company	name	address	city	state	zip	amount	last payment
Industrial Mining Co.	Michael Townsend	P.O. Box 4110	Cambridge	MA	02139	127.53	7/21/92

To start the next record, be sure the insertion point is in the last cell (the one under "last payment") and press (TAB):

company	name	address	city	state	zip	amount	last payment
Industrial Mining Co.	Michael Townsend	P.O. Box 4110	Cambridge	MA	02139	127.53	7/21/92

Fill in the second record as well:

company	name	address	city	state	zip	amount	last payment
Industrial Mining Co.	Michael Townsend	P.O. Box 4110	Cambridge	MA	02139	127.53	7/21/92
City of Olsenburg	Tamara Fine	91 Oak Avenue, Suite 320	Olsenburg	IL	60606	118.18	7/31/92

If you want, you can add other records to see how they print out.

Give the Save command to save this work on disk, and switch to the main document, the Balance 1 letter. You want to replace each "XX" with the name of the appropriate field. You cannot simply type in the field names, however; you need to put in the special merge characters. The easy way to do this is to use the Print Merge Helper bar at the top of the window.

Switch to the Balance 1 file, select the first "XX", which will be the person's name (don't select the paragraph mark after the "XX"). You want to replace this with the field called "name", so pull down the Insert Field Name drop-down list in the Print Merge Helper bar, select "name", and release the mouse. Word then replaces the "XX" with "NAME" surrounded in the field markers, as shown in Figure 14-5.

Select the second "XX", which you want to be the company, and select "company" from the Print Merge Helper bar. Keep doing this until your document looks like Figure 14-6.

You can add formatting, such as italics, to the field names if you wish. This causes the information in the fields to be printed with the formatting. Note that you add formatting to the main document; formatting in the datafile is ignored.

Figure 14-5. *Field name inserted in the document*

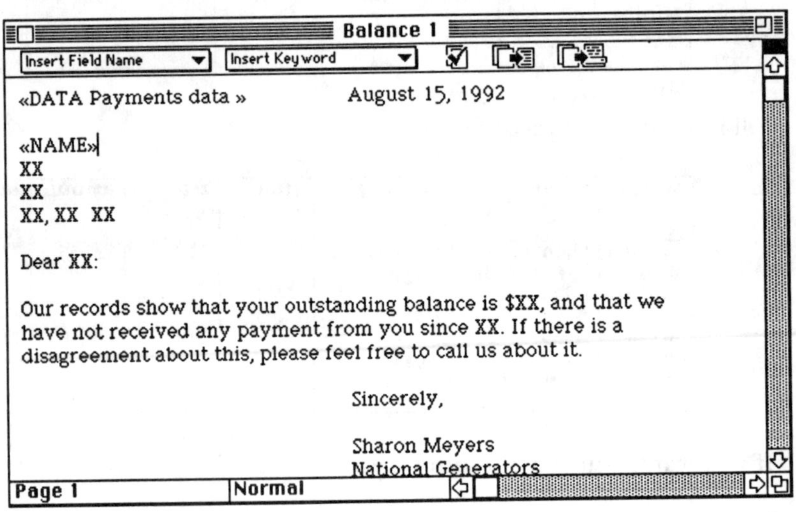

Figure 14-6. *Completed main document*

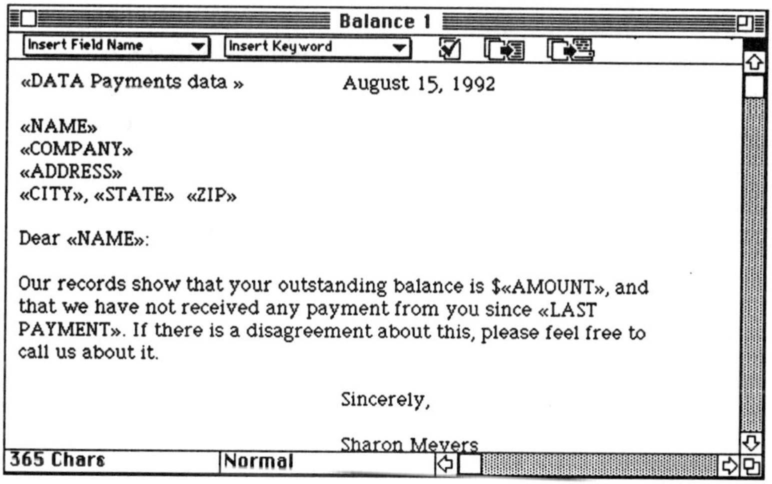

14

Lesson 67: Printing Form Letters

Printing with merge is very similar to regular printing. Give the Print Merge command from the File menu after setting up your printer with the Page Setup and Chooser commands. You see the dialog box shown in Figure 14-7.

Figure 14-7. *Print Merge dialog box*

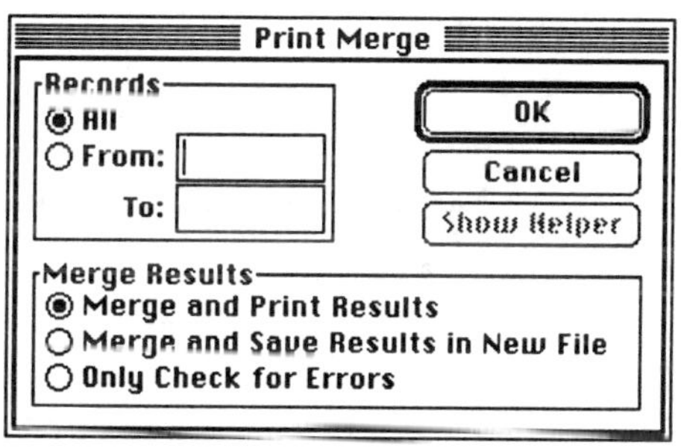

The Records choice lets you specify which records in your datafile you want to use. You can enter record numbers in the From and To choices to restrict the records you print.

The three choices in the Merge Results section define what happens when you click OK. Merge and Print Results causes the results to be sent to the printer, while Merge and Save Results in New File causes the results to be saved in a new file. You can use the latter choice if you want to make some changes in the letters before printing them out.

Figure 14-8 shows the letters Word prints out when you merge the Balance 1 letter. As you can see, Word fills in the fields in the body of the paragraph and correctly wraps the text.

Figure 14-8. *Letters printed by the Print Merge command*

August 15, 1992

Michael Townsend
Industrial Mining Co.
P.O. Box 4110
Cambridge, MA 02139

Dear Michael Townsend:

Our records show that your outstanding balance is $127.53, and that we have not received any payment from you since 7/21/92. If there is a disagreement about this, please feel free to call us about it.

Sincerely,

Sharon Meyers
National Generators

August 15, 1992

Tamara Fine
City of Olsenburg
91 Oak Avenue, Suite 320
Olsenburg, IL 60606

Dear Tamara Fine:

Our records show that your outstanding balance is $118.18, and that we have not received any payment from you since 7/31/92. If there is a disagreement about this, please feel free to call us about it.

Sincerely,

Sharon Meyers
National Generators

Lesson 68: Using Merge Instructions

The previous example showed a simple merge file with a DATA instruction and many fields. A unique feature of Word that makes letter writing even easier is *conditional insertion*. You can check the value of a field and insert different text depending on the value of the field. For example, if the information in the amount field is over 1000, you can insert a sentence describing the dire consequences of not paying promptly. Your datafile can also have a field called "regular customer" that contains a "Y" or "N", and you can use this to decide what type of salutation to use.

The merge feature has many instructions that you can use; these are listed in Table 14-1. Some are described in this lesson, but the full use of merge instructions is beyond the scope of this book.

The main document in Figure 14-9 is similar to the Balance 1 document except that it has an IF instruction used with a text field. The IF instruction checks the value of the "sales rep" field and prints one of two possible sentences, depending on whether the information in "sales rep" is "none" or some other value. The datafile, shown in Figure 14-10, is also similar to the

Table 14-1. *Word Merge Instructions*

Instruction	Use
ASK	Has Word prompt you to fill in a field when each letter is printed
DATA	Identifies the datafile
IF...ENDIF or IF...ELSE...ENDIF	Conditionally inserts text if a field in the datafile has a particular value. You can use the =, >, or < operators for numeric fields or the = operator for string fields.
INCLUDE	Inserts another Word file in the main document
NEXT	Has Word read the next record in the datafile
SET	Sets the contents of a field or has Word prompt you for the value once at the beginning of printing

Figure 14-9. *Main document with IF instruction*

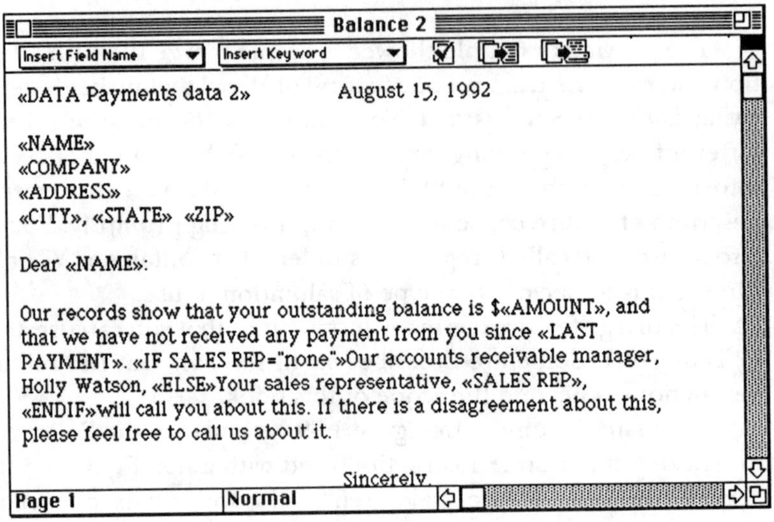
Balance 2

Insert Field Name | Insert Keyword

«DATA Payments data 2» August 15, 1992

«NAME»
«COMPANY»
«ADDRESS»
«CITY», «STATE» «ZIP»

Dear «NAME»:

Our records show that your outstanding balance is $«AMOUNT», and that we have not received any payment from you since «LAST PAYMENT». «IF SALES REP="none"»Our accounts receivable manager, Holly Watson, «ELSE»Your sales representative, «SALES REP», «ENDIF»will call you about this. If there is a disagreement about this, please feel free to call us about it.

Sincerely,

Page 1 | Normal

previous one. Figure 14-11 shows the new output. You will see in Chapter 15 how to add columns to a table.

To enter merge instructions, put the insertion point where you want the instruction and use the Insert Keyword drop-down list in the Print Merge

Figure 14-10. *Datafile for Balance 2*

company	name	address	city	state	zip	amount	last payment	sales rep
Industrial Mining Co.	Michael Townsend	P.O. Box 4110	Cambridge	MA	02139	127.53	7/21/92	Jan Philips
City of Olsenburg	Tamara Fine	91 Oak Avenue, Suite 320	Olsenburg	IL	60606	118.18	7/31/92	none

Figure 14-11. *Output from Balance 2 letter*

August 15, 1992

Michael Townsend
Industrial Mining Co.
P.O. Box 4110
Cambridge, MA 02139

Dear Michael Townsend:

Our records show that your outstanding balance is $127.53, and that we have not received any payment from you since 7/21/92. Your sales representative, Jan Philips, will call you about this. If there is a disagreement about this, please feel free to call us about it.

Sincerely,

Sharon Meyers
National Generators

August 15, 1992

Tamara Fine
City of Olsenburg
91 Oak Avenue, Suite 320
Olsenburg, IL 60606

Dear Tamara Fine:

Our records show that your outstanding balance is $118.18, and that we have not received any payment from you since 7/31/92. Our accounts receivable manager, Holly Watson, will call you about this. If there is a disagreement about this, please feel free to call us about it.

Sincerely,

Sharon Meyers
National Generators

Helper bar. For example, when you choose IF...ENDIF... from the Print Merge Helper bar, you see the following dialog box:

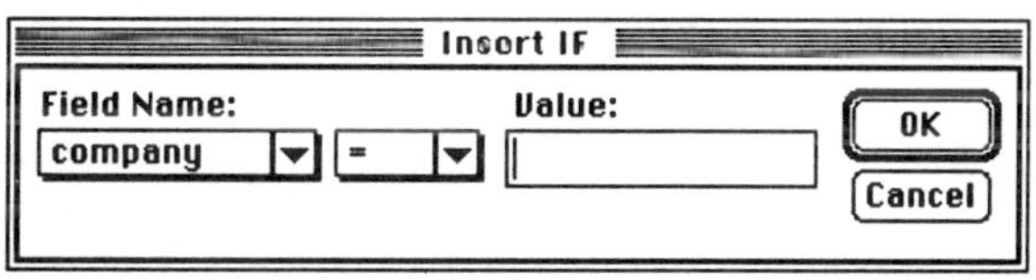

Choose the appropriate field name, the equal sign, and type **none** for the value. Word inserts the correct merge instruction.

You can also use the IF instruction with integer fields to test whether a number is greater than, less than, or equal to a field value. For instance, if your datafile has a field named "cust years" that is the number of years a customer has been with your firm, you might include the following sentence in a letter:

«IF cust years>5»We value your long-standing relationship with us.«ENDIF»

The IF instruction can be used to check whether or not there is anything in the field. For example, the following command determines if there is any value in the owner field:

Dear «IF owner»«owner»«ELSE»Store Owner«ENDIF»

This prints the contents of the owner field, if it exists, or the phrase "Store Owner", if it does not.

The SET and ASK instructions allow you to enter information when you print. The SET instruction sets a field once for all letters, whereas the ASK instruction prompts you for a new value for each letter. You can include a string with which Word prompts you.

Review

Imagine you have an office supply business. Create a client order list including name, title, address, phone, item, and quantity purchased. Next, create a billing letter template and customized bills for each client.

Think about how to use the information in the order list with the merge instructions. For example, think about how to thank a client for a large order.

15

Working with Tables and Footnotes

Lesson 69: Introduction to Tables

Although Word's table feature is a bit more complicated than just using tabs, you will find that the tables it produces are better looking and easier to manipulate. With the table feature, the sizes of the lines of text in your tables shrink and grow naturally as you delete and add text to items, and the formatting within a column or row can be controlled more carefully. Since most business writing includes tables of many sorts, you should learn to use the table feature so that you can create more attractive and informative tables.

You have already seen an example of tables in Chapter 14. The Print Merge Helper feature creates a table for the datafile. Most often, however, you will create and format tables yourself using a small number of Word commands.

A table is made up of cells. A *cell* is a block in the table. A horizontal line of cells is a *row*; a vertical line of cells is a *column*. For example, the table in Figure 15-1 has six cells: three in the first row and three in the second row.

Figure 15-1. *Table with two rows and three columns*

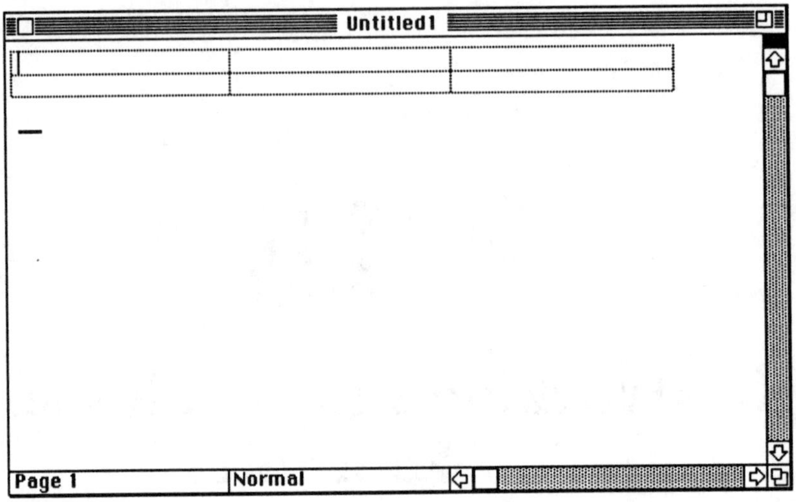

Usually, the information in a row pertains to a single item. All the cells in a column usually deal with one type of data (such as dates, amounts of money, descriptions, and so on). You can manipulate tables by individual cells, rows, and columns. As you will see, rows do not have to be identical or have the same number of columns.

You can specify the format of the information within a cell just like you can in a paragraph. In fact, a cell can contain more than one paragraph. Within a cell, Word automatically wraps words just as it does in the paragraphs in your document, as shown here:

Notice how this text wraps naturally within the cell		

The table feature uses many Word commands. To start a table, give the Table command from the Insert menu. To change the formatting of cells or of rows and columns of cells, use the Table Cells command from the Format menu. As you will see later in this chapter, you use the Table Layout command from the Format menu to add or remove cells. You can also convert text that is in tabular format (such as text separated by tab characters) to a table by using the Text to Table command from the Insert menu.

When you work with tables, it is often useful to see the boundaries on cells. The default is for you to see a grid for all the tables in your text (note, however, that the grid will not print). You can turn this off with the View option of the Preferences command from the Tools menu, but you should have table gridlines visible as you experiment with the tables in these lessons.

Lesson 70: Creating Tables

In a new document, give the Table command from the Insert menu to start a new table. You will see the dialog box shown in Figure 15-2. Change the value for Number of Columns to 3, the Number of Rows to 1, and click the OK button. Word displays the table with one row:

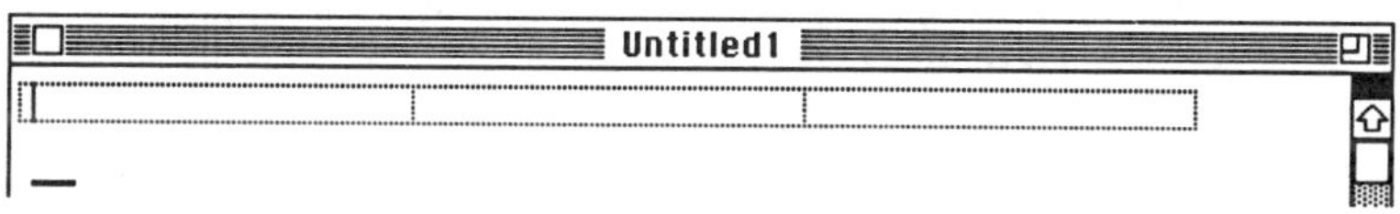

For this example, you want to make two narrow columns and one wide one. You can put the insertion point in a cell by clicking in it. In this case, it is already in the first cell, as you want. Give the Table Cells command from the Format menu. The dialog box in Figure 15-3 shows you the choices you have in the Table Cells command. The following are the choices in this dialog box:

- Apply To tells the command what you want to act on if you have more than one cell selected.
- Column Width lets you change the width of the selected column.
- Height is the height of the row. Usually you will leave this set to Auto, indicating that Word should adjust based on the contents of the cells. You can also enter an exact amount such as **1 in** if you wish.

Figure 15-2. *Insert Table dialog box*

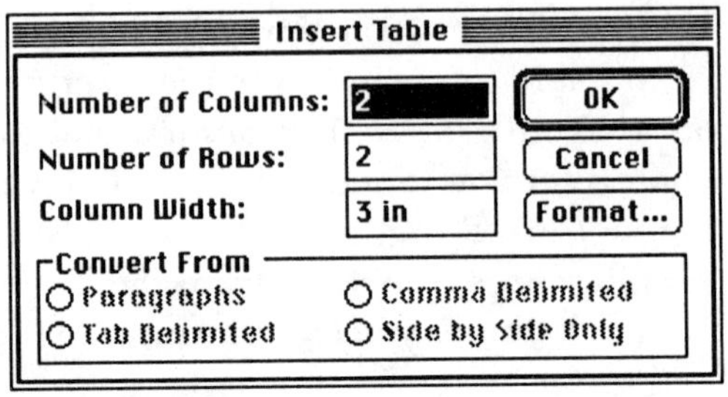

- Space Between Columns indicates the space between each column in the row. It is usually best to leave a little room between the columns so that the text of the columns does not run together.
- Indent sets the indentation for the first cell in the row from the left margin.
- Alignment tells Word how to align the row between the margins (left, right, or center).

Figure 15-3. *Table Cells dialog box*

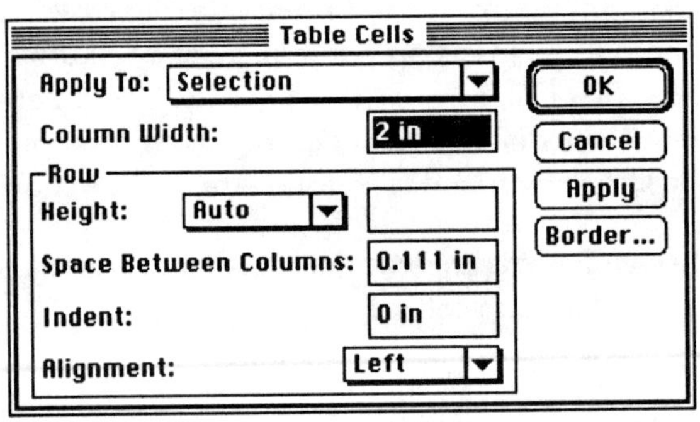

Note that the Row choices apply to the entire row, not just the cell you selected. All cells in the row change if you change one of these settings. The Border button lets you set the borders for the cell, as shown later in this chapter.

For this example, use the Table Cells command to set the width of columns 1 and 2 to 1.5 inches and the width of column 3 to 3 inches. To do this, click in the first cell, give the Table Cells command, change the column width to 1.5 inches, and click OK. Click in the second cell, and so on. The table grid looks like this:

You can now see how to enter text in a table. Put the insertion point in the first cell and type **Task**. Press the (TAB) key to move to the next cell, type **Who**, press (TAB), and type **Comments**. The table should now look like this:

Task	Who	Comments

Be sure the insertion point is at the end of the third column, and press (TAB) to create the next row. Note that you do not press (RETURN) in the third column, because a cell can have more than one paragraph in it. When you press (TAB) (from the rightmost cell), Word creates another row:

Task	Who	Comments

In the first cell in the second row, type **Select new fan supplier.** Note how Word automatically wraps the text within the column. Fill out the rest of the column as shown in Figure 15-4, and then add the next two rows. Remember to add new rows by pressing (TAB) at the ends of the rows.

Figure 15-4. *Table filled in*

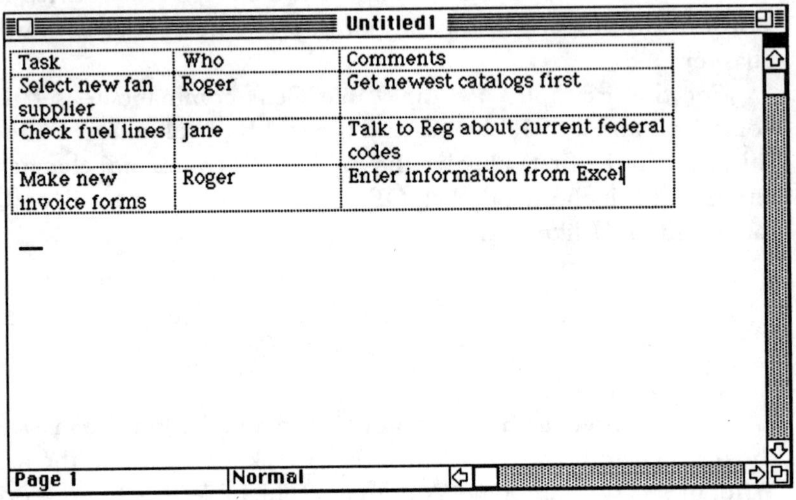

You can also set the column widths on the ruler without the Table Cells command. With the ruler showing, put the insertion point in the cell whose width you want to change, and click the scale icon on the ruler, as shown here:

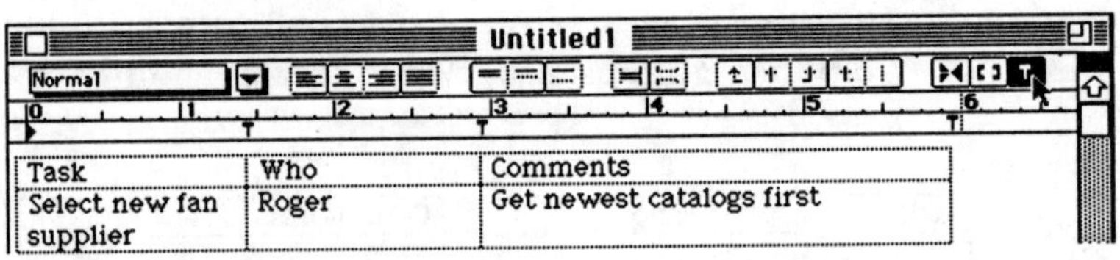

You can then drag the column marks—the "T" characters—to change the width. If you want an entire column to have the same width, select the column and use these marks to change the table.

Since each cell has a paragraph in it, you can change the character and paragraph formatting easily. To select a column, move the pointer near the top of the cell in the first row. The pointer becomes a downward-pointing arrow:

Click this pointer to select the column:

Task	Who	Comments
Select new fan supplier	Roger	Get newest catalogs first
Check fuel lines	Jane	Talk to Reg about current federal codes
Make new invoice forms	Roger	Enter information from Excel

For example, assume that you want to center the text in all the cells in the second column. Select the column, give the Paragraph command from the Format menu, and select the centered alignment icon from the ruler. (You could also center the paragraph by pressing ⌘-SHIFT-C, as you do in text.) The paragraphs in those cells become centered, as in Figure 15-5.

Figure 15-5. *Cells with centered text*

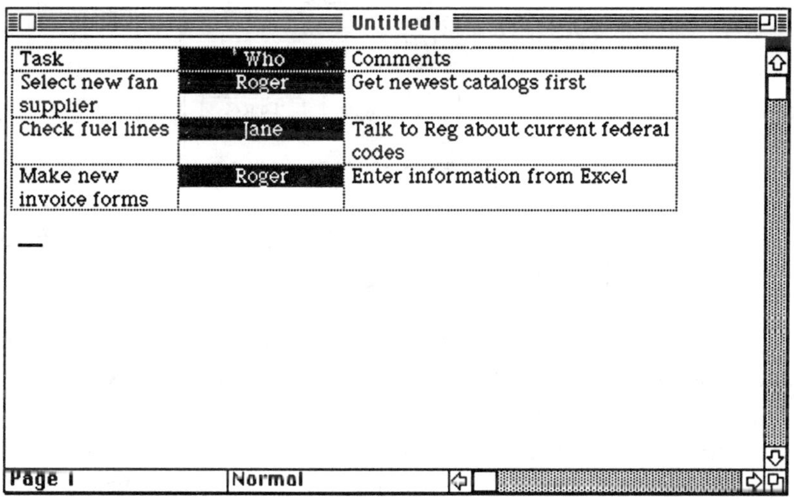

There are many other formatting choices you might want to make for whole rows or columns of cells. For example, you might want to make the whole first row bold. To select the row, double-click in the row's selection bar at the left of the window. You might also want to right-align or decimal-align numbers in some columns.

If you experimented with selecting and moving in your table, you may have noticed that the actions are somewhat different than in regular paragraphs. To select a cell, you click within the cell's *selection bar*—the thin area to the left of the text of the cell. To select a row, you double-click in the selection bar of any cell in the row. You saw that to select a column, you select from the top of the column when the pointer turns to a downward-pointing arrow.

Lesson 71: Advanced Table Handling

To add or delete rows or columns in your table, you need to use the Table Layout command from the Format menu. Word displays the dialog box shown here:

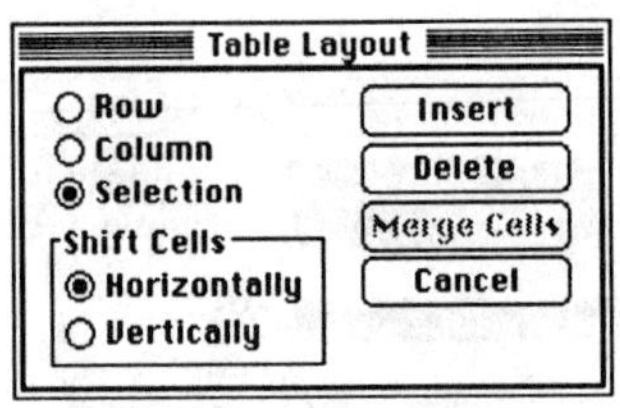

You choose what you want to work on at the left of the dialog box, and then click one of the buttons on the right.

For instance, assume that you want to add a row between the first and second row in the table. Select the second row (or any part of a cell on the second row), give the Table Layout command, select Row at the left of the dialog box, and click Insert.

In the Table dialog box, you must specify whether you want to insert or delete rows or columns. Adding rows or columns always adds before the selection.

If you have selected some cells that are not a row or column, you can delete them by specifying Selection and Delete. For example, if you want to delete a single cell from the second row, first select it or put the insertion point in it:

Task	Who	Comments
Select new fan supplier	Roger	Get newest catalogs first
Check fuel lines	Jane	Talk to Reg about current federal codes
Make new invoice forms	Roger	Enter information from Excel

Give the Table Layout command, select Selection, indicate that you want to shift the cells horizontally (to move the cells that are to the right of the deleted cell to the left when it is deleted), and click Delete.

Task	Who	Comments
Select new fan supplier	Get newest catalogs first	
Check fuel lines	Jane	Talk to Reg about current federal codes
Make new invoice forms	Roger	Enter information from Excel

Notice that the second row now has only two cells instead of three. Word's tables do not have to have the same number of cells in each row.

If you have selected some cells that are not a row or column and you are inserting cells, you can specify whether the added cells should shift the other cells horizontally or vertically. For example, if you want to add a cell to a row, select the cell that will be positioned before the one you want to add, give the Table Layout command, select Selection, select Horizontally, and click Insert. If you need to combine the information in adjacent cells and turn them into a single cell, you can merge them by selecting them and clicking Merge Cells.

The Delete button on the Table dialog box is necessary because Word does not let you remove cells from a table with the DELETE key or the Cut command. If you select some cells and give the Cut command, Word copies the contents of the cells to the Clipboard, but does not remove the cells from the table; it leaves the table's cells blank. Thus, to remove cells from the table itself, you must use the Table Layout command.

If you use the Paste command when there are cells in the Clipboard, Word replaces the cells in the same-shaped area as the cells in the Clipboard. For example, if you select a 2 x 2 section of cells, give the Copy command, and then put the insertion point in a cell and give the Paste command, Word replaces the contents of that cell with the upper-left cell in the Clipboard. Word also replaces the cell to the right of it, as well as the cell below it and the cell kitty-corner to it.

You may already have text that has tab characters in it that you want to convert to tables. (Also, if you have been using Word version 3 or before, you may have some paragraphs that are formatted with the Side By Side option; these can be converted too.) The Text to Table command makes it easy to convert old-style tables into new tables.

To convert these types of text into a table, select the text to be converted and give the Text to Table command from the Insert menu. The choices in the Convert From area of the dialog box now become much more important:

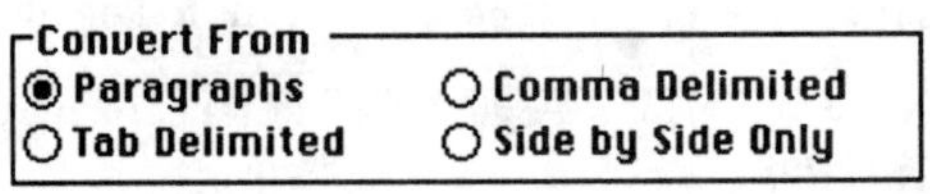

Select either Tab Delimited or Side by Side Only, depending on the type of text you have selected. When you click the OK button, Word changes the text into a table.

The other two choices in the Convert From box of the Insert Table dialog box are also useful. You can take any text in your document and turn it into a table with the Paragraphs choice. The Comma Delimited choice lets you change comma-delimited records (such as ones imported from some databases) into a table.

For instance, you might have formatted a list of names and participants in some seminars as follows:

Keller, Stanley, Anderson, Thatcher

Customer service seminar for all C.S. staff. Receptionists are invited to this seminar.

Nolan, Timmer, Fellston

Group dynamics seminar for engineering staff and quality control technicians.

In this case, each paragraph has a spacing of 12 points between it and the next paragraph. To turn this into a table, simply select the paragraphs, give the Text to Table command, select Paragraphs, and type **2** as the number of columns. Word forms the table:

Keller, Stanley, Anderson, Thatcher	Customer service seminar for all C.S. staff. Receptionists are invited to this seminar.
Nolan, Timmer, Fellston	Group dynamics seminar for engineering staff and quality control technicians.

Lesson 72: Borders for Cells

Remember that the gridlines you see around tables on the screen do not print. You can, however, add borders to tables just as you can to paragraphs (as you saw in Chapter 11). You can add borders to just some cells or to the entire table, depending on what you select. You can add borders by giving the Border command from the Format menu or by clicking the Border button in the Table Cells command. The Borders dialog box is shown in Figure 15-6. The choices are the same here as they were for paragraphs.

You can put borders to the left, right, above, or below a cell. You can also add borders between cells vertically or horizontally. For example, if you select

Figure 15-6. *Borders dialog box for cells*

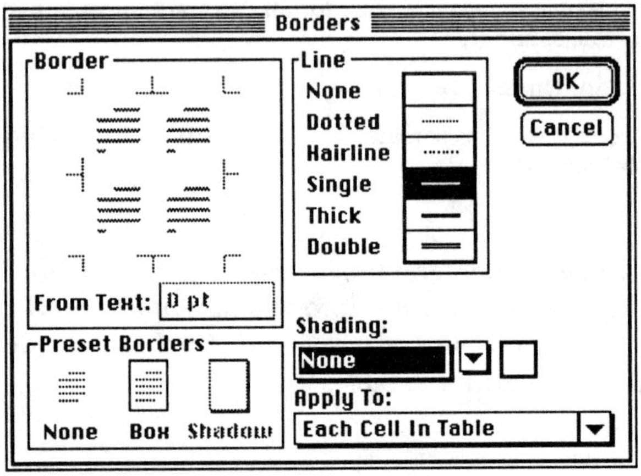

a row of cells, give the Border command, and select the vertical line between the middle guides, as shown in Figure 15-7, Word draws vertical and horizontal lines between the cells in that row.

The choices in the Apply To list give you a great deal of flexibility on deciding how to add borders. The Selected Cells choice adds the borders to just the selected cells while Each Cell In Table applies the border to the whole table, regardless of what you selected. You can also use Entire Rows Selected and Entire Columns Selected to make the formatting apply to more than the cells you select.

Lesson 73: Using Footnotes

Many writers find footnotes hard to incorporate in text correctly; however, Word lets you include footnotes easily. In general, footnotes are used for two purposes: to give the reference for a quotation or an idea, or to give a supplementary note. They are commonly used in academic and scholarly papers, but are becoming more common in financial reports.

Figure 15-7. *Specifying a vertical border between cells*

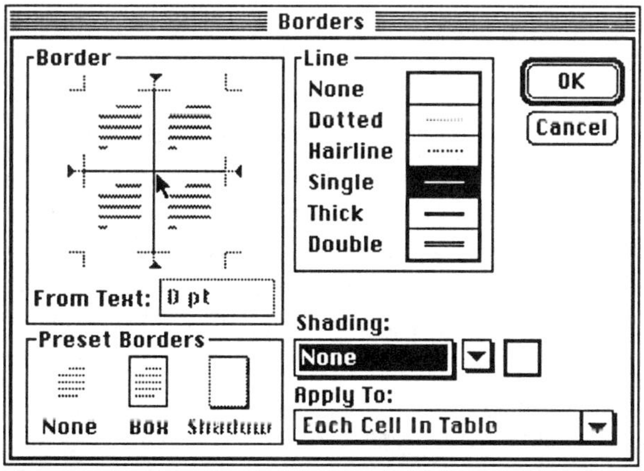

Footnotes consist of the *reference mark* (usually an asterisk or a number) and the *footnote text.* To enter these, use the Footnote command from the Insert menu. Most people prefer to use sequentially numbered footnotes. Word keeps track of the current footnote number and even renumbers your footnotes if you take one out. Using the Document command from the Format menu, you can choose whether you want the footnotes printed on the page where they are referenced, at the end of each section, or at the end of the document (using the Document command).

To insert a footnote, put the insertion point at the place where you want the reference mark and give the Footnote command from the Insert menu. The dialog box that appears is shown here:

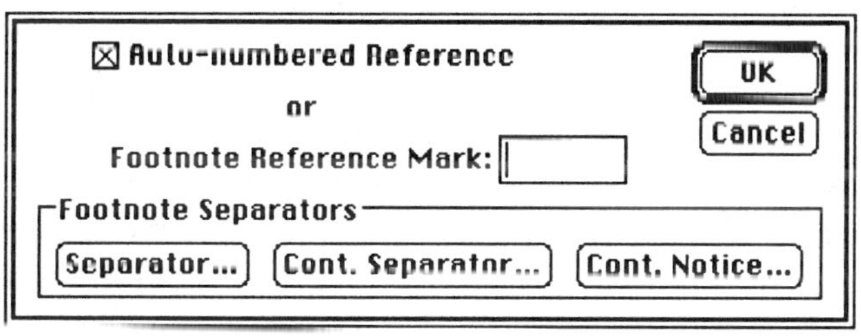

If you enter a character (or up to ten characters) for the footnote reference mark, Word uses that as the reference mark. If you leave the Auto-numbered Reference option selected, Word automatically numbers the footnote in sequence.

When you click OK, Word splits the main text window, creating a footnote area at the bottom. You can then enter and edit the footnote text in this area, and return to where you were before you entered the footnote by clicking in the top pane. You can also drag the split bar to the bottom of the window or press ⌘-OPTION-Z if you want to leave the Footnote window open.

If you want to open the Footnote window without creating a footnote, press the SHIFT key when you drag down the split bar. If you leave the Footnote window open as you scroll through your document, Word scrolls the Footnote window to the first footnote of the page you are on. You can also open the Footnote window by double-clicking on an existing footnote marker.

To see how footnoting works, assume that you want to add another footnote to the report you saw in earlier chapters. (Remember that the report already had some footnotes in it.) Move the insertion point to just after the period following the words "trade shows" at the end of the third section. Give the Footnote command and click the OK button, since the automatic numbering choice is already selected by default. Now enter the text for the additional footnote:

Notice that Word automatically renumbers the footnote that follows your new footnote. If you use automatic numbering, Word keeps track of footnotes that you insert or delete and correctly numbers them. To delete a footnote, simply delete its reference mark in the text.

Word lets you change the appearance of the footnotes, the footnote markers, and the separators between the text and the footnotes. This gives you flexibility in determining how your documents appear. You can change the formatting of the footnote text and footnote markers with the direct formatting commands. In addition, you can change their appearance with the Style commands that you learned about in Chapter 13.

The three buttons in the Footnote dialog box allow you to change the characters Word uses to separate the text and the footnotes at the bottom of the page. It is unlikely that you will want to use these.

The Footnotes section of the Document command lets you change how footnotes appear in the printed document. The choices are shown in the following dialog box:

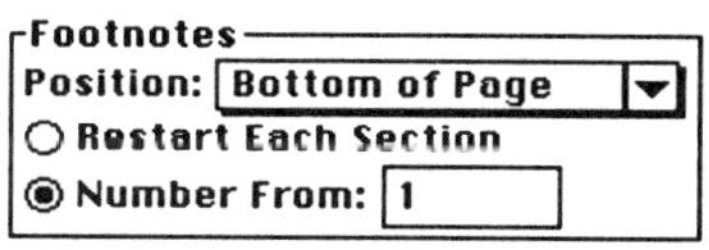

The Restart Each Section and Number From choices let you choose how the footnotes are numbered. You would want to restart the numbers in each section if each section of your document represents a chapter and you want the numbers to start at 1 for each chapter.

There are four choices in the Position drop-down for where footnotes appear in your printed document:

- Bottom of Page puts the footnotes at the bottom of each page, even if there is white space (such as the end of a section or if you have inserted page breaks).
- Beneath Text puts the footnotes directly under the text. If you have white space at the bottom of a page, Word puts the footnotes higher on the page.
- End of Section puts the footnotes on the last page of the section.
- End of Document puts all the footnotes at the end of the document.

These choices allow you to conform to different standards, such as those for academic papers.

Review

Find a table in a magazine article and add it to your Magazine file. Be sure to use the same character and paragraph formatting that appears in the original table.

Add a border with a double line to just the cells in the heading of the table. Then add a border with a single line to the other cells.

Add a footnote to some text near the middle of the document. Go back to the beginning of the file and add another footnote. Note how Word changes the number of the other footnote.

16

Customizing Word

Word has commands that allow you to set various options for the way you use Word. For example, you can adjust the way Word's screen looks and the amount of information that Word gives you.

Most Macintosh programs only let you work with the menus that come with the program. Word, on the other hand, lets you add and remove items on the menus and also lets you add a special menu, called the Work menu, to make using Word easier. You can also change the keyboard combinations used to issue Word's commands.

The settings described in this chapter are remembered when you quit from Word and are automatically used when you start Word again. You can also save different sets of settings and use them at different times, for example, if two people use the same Macintosh and want to use different settings.

Lesson 74: Setting the Options

The Preferences command from the Tools menu lets you specify many different types of settings. You have already seen some of these in earlier chapters because the settings affect a wide range of Word's commands. The initial dialog box is shown in Figure 16-1.

There are many icons in the scrolling list on the left of the dialog box. Each icon represents a set of settings. When you click an icon, those settings appear on the right. For example, when you click the Open And Save icon, the third in the list, the dialog box changes to show those choices.

The rest of this chapter explains the contents of the dialog box for each icon.

General Settings

You see the general settings when you give the Preferences command.

Your name and initials are used by the Summary Info dialog box. These are described in Chapter 21.

You can add a custom paper size that will be used in the Page Setup command, described in Chapter 8. Use this if you regularly use a nonstandard paper size.

The Measurement option lets you set the units that Word uses when it prompts you for linear measurement, such as in the Paragraph command and

Figure 16-1. *Initial Preferences dialog box*

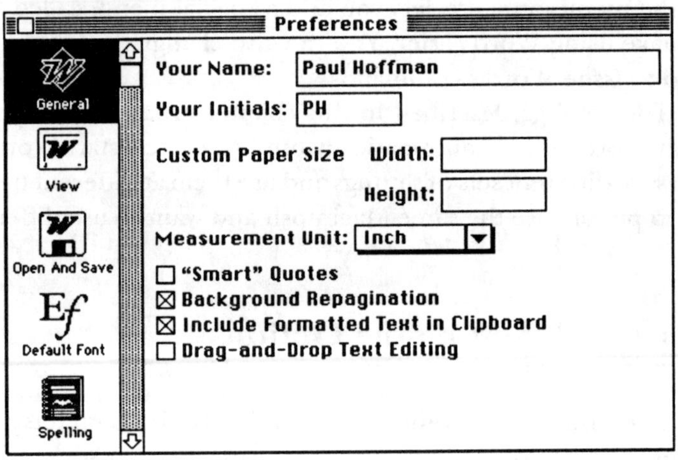

on the ruler. You select the choice you want to use when you give measurements. The choices are

Choice	Meaning
Inch	Inches (1 in. = 2.5 cm.)
Cm	Centimeters (1 cm. = 0.4 in.)
Points	1 point = 1/72 in. (Points are used for measurement by typesetters and are described in Chapter 10.)
Pica	6 picas = 1 in.

"Smart" Quotes cause Word to type curved single and double-quotes when you enter straight ones. An opening quote is entered if there is a space before the straight quote you type. This option is an alternative to using the OPTION and SHIFT keys in order to use curly quotes. If you want to type curly quotes directly, you have to use the following key sequences:

Character	Keystroke
“	OPTION-[
”	OPTION-SHIFT-[
‘	OPTION-]
’	OPTION-SHIFT-]

Background Repagination turns on automatic repagination. This is described in Chapter 12.

You would only want to turn off the Include Formatted Text in Clipboard feature if you are having a problem transferring text to another program. This is rare, and it is always better to transfer text with formatting when possible.

The Drag-and-Drop Text Editing choice tells whether you want to use this option. See Chapter 4 for more information on drag-and-drop editing.

View Settings

Figure 16-2 shows the view settings—how things look, what you see, and what you don't. The first four choices tell Word whether or not you want to

Figure 16-2. *View settings*

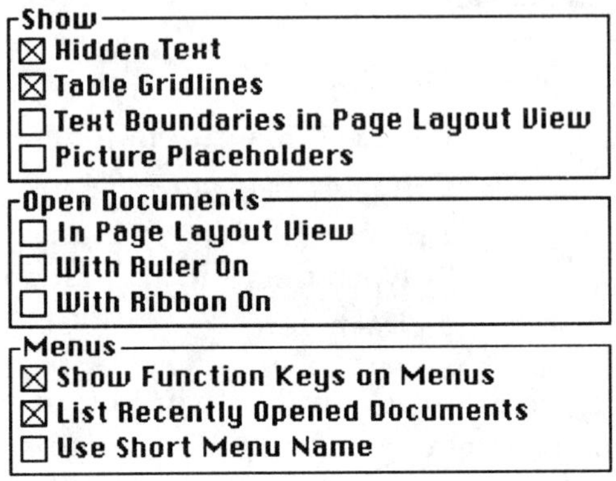

see special features on the screen. The Open Documents choices specify how the document window looks when you give the Open or New commands.

Hidden Text tells Word whether or not to display hidden text on the screen. Hidden text, described in Chapter 18, consists of remarks or instructions that are about the document but not to be printed as part of it. When you are entering a great deal of hidden text, such as when you are putting in index and table of contents entries, you usually want this option turned on. However, you usually want this option off when you are repaginating, because Word counts the text in its measurements when you repaginate. Note that this choice does not cause the hidden text to show up in your printed output. For that, you must select the option in the Print command or in the Document command. Hidden text is off by default.

Table Gridlines displays lines between the cells in a table, as described in Chapter 15. It does not, however, cause these lines to be printed. This option is on by default.

Text Boundaries in Page Layout View is useful when you have positioned paragraphs and tables in a document and you are in page layout mode. This option causes each text box to be surrounded by a dotted border. This option is off by default.

Turning on the Picture Placeholders option makes scrolling faster, because Word does not show the actual graphic in your documents, only a gray rectangle. This can be especially useful on Macintoshes with small amounts of memory or when you have very complex pictures because of the time spent in redrawing each view of the picture.

The In Page Layout View option causes the New and Open commands to use page layout mode instead of normal mode by default. If you use page view often, you might want to select this option. Page view is off by default.

With Ruler On and With Ribbon On start documents with the ruler and ribbon showing. People with small screens sometimes prefer not to select these options, while people with large screens often select these options. These are on by default.

Show Function Keys On Menus tells Word to show the keyboard equivalents to the right of the command names. This option is normally selected, since it takes very little space, it does not slow down Word, and is a very useful and handy reference. Keyboard equivalents are discussed in detail later in this chapter.

List Recently Opened Documents causes the last four files that you open to appear in the File menu. If you work on only a few files, this is very handy, since you can select these to open a file, rather than going through the various open windows and folders to find the file.

The Use Short Menu Name option shortens a few of the names on the menus. Only use this if your menu bar is too crowded.

Open and Save Settings

The Open and Save settings change the way that the Open, New, Save, and Save As commands work. The options are

☒ Always Interpret RTF
☐ Always Make Backup
☒ Allow Fast Saves
☒ Prompt for Summary Info
☐ Save Reminder Every [ ] Minutes

Always Interpret RTF causes Word to check text files to see if they are in *Rich Text Format* (also called *RTF* or *interchange format*) when opening them. RTF files are special text files that keep formatting information. You should always leave this option on.

Always Make Backup causes Word to create a backup copy of a file when you give the Save or Save As commands. The backup is called "Backup of" and the document name. You can also change this option in the Save As dialog box.

The Allow Fast Saves option lets Word save files in a faster manner. This is generally good (especially if you are editing long files), but some programs that can read Word files can only read those that have been saved in the slower method. Also, files saved with the fast save method often are larger than files saved with the slower method. After a few fast saves, Word normally reverts to a slow save to bring down the size and complexity of a file.

The Prompt for Summary Info option tells Word whether or not to display the Summary Info dialog box you see the first time you save a file. This is described in detail in Chapter 21. This is on by default.

Save Reminder Every () Minutes instructs Word to remind you to save your work at regular intervals. This is useful if you often forget to save your work and end up working for long stretches without saving. If you select this option, after the time period, Word prompts you:

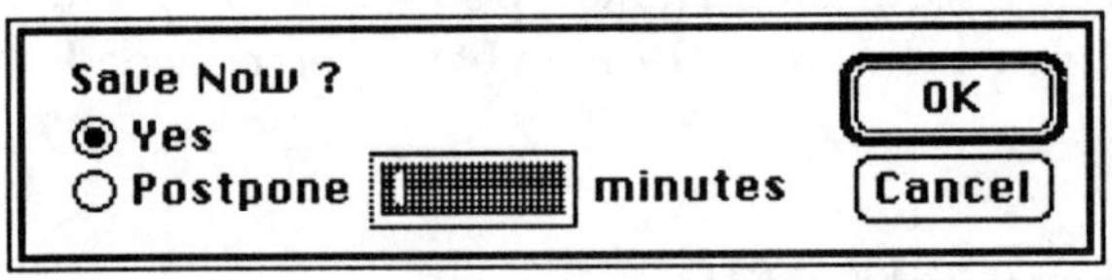

Default Font

You can specify a default font and size to be used when you open a new file. The choices are in a drop-down list like this:

Choose the font name and font size from the drop-down lists.

Figure 16-3. Spelling settings

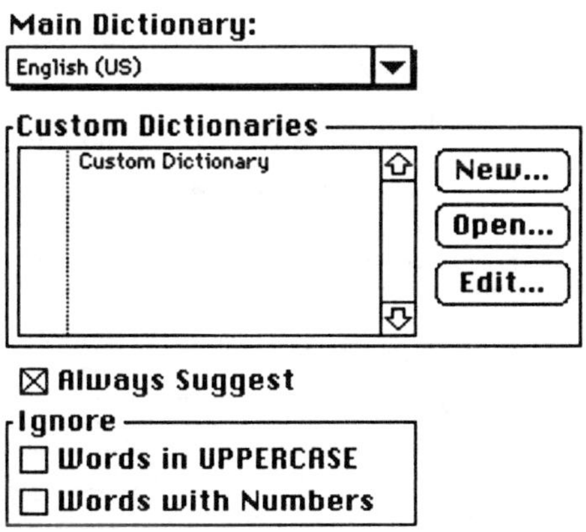

Spelling Settings

The spelling settings are shown in Figure 16-3. You can also get to this dialog box by clicking the Options button in the Spelling command. The spelling options are covered in Chapter 19.

Grammar Settings

The grammar settings are shown in Figure 16-4. You can also get to this dialog box by clicking the Options button in the Grammar command. The grammar options are covered in Chapter 19.

Thesaurus

The single choice for the thesaurus is for the language:

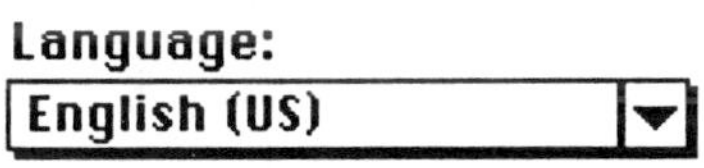

Figure 16-4. *Grammar settings*

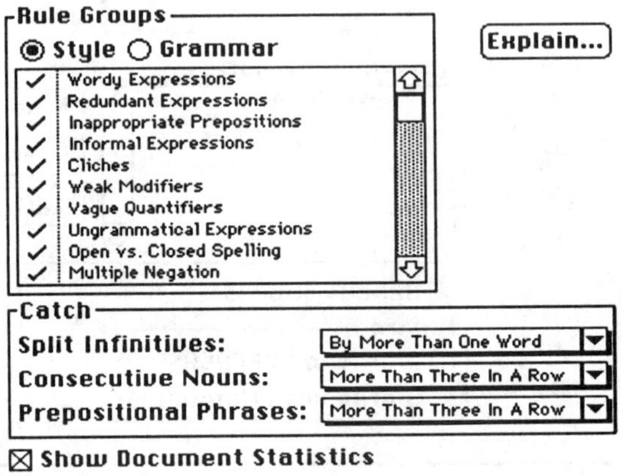

The languages listed are those for which you have dictionaries on your hard disk. The thesaurus is covered in Chapter 19.

Hyphenation

The single choice for hyphenation is for the language:

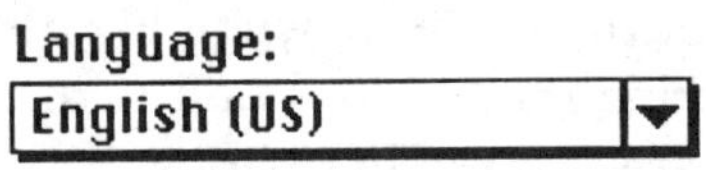

The languages listed are those for which you have dictionaries on your hard disk. Hyphenation is covered in Chapter 19.

Lesson 75: Customizing Menus in Word

Use the Commands command from the Tools menu to add items to menus, remove items from menus, or change the key combination used for a menu item. This is a very powerful tool for customizing Word to your needs. The dialog box for the Commands command is shown in Figure 16-5.

The list at the top left contains all the commands that are available to you in Word. These include all the commands normally found on the menus, as well as the names of dialog boxes directly available (such as the Tabs dialog box), choices in some dialog boxes (such as Fractional Widths), some formats, and some actions that are usually accessed only through key combinations.

The Description box at the right gives a brief description of what the command you've selected from the list does.

To add a command to a menu, select the command from the list and look in the Menu section near the bottom left of the dialog box. If the command is already in a menu, the Add button becomes gray and the Remove button becomes available. Click Remove to take the command off of the menu. If the command is not in a menu, the Remove button becomes gray and the Add button becomes available. Word chooses a menu where the command would logically go in the drop-down list of menus. To change this, simply choose a new menu from the drop-down list. Click Add to add the command to the menu. If a menu becomes too long for all the commands to show at once, it becomes a drop-down—scroll down to the entry you want.

Figure 16-5. *Commands dialog box*

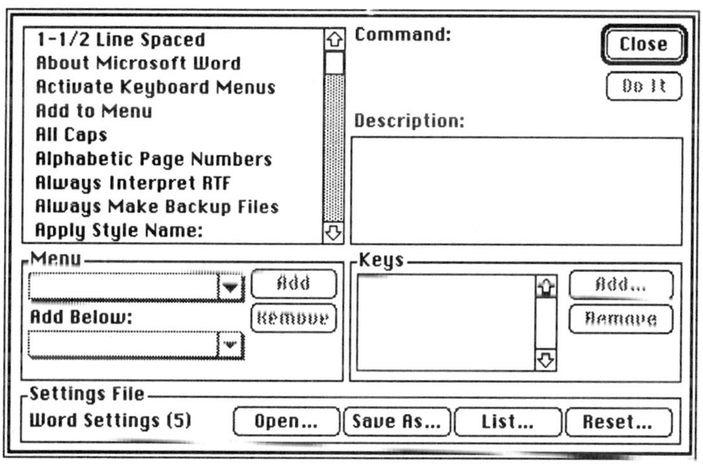

Figure 16-6. *Cell Shading command being added to the Format menu after the Border command*

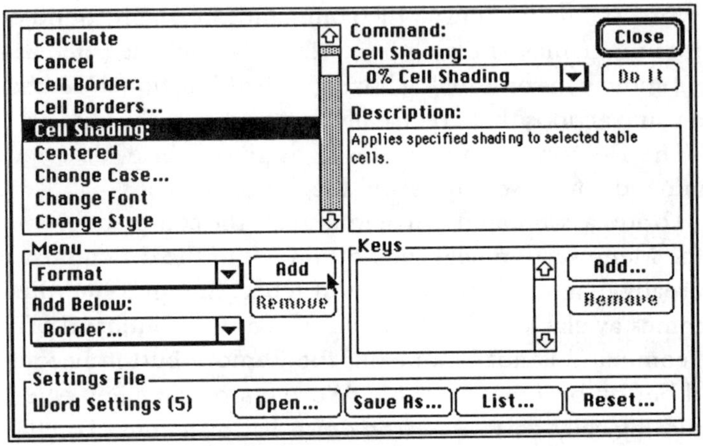

You also specify where on the menu you want the command to appear in the Add Below drop-down list. The Auto choice tells Word to put the command in a predefined location on the menu, or you can choose a specific command to put the new command after. Click the Add button in order to add the command to the desired menu.

Figure 16-6 illustrates the Cell Shading command being added to the Format menu after the Border command. You might use this to visually emphasize a frequently used command.

You can add, remove, or change the key combination for a command in a similar way. After you select the command from the list in the upper-left corner, the Keys section shows the current keys for the command. To add a new combination, click the Add button. Word displays a dialog box with the name of the command. For example, if you are adding a key combination to the Centered command, you will see the following:

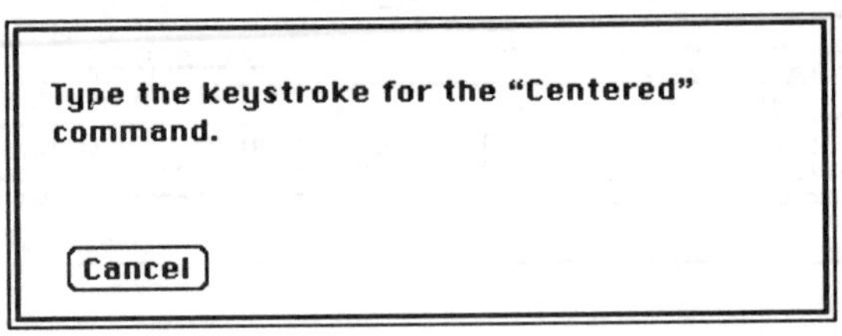

Press the key combination you want. To remove a key combination, select it from the list and click the Remove button.

When you have finished adding menus and keys, click the Cancel button to make the dialog box disappear.

The Do button in the Commands dialog box lets you execute a command from the list at the left without adding it to a menu. Simply select the command from the list and click the Do button.

Lesson 76: The Work Menu

The Work menu holds the names of documents, the names of glossary entries, and the names of styles. It is a handy place to hold all of your personal items that are not general Word commands. The Work menu appears to the right of the Window menu on the menu bar.

To add a document, glossary entry, or style to the Work menu, press ⌘-OPTION-+. The pointer turns into a bold plus sign:

+

Then select the item you want added, and Word adds it to the menu.

For example, assume that you want to add the Sample 1 file to the Work menu. Press ⌘-OPTION-+ and give the Open command. Select Sample 1 from the list box and click the Open button. Although the Sample 1 file is not opened, it is added to the Work menu. You can remove a menu item by pressing ⌘-OPTION-- and selecting the menu item.

You add glossary entries and style names to the Work menu in a similar way. Press ⌘-OPTION-+ and give the Glossary or Styles command.

Lesson 77: Storing Your Settings

The options you specify in this chapter are stored in a file that is kept in the Preferences folder in your System Folder on your disk. Normally the file is called Word Settings (5). You also can store your settings in other files and open those files whenever you feel like it. This is useful if you have different people using Word on one Macintosh and they have different choices they want for the settings. To store the current settings in a different setting file, give the Commands command and click the Save As button near the bottom of the dialog box.

To open a settings file other than Word Settings (5), click the Open button in the Command dialog box.

Use the Reset button to remove any changes you have made during the current session and restore the settings to those in the open settings files.

The List button creates a new document with a list of all the commands, their menus, and their key combinations in a table. This button displays the following:

The All Word Commands choice creates a long table that lists all of the possible Word commands. The table makes a good reference chart.

Review

If you work in normal mode most of the time, you may want to make a key combination for the Header command from the View menu so that you can change the header text without using the mouse. Choose a key combination that makes sense to you for this action (such as ⌘-OPTION-H) and assign that key combination to that command.

Add the Insert Columns option (normally only available in the Table Layout command) to the Insert menu. Look for other actions that you might want on the Insert menu.

17

Outlining

There are many circumstances where outlines help you organize your thinking. Outlines can assist you in determining how important thoughts relate to each other. Writing an outline is also a good way to be sure you have covered all the topics that are relevant to your subject.

If you wish, you can use the features of Word you have already learned to make an outline. If you set the tabs for a document at half-inch increments, you can enter text in a standard outline format. You can use Word's selection features to move groups of items around; you can even use an outline style sheet to specify a different emphasis for each level of your outline. However, Word's new outlining features allow you to do much more.

This chapter shows you how to create and modify outlines using special outlining features. With these new features you can even turn existing documents into outlines. If you are familiar with other outlining programs for the Macintosh, you may see similarities between those programs and Word. Once you've learned how to outline with Word, you will find many situations in your daily work where outlines are very useful.

Lesson 78: Introduction to Word's Outlining Features

Every document in Word can also be viewed as an outline. Until now, you have used the normal and page layout modes for editing; since you haven't used any of Word's outlining features, you haven't needed to see your document in outline mode.

It is important to understand that outlines are not different from text documents in Word. Most outline programs create files that can only be used as outlines. Word, on the other hand, lets you create an outline and then fill in its parts with text. When you want to see the text, you use normal mode; when you want to see the outline, you use *outline mode*. Outline mode is just a different, more streamlined way to look at your document.

You use the outline mode and the normal mode for different purposes. You edit and format in normal or page layout mode, as you have seen. You use outline mode to review and change the structure of your text, just as you might decide to switch the position of two major ideas after writing an outline on paper.

In Word's outline mode, when you move a heading, all the text under that heading moves, too. To achieve this result in normal mode, you would have to select a huge amount of text, delete it to the Clipboard, move to the new location, and insert the text there. In outline mode, you just move the heading, and the associated text moves with it.

There is a price for the convenience of using outline mode: you cannot select text across paragraph boundaries. Because of this limitation, you are usually restricted to editing a single paragraph. (In outlines, each heading is a separate paragraph.)

If you have a complicated and detailed outline, you may have dozens of subheads under a main heading. When you are working with this kind of outline, you can get lost in the lower-level headings and miss the overall picture. Word lets you *collapse* an outline so that lower-level headings are invisible.

Moving between normal mode and outline mode is very easy. You can switch between normal mode and outline mode by using the Outline command from the View menu or by pressing ⌘-OPTION-O.

You can tell which view you are in by looking at the top of the window. In normal mode, the page looks normal. In outline mode, the outline bar at the top of the window looks like this:

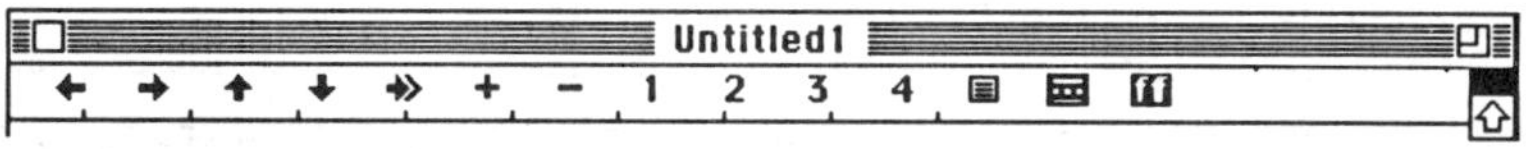

Outlines can have both *headings* and *body text* (body text is like regular text). Each heading has a level, starting with level 1. Body text does not have a level. As you make an outline, Word remembers the level of headings by saving a paragraph style with each one. These styles are "heading 1", "heading 2", and so on. Body text is formatted as Normal. As long as you enter your outline in outline mode, you do not have to add these styles; Word does it for you. (Styles are covered in Chapter 13.)

Because outlines are just like regular documents, Word treats them very similarly. You can print an outline with the Print command from the File menu, and you can save it with the Save command from the File menu. In fact, you will find that handling outlines is almost identical to handling regular text files.

Lesson 79: Creating an Outline

You can enter the text for a new outline in either document mode or in outline mode. It is usually better to enter and edit outlines in outline mode.

When you want to create a new outline, be sure that you use a new document. Switch from normal mode to outline mode by choosing the Outline command from the View menu. Your screen looks like Figure 17-1.

Figure 17-2 shows the outline you will work with in this chapter. Begin by entering the first heading, **Contract preparation**, and press (RETURN). Word assumes that you want to start at level 1 (the level indicator is shown in the style box at the bottom of the window).

Next type the line **Use standard contract as basis**. However, this entry is level 2, not level 1. To tell Word that this line is level 2, click the right-arrow icon in the outline bar, the second icon from the left:

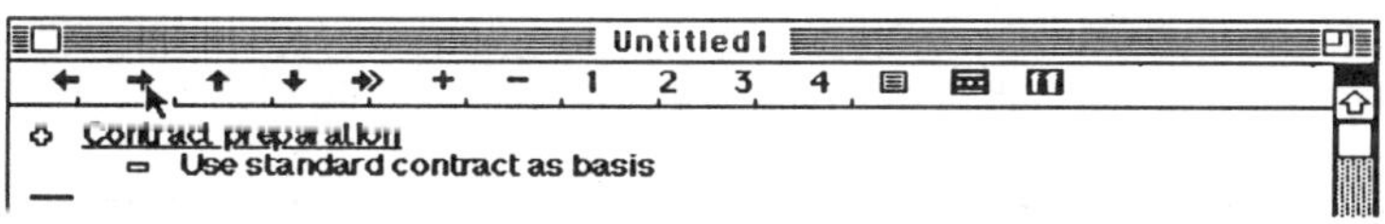

Figure 17-1. *Outline mode*

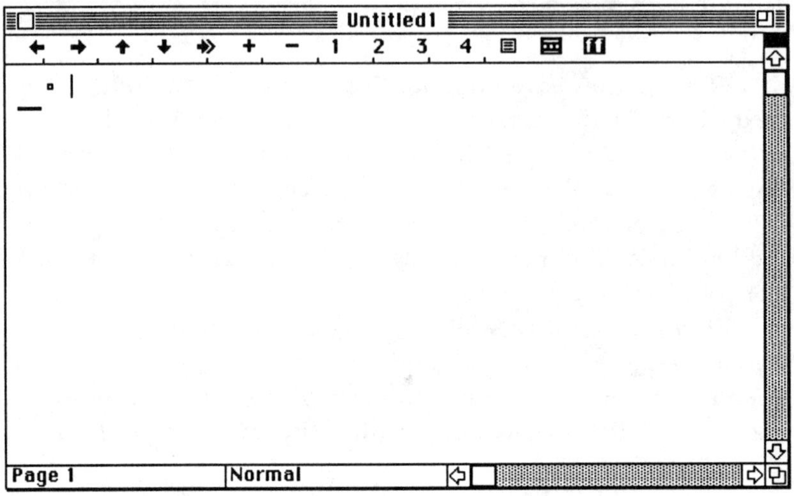

Figure 17-2. *Sample outline*

- Contract preparation
  - Use standard contract as basis
  - Add union work clause
    - Local 112 for installing
    - Local 112 and 427 for maintenance
  - Add outdoor setting clause
- Contract signing
  - Phillips at National Generators
  - Martinez and Washington at fair
- Site preparation
  - Verify space requirements
  - Erect shelters
  - Cable to main sections
    - 4 500' spans
    - Check with Martinez for exact locations
- Install generators
  - 2 30G's for main supply
    - 2 fuel tanks
  - 1 33G for backup
    - 1 extra fuel tank
  - Operations shack
- Test
  - Load to full power

Word indents the line, and the level indicator reflects the level you have chosen.

Note that the first line you entered has a hollow plus sign next to it and the second line has a hollow minus sign:

The plus sign indicates that the heading has a subhead beneath it, while the minus sign indicates that the heading does not have any subheads.

Continue by typing the next line, **Add union work clause**, press (RETURN), and then click the right-arrow icon again to tell Word that the next line is at level 3. If you prefer to use the keyboard instead of clicking the icons, you can press the (OPTION)-(→) key instead of clicking the arrow in the outline bar.

After you add the two level-3 lines, go back to level 2. To do so, click the left-arrow icon or press (OPTION)-(←). You can see how the left-arrow and right-arrow icons move the levels up and down. Finish entering all the text and save the file as Fair Organization with the Save command.

So far, you have only entered headings. Many outlines contain body text, such as paragraphs under headings or a title. For this example, use body text to add a title to the outline. To do this, move to the top of the outline, press (RETURN) twice to add some space, and type **Millerton Art Fair** on the first line. To tell Word that this is body text, click the double-right arrow between the down-arrow icon and the plus icons:

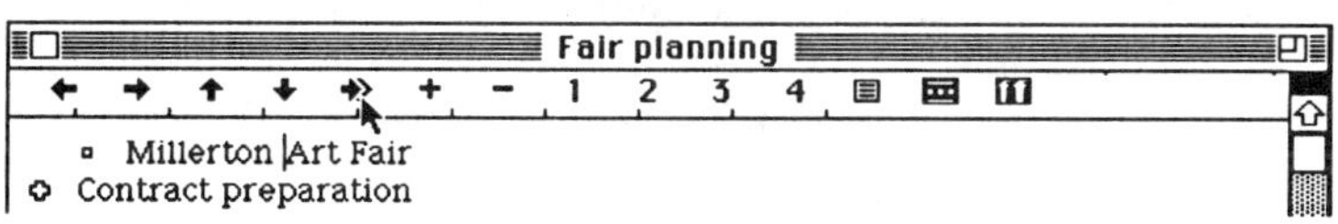

You can insert topics in the middle of an outline by moving to the beginning of a line, typing in new characters, and pressing (RETURN). You can change the level of a heading by selecting any part of the heading and clicking the left- or right-arrow icons. You can change a heading into body text by selecting any part of the heading and clicking the double-right arrow.

It is important to remember to use the left- or right-arrow icons or (OPTION)-(←) or (OPTION)-(→) to shift headings. You should not use the (TAB) key to do this because Word does not recognize it.

Lesson 80: Collapsing and Expanding

A detailed outline can be very hard to follow, especially if it includes body text. When outlining a complex business report, for example, you can quickly lose track of the outline among all the text.

To avoid this problem, you often want to see only higher-level portions of an outline. Word allows you to hide lower-level heads and body text by collapsing them. To collapse all of the headings below a particular one, simply select that heading (or any part of it) and click the minus icon on the outline bar. To restore these headings, click the plus icon on the outline bar.

For example, select first the entire level-1 heading, "Contract preparation". Click the minus icon in the outline bar to hide the subordinate headings. You can also press the (-) key on the keypad. The result is this:

```
    ▫ Millerton Art Fair
  ✪ Contract preparation
  ✪ Contract signing
        ▭ Phillips at National Generators
        ▭ Martinez and Washington at fair
```

When you collapse a heading, Word puts a gray bar where the collapsed material is, to remind you that there is more under that heading:

```
✪ Contract preparation
```

You can *expand* a collapsed heading by clicking the plus icon in the outline bar or pressing the (+) key on the keypad.

Expanding a heading shows only the level immediately below it. For example, if you collapse a level-1 heading and some of the level-2 heads below it have subheads, expanding the level-1 heading does not expand the level-2 heads at the same time. If you have collapsed different levels of headings and you want to expand them all at once, use the * on the keypad or click the box with three lines near the right side of the outline bar. This expands all the headings.

Note that the minus and plus on the outline bar collapse and expand the lowest level of heading under the selected paragraph. Thus, if you have a level-3 outline and have selected a top-level heading, clicking the minus on the outline bar hides the level-3 entries only.

It is likely that you will want to view your outline as a whole from various levels. To do this, click the numbers in the outline bar. For example, clicking on 2 in the outline bar collapses everything except level-1 and level-2 headings. Collapsing lower-level headings in this way is useful when you are analyzing whether points in your outline are properly arranged and have equal weight.

Lesson 81: Rearranging Your Outline

If you could write an outline correctly the first time you tried, there would not be much use for Word's special outlining commands. Because you use outlines to organize your thoughts, you need to rearrange headings as you decide to change their position or importance. The outline edit mode makes these adjustments especially easy.

If you are moving a heading, it is likely that you also want to move all the ideas associated with it. Word lets you do this. In outline edit mode, when you delete and send a heading to the Clipboard, all subheads and body text under that heading are included, so moving whole ideas is easy.

For example, suppose that you want to move "Add union work clause" and its related subheads to follow "Add outdoor setting clause". To quickly select the head and its subheads, click the hollow plus icon next to "Add union work clause":

```
✥ Contract preparation
    ▭ Use standard contract as basis
    ✥ Add union work clause
        ▭ Local 112 for installing
        ▭ Local 112 and 427 for maintenance
    ▭ Add outdoor setting clause
```

Click and drag the plus icon down to after "Add outdoor setting clause", as shown in Figure 17-3. A dotted line appears, showing you where the selected text moves when you release the mouse button.

The ability to move a head along with the ideas associated with it is especially useful if you have a lot of body text. Instead of scrolling through many screens of text, you can simply select all the subordinate headings under the heading by clicking the hollow plus icon in the selection bar.

Lesson 82: Numbering Your Outline

Up to this point, all the outlines discussed have been simple outlines without numbers and letters. If you create an outline with numbered headings, you cannot move one of these headings somewhere else in the outline without affecting the numbering. Word gives you a simple way of numbering and renumbering outlines.

Figure 17-3. *Moving the heading down*

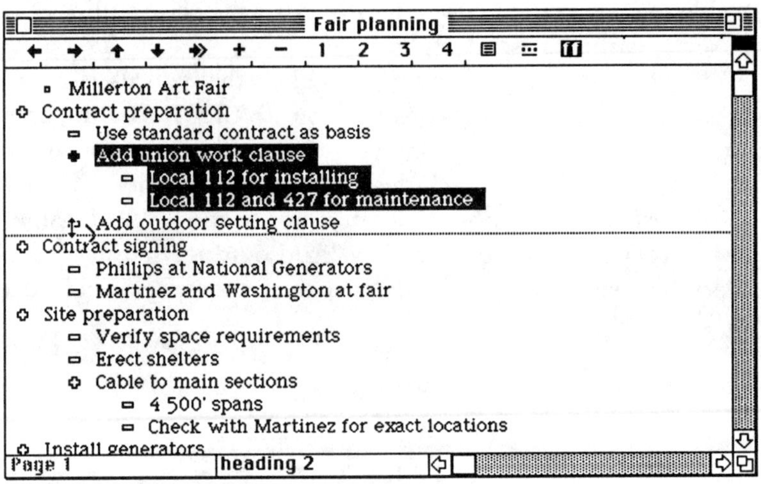

This lesson shows you how Word numbers and renumbers outlines. Numbering regular text in normal mode is very similar. Word will, in fact, number anything, not just outlines.

You can add numbering with the Renumber command from the Tools menu. Word can number in cascading numeral format: 1, 1.1, 1.2, 1.2.1, and so on. If you are numbering an outline, Word does not number body text.

For an example of how the Renumber command works, select the entire outline (not including the title), and then give the Renumber command:

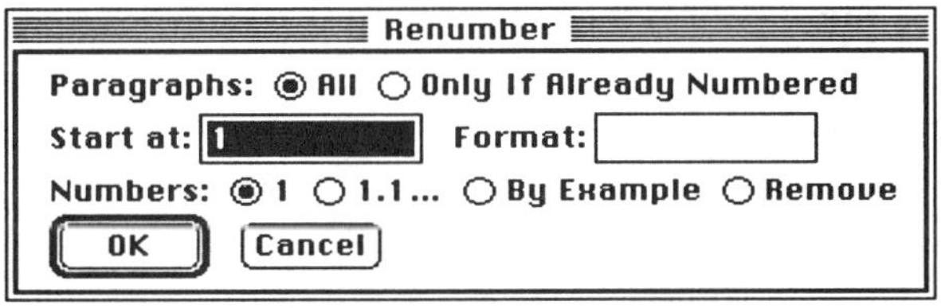

Select Numbers 1.1... and click OK. The outline is now numbered as shown in Figure 17-4.

Figure 17-4. *Renumbered outline*

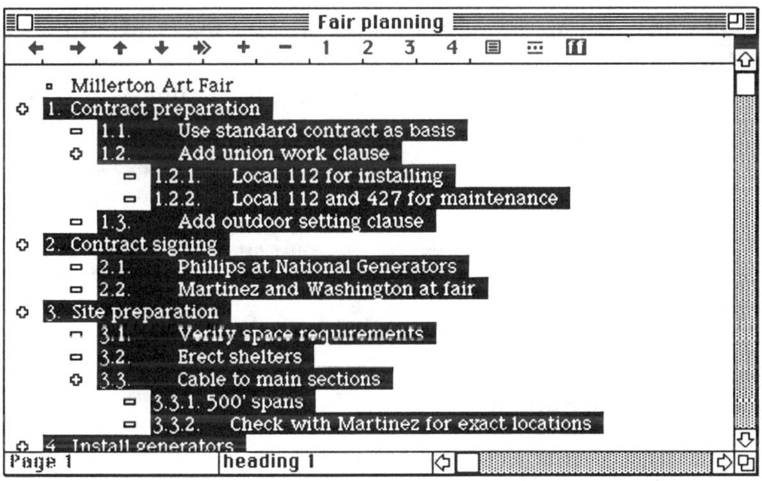

If you want to use a different form of numbering, you have to indicate what form you want. In the Format box in the Renumber dialog box, enter the format using the type symbols shown in Table 17-1. If you want to have different types of numbers for different headings, put a punctuation mark between the types for the different levels.

Standard outline style is to have uppercase Roman numerals for level-l heads, uppercase letters for level-2 heads, Arabic numbers for level-3 heads, and lowercase letters for level-4 heads. Each of these would have a period (.) after it. To do this enter **I.A.1.a.** in the format box. You can use any of the following punctuation marks between the levels:

,	comma
-	hyphen
/	slash
;	semicolon
:	colon
( )	left and right parenthesis
{ }	left and right brace
[ ]	left and right bracket

Word also renumbers your outlines if you move headings around. For example, if you move the "Add union work clause" heading and give the Renumber command, Word correctly renumbers that heading and all the subsequent heads.

If you use the Renumber command to renumber a regular document, Word adds a tab between the number and text. Thus, you should be sure that you have set up your document with proper tab settings before you renumber.

Table 17-1. *Format Symbols for the Renumber Command*

Type of numeral	Symbol
Arabic	1
Uppercase Roman	I
Lowercase Roman	i
Uppercase letter	A
Lowercase letter	a

For example, you may want to use hanging indents, which would make the numbers stand out.

Review

Make an outline that explains the advantages and disadvantages of three possible sites for an annual convention. First list the sites, then add the advantages and disadvantages as subheads, and add more detail under some of the advantages. Rearrange the order of the sites in the outline.

18

Tables of Contents and Indexes

Tables of contents and indexes are not only time-consuming and tedious to prepare manually, but they also must be updated whenever you modify your document. Few word processing packages automatically compile tables of contents or indexes. Those that do usually restrict you to a preset style of printout that may not meet your needs.

With Word, however, you can easily create entries for the table of contents or index, and you have great flexibility in styling your printout. In addition, you can generate a new table of contents or index whenever you choose. These features make Word one of the most popular programs for business and academic use.

The methods used for creating a table of contents and an index are similar. You indicate what you want in your table of contents or index as you edit your document. When you have finished editing and formatting, you give a command that collects the entries and generates a table of contents or index based on the entries and their page numbers. Thus, the table of contents and index are not made "automatically," but you can create them or update them at any time with a single command.

Lesson 83: Planning a Table of Contents

Before you start using Word to generate tables of contents for your documents, you should consider the purpose and structure of a table of contents. A table of contents appears at or near the beginning of a document. It tells the reader what is presented in the document and in what order. A document that is only one or two pages long generally does not need a table of contents.

A table of contents can be a simple list of where each section of the document begins, or it can be a detailed road map of the document. For example, the table of contents of most books contains only the chapter names and beginning page numbers. This keeps the table of contents short (it usually fits on one page) and gives the reader a feel for the general categories and progression of subjects.

Some tables of contents are meant to show almost the entire contents of a document. These are much longer than simple tables of contents and are often hard to browse through. Of course, someone looking for a particular subject will be more likely to find it in a detailed table of contents. However, many authors prefer to create an index for detailed listings and keep the table of contents brief.

The format of a table of contents is also important. If you list two or more levels of headings in a table of contents, using paragraph and character formatting (or styles) makes the table of contents significantly easier to read. Compare the unformatted and formatted tables of contents shown in Figure 18-1.

Lesson 84: Indicating Table of Contents Entries

There are two methods for indicating to Word what you want in your table of contents:

- Use the predefined styles "heading 1", "heading 2", and so on. You can specify these styles yourself or you can use the outlining feature, which uses these styles automatically. Styles are covered in Chapter 13 and outlining is covered in Chapter 17.

Figure 18-1. *Tables of contents without and with formatting*

Unformatted:

Installing	1
Unpacking	2
Checking the crates	2
In case of damage	3
Removing the main unit	4
Other units	8
Connecting to equipment	10
Adding fuel	10
Testing	13
Starting for the first time	14

Formatted:

Installing 1
  Unpacking 2
    Checking the crates 2
    In case of damage 3
    Removing the main unit 4
    Other units 8
  Connecting to equipment 10
  Adding fuel 10
Testing 13
  Starting for the first time 14

- Mark the paragraphs you want to include in the table of contents with hidden text.

The styles method is much easier than the hidden text method and is described here first. Using styles, particularly if you also use outlining, is natural–since all of your chapter titles have the same formatting, all your top-level headings have the same formatting, and so on.

To indicate the paragraphs you want in the table of contents, use the predefined styles "heading 1", "heading 2", and so on. For example, in this book, the chapter names would be "heading 1", and the lesson names "heading 2".

You can check the organization of your table of contents by viewing your document in outline mode, as described in Chapter 17. When you click one of the numbers in the outline bar, Word hides all of the headings and text at a level below that number.

Note that you have to use styles to mark entries this way. You cannot simply apply direct formatting to the headings. If you do not want to use styles, you must use the hidden text method for indicating entries. The hidden text method is described later in this chapter in the lesson on using hidden text.

Lesson 85: Creating the Table of Contents

Once you have marked all of the entries, you can create a table of contents with the Table of Contents command from the Insert menu. Briefly, this command performs the following steps:

1. Repaginates your document
2. Searches through your document from the beginning for entries
3. Collects copies of those entries and their associated page numbers
4. Creates a new section at the beginning of your document containing the entries

The Table of Contents command has many interesting features that are described in this lesson and later in the chapter. Even if you skip these descriptions, you can quickly generate a simple table of contents just by giving the Table of Contents command. With a bit more planning and work, however, you can create more complex tables of contents and figure lists.

You can give the Table of Contents command at any time. If you change your document by adding, deleting, or moving text, you should give the command before you print your document so that the table of contents reflects the most current revision. If you have already created a table of contents, Word replaces the old copy with the new one after you verify that you want this done.

When you give the Table of Contents command from the Insert menu, you see the following dialog box:

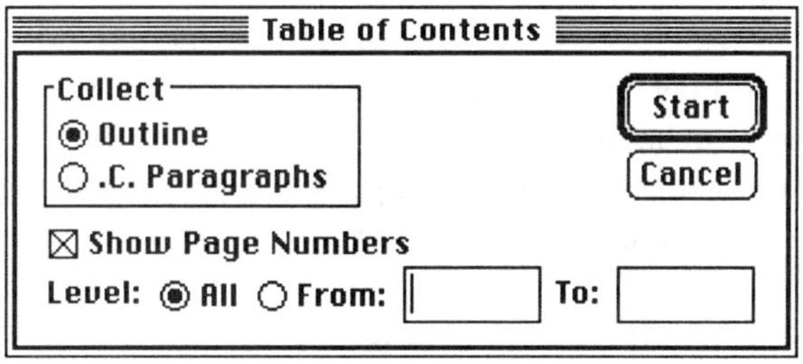

Choose Outline and Show Page Numbers, and then click the Start button. Word creates a new section at the beginning of your document containing the table of contents. Your table of contents will be similar to the one shown in Figure 18-2. Word formats the table of contents with the predefined styles "toc 1", "toc 2", and so on.

Word puts the table of contents at the beginning of your document in its own section so that it does not affect the numbering of the pages in the

Figure 18-2. *Sample table of contents*

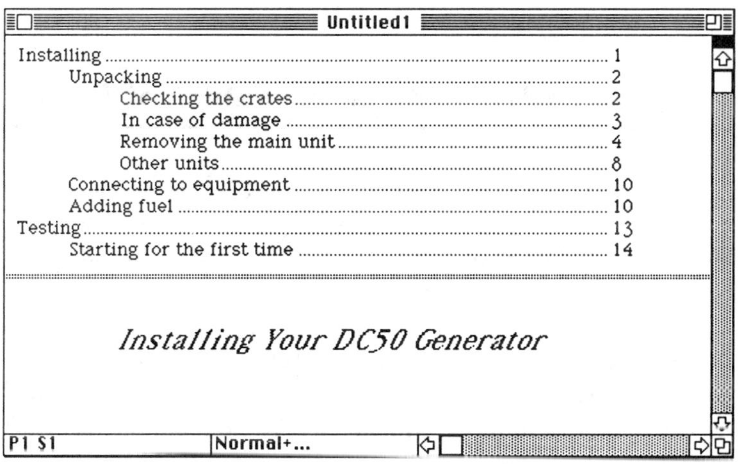

main part. Unless you have a specific reason to move it, it is best to leave the table of contents there. However, if you have a title page and other front matter, you may want to move the table of contents after it.

Once you have this text at the beginning of your document, you can format it any way you want. In general, you use the predefined styles. You can use normal character and paragraph formatting on the text, but it is much better to change the formatting on the styles instead. You can also use section formatting on the table's section. Note, however, that if you use direct formatting instead of style formatting and remake the table of contents, any direct formatting changes you made are lost.

If you are making a table of contents from hidden text instead of from the heading styles, simply select .C. Paragraphs instead of Outline in the Table of Contents command.

Word knows where previous tables of contents are in your document. When it re-creates a table of contents, Word only erases the table of contents entries, not any text you have added before or after the entries in the same section.

You can add text at the top of your table of contents, such as the title "Table of Contents." You can also format the section marker for the table of contents after the first time Word creates it. Word won't change it after that.

Lesson 86: Advanced Use of Tables of Contents

Many reports have numerous figures and tables. It is useful to list these elements and let the reader know what pages they appear on. In the same way that you create tables of contents, you can also create other lists.

For example, assume that you have a figure listing like the one in Figure 18-3. To create this, you should format your figure titles with the "heading 9" style. You use this style because the Table of Contents command looks for any of the "heading" styles. Since it is very unlikely that your document uses nine levels of headings, "heading 9" will be safe to use for your figure captions.

Next give the Table of Contents command. In the Level option, type **9** for the From option. When you execute the command, Word creates a new list consisting of the entries that had the "heading 9" style.

Figure 18-3. Sample figure listing

Figures

Because level-9 entries for figure lists would normally appear in your regular table of contents, when you create your regular table of contents, type **1** for From and **8** for To. Thus, you will have two lists: the main table of contents, which is levels 1 to 8, and a figure list, which is level 9.

You can use this technique to create lists of figures, tables, charts, and so on. All other aspects of creating tables of contents are identical to those for creating other lists.

Lesson 87: Hidden Text

To create a table of contents without using styles, you must tell Word what you want in the table. You do this by flagging the headings you want included with a special marker that is formatted on the screen as *hidden text.*

Hidden text is similar to other text that has any character format applied to it. You know that you can give the Character command from the Format menu to make text bold; you can also use the command to make text hidden.

To make a section of text hidden, simply select it and give the Character command with the Hidden option, or press ⌘-SHIFT-X. You can also press ⌘-SHIFT-X, type the letters you want in hidden text, and press ⌘-SHIFT-SPACEBAR to continue typing.

Once you mark something as hidden, you cannot see it on the screen unless the Hidden Text option in the View section of the Preferences command is selected. Since you will probably only use hidden text for table of contents and index marking, it is likely that you will not show it most of the time.

Do not get into the habit of showing hidden text on the screen. Should you print or repaginate a document that has hidden text showing, Word would include that text in its calculations for the ends of pages and so on. Then, were you to generate a table of contents or an index, Word would have incorrect page numbers. Remember to turn off the viewing of hidden text before you generate a table of contents or index.

If you want to see hidden text, you can open up a second window and use the Preferences command in that window to do so. This lets you see the document both with and without the hidden text. You will get used to typing hidden text fairly quickly, and most of the time you won't need to see it.

Hidden text has two primary uses: marking table of contents entries (when you are not using styles) and marking index entries. Marking index entries is described later in this chapter. Some people also use hidden text for making notes to themselves or others, although this is not common.

To mark table of contents entries with hidden text, type **.c1.** in front of each level-1 entry, type **.c2.** in front of each level-2 entry, and so on. For example, Figure 18-4 shows two entries marked this way. Note the dotted underline under the marks, indicating that they are hidden text. (If you want, you can use **.c.** for level-1 headings.)

When you give the Table of Contents command, Word scans your document for the hidden text codes and identifies them as indicating an entry. The entry itself can be either hidden or regular text. Word assumes that the first character after the mark is the first character of the entry.

Assume that you want to add the level-2 heading shown here to the table of contents:

II. Market Analysis

National Generators currently has a 42% share of the markets we now serve. Our nearest competitor, Regional Outdoor Electricity,

Put the insertion point before the first character. Press ⌘-SHIFT-X to turn on hidden formatting, type **.c2.**, and press ⌘-SHIFT-SPACEBAR to turn off hidden formatting.

Word ends the entry when it sees the end of the paragraph or a semicolon. Because most tables of contents contain headings from the document and most headings are paragraphs with no other text in them, you can generally just add the hidden mark at the beginning of lines you want included in the table.

Some headings are *run in* with text on the same line, like this:

generator for heavy construction projects that can replace several smaller ones.

Market Analysis National Generators currently has a 42% share of the markets we now serve. Our nearest competitor, Regional Outdoor

Figure 18-4. *Table of contents entries marked with hidden text*

.c1.Excerpts from a Proposal for Bank Funding

.c2.I. Introduction

National Generators has the opportunity over the next five years to take a commanding lead in our established markets and to penetrate a new market, the construction industry, where our products will be particularly attractive. This report is intended to provide an overview of the company's business development strategies along with a description of those areas for which we require funding.

In this case, you need to use a hidden semicolon after "Analysis" to mark the end of the heading:

```
generator for heavy construction projects that can replace several
smaller ones.

.c2.Market Analysis; National Generators currently has a 42%
share of the markets we now serve. Our nearest competitor, Regional
```

Unfortunately, when you are specifying entries, there are many special cases. If your heading contains a semicolon, you have to tell Word exactly what text you want included. Any entry that includes a semicolon must have quotation marks at the beginning and end of the entry. Of course, these quotation marks should be formatted as hidden characters or they will show up in your document.

If your entry contains quotation marks, the situation is even trickier. First, you must enclose the entire entry in quotation marks, just as if it contained a semicolon or a colon. Next, you must precede any quotation mark in the entry by another quotation mark. Again, use hidden formatting for all of these special quotation marks. Needless to say, this can be tedious, and it illustrates another advantage of using styles to mark tables of contents.

Lesson 88: Marking Index Entries

The steps used to make an index are almost identical to those used for a table of contents, and the results are also similar. However, you cannot mark index entries with styles; they must be marked with hidden text.

To mark an entry for the index, use **.i.** in hidden text format instead of the **.c.** for contents. The same rules apply for ending the entry: use either a semicolon or the end-of-paragraph mark. If you are marking a visible part of your text, you will probably use hidden semicolons almost all the time. The rules for special characters apply here as well.

You can also give the Index Entry command from the Insert menu to mark entries. Select the text you want to index and give the Index Entry command. Word puts the correct hidden text before and after the text you have selected.

For example, assume you want to mark index entries in the following paragraph:

> National Generators can become the premier producer of electrical generation equipment for the entertainment and exposition industries. Our portable yet sturdy generators have acquired a solid reputation in these fields. As the number of outdoor concerts, large conventions, and other events that use portable generators continues to increase each year, we will be better able than our competitors to satisfy the demand for reliable equipment.

To mark "entertainment", put the insertion point before the word, press ⌘-SHIFT-X, type **.i.**, move the insertion point to the end of the word, press ⌘-SHIFT-X, and type a semicolon. The Index Entry command is much simpler to use. To mark "exposition", you need only select the word and give the Index Entry command from the Insert menu.

Subentries are created somewhat differently. Because there is a predetermined order to an index, you must specify a main entry when you specify a subentry. Separate the two with a colon. For example, to include an index entry for "portable" under "Generators", type **.i.Generators:** in hidden text before the word "portable" and a hidden semicolon after, so the result is

> National Generators can become the premier producer of electrical generation equipment for the .i.entertainment; and .i.exposition; industries. Our portable yet sturdy generators have acquired a solid reputation in these fields. As the number of outdoor concerts, large conventions, and other events that use .i.Generators:portable; generators continues to increase each year, we will be better able than our competitors to satisfy the demand for reliable equipment.

Word allows up to five levels of entries. However, indexes rarely have more than three levels, and most have only two.

As you become proficient at determining what a reader needs in an index, you will find that the words and concepts you want to refer to on a page may not be stated specifically. Thus, many of your index entries consist entirely of hidden text. For instance, imagine that you are discussing religion and you also want a reference to theology, although that word does not appear in the text. You can enter **.i.theology** in hidden text to make the entry.

Lesson 89: Creating an Index

When you give the Index command, the following dialog box appears:

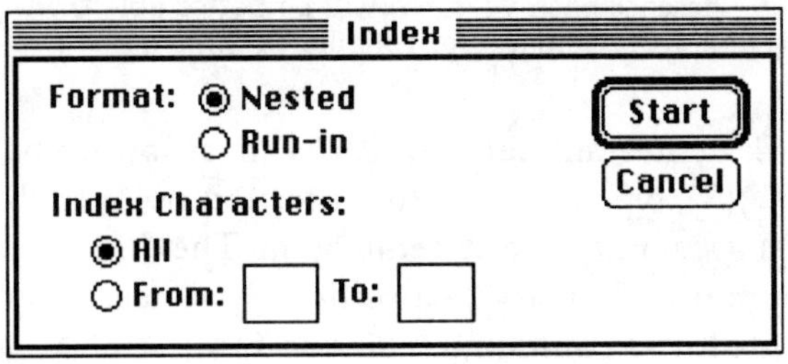

You generally use only the Nested and All options.

When you execute the Index command from the Insert menu, Word creates a new section at the end of your document and places the alphabetically sorted index entries in it. You can format the output any way you want, just as with the table of contents. Word uses styles "index 1", "index 2", and so on for the entries, so it is best to change those styles instead of using direct formatting.

It is common practice to have multicolumn indexes. Recall from Chapter 12 that Word can make columns easily with the Section command. Since most index entries are short, a two-column index usually looks fine. Be careful, however, to check that none of the page numbers in the entries wrap around in a confusing fashion.

You can use special characters in the .i. mark to make the page number come out in a special form when the index is created. For instance, using **.ib.** instead of **.i.** causes the page number to come out in bold. This might be useful if you have many index instances for one word, but one of them is the most useful (for example, the one that defines the word). Table 18-1 lists the special characters you can use.

The range and text options make creating complex indexes much easier. To use the range characters (the left and right parentheses), simply type **.i(.** at the first occurrence of the topic and **.i).** at the last. For example, the following illustration shows how to make a range for the entry "Durability":

(on page 21 of the document) .i(.Durability;
(on page 26 of the document) .i).Durability;

The result in the index is

Durability 21-26

To use the text option, put the pound sign (#) and your text at the end of the entry and place a semicolon at the end. This is especially useful for "see" references. The following illustration shows an example of this.

.i.Gasoline#(See Fuel);

The result in the index is

Gasoline (See Fuel)

Table 18-1. *Index Entry Characters*

Entry	**Result**
.ii.	Italic page number
.ib.	Bold page number
.i(.	First page in a range
.i).	Last page in a range
.i.entry#*text*	Replace page number with *text*

Review

Look in a few books and reports and note how the table of contents is formatted. Pay attention to whether all headings are included or just higher-level headings.

In the same books and reports, look at the indexes. How complete are they? Do they use second-level headings?

19

Proofing Your Documents

Most of the time you spend writing is taken up by editing and formatting your document. Good writers know that you also need additional help in making your document look just right. Word includes many tools that let you improve your writing and make it look as good as possible on the page.

Because most people are not perfect spellers, Word has included an easy-to-use spelling checker that works closely with the other parts of Word.

The thesaurus that comes with Word allows you to find synonyms for words and to look at the many meanings that a word can have.

A new feature in Word 5 is a grammar checker that can find common mistakes in your writing. It looks for things such as overused phrases and incorrect tense.

Word also includes a hyphenation program to help your text look better when printed. Justified text looks significantly better if the long words in the text are hyphenated to reduce the amount of white space between words. Of course, inserting hyphens yourself is tedious. The hyphenation feature frees you from the task of putting hyphens in the words that need them and uses the same dictionary that the spelling checker uses.

Lesson 90: Introduction to Spelling Checking

The second most useful program for writers is a spelling checker (the first, of course, is a word processor). Even if your spelling is nearly flawless, it is likely that your proofreading is not, and a single spelling mistake in a report or memo can have a very negative effect.

The idea behind spelling checkers is fairly simple. When you run a spelling checker, it reads your document and compares the words in it against a list of all the English words it knows. It then tells you the words that it does not recognize. You can correct the words or, if they are proper words that the spelling checker did not know, add the words to the dictionary so the spelling checker recognizes them the next time.

Of course, even a good spelling checker is not perfect; you will probably use words that it does not know, and it will indicate that you have misspelled them. Most dictionaries that come with spelling programs do not include proper names, so a program may think that you misspelled something if, for example, it sees the word "Jones" in your text. Also, spelling checkers cannot spot words that are used incorrectly in context, as in "I son the race."

The dictionary in Word's spelling checker is quite comprehensive. This makes it unlikely that it will not recognize a correctly spelled word. It is easy to "teach" the spelling checker new words, such as proper names or obscure words.

If Word thinks you have misspelled a word in your document, it can offer help by checking through its dictionary and making a few suggestions for what you intended. For example, if you have the misspelled word "postion" in your document, Word has many guesses, including "position" and "positron."

The spelling checker uses two types of dictionaries when it checks a document. It searches these dictionaries invisibly so that you need not keep track of the names.

- The *main dictionary* contains all common words. You cannot add words to this dictionary. It comes standard when you install Word.
- *User dictionaries* are for words that do not appear in the main dictionary but are still valid. You can tell the speller to check one or

more user dictionaries. You create user dictionaries in the Preferences command from the Tools menu.

Most people use the English (US) dictionary as their main dictionary and have just one user dictionary that has all their additional words.

As it checks your document, Word lists the unrecognized words (those not found in the dictionaries) one at a time. For each word, you have the following choices:

- Add the word to one of the user dictionaries.
- Correct the word in your document by typing in the correct spelling or by selecting one of the guesses.
- Ignore the word, indicating that you know it is not recognized, but you don't care to add it to the user dictionary.

The spelling checker is easy to use. If you are creating a large document, you may want to check the spelling after you enter, but before you edit, all the text, and again just before you print the text.

Lesson 91: Using the Spelling Checker

Before you give the Spelling command, you need to set up the spelling checker. Give the Preferences command from the Tools menu, and select the Spelling icon. You see the dialog box shown in Figure 19-1.

The Main Dictionary option lets you select the main dictionary. If you installed more than one (for example, if you have an international version of Word), you can choose the one you want from the drop-down list.

The Custom Dictionaries option lets you choose which custom dictionaries you want to use. To create a new custom dictionary, click the New button and give a filename. To select a custom dictionary to be used, you must click in the column on the left of the Custom list so that the dictionary in the list is checked. For example, if you have added a custom dictionary called "New Words," you would have to click to the left to select it:

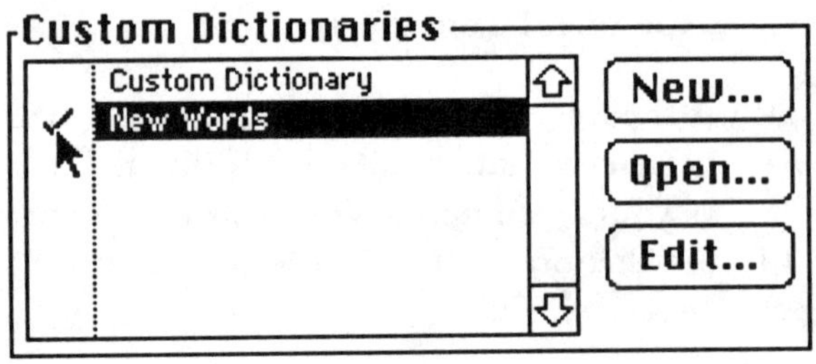

The Always Suggest option tells Word that you want it to always make suggestions when Word finds a word that it does not recognize. This is handy, but it also slows down the process of spelling checking. If you find that most of the words that are not recognized are words you are adding to a custom dictionary, you should probably not select this.

The Ignore choices tell Word to ignore certain types of words when it is checking. If you have many acronyms, in all uppercase letters, you may want Word to ignore them (although it is safer to add them to a custom dictionary

Figure 19-1. *Spelling preferences dialog box*

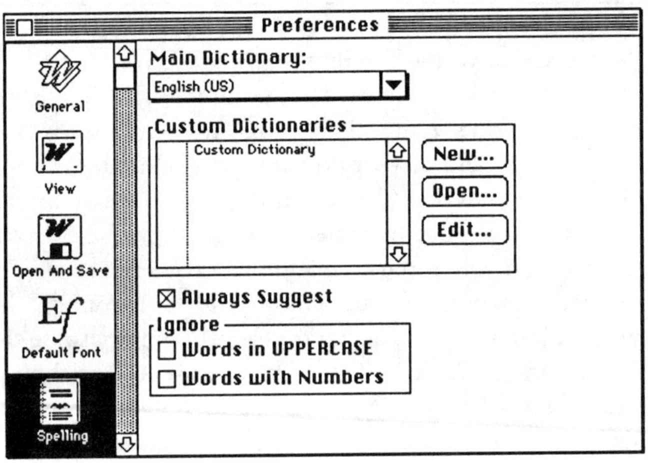

instead). If you have many words that include numbers, such as in technical literature, you may want to select Words with Numbers to be ignored.

When you are ready to check the spelling of a document, give the Spelling command from the Tools menu. Word displays the dialog box shown in Figure 19-2. Word automatically starts checking your document and shows the first word it does not recognize, in this case "Chris." If the Always Suggest choice in the Preferences dialog box is on, you also see a list of suggestions.

You now have many choices:

- If you want to change the word in your document to something else, type the new word in the Change To option. Word puts the first suggestion in the list in the Change To option by default, but you can type over that if you want. You can also select another suggestion from the list, and Word automatically puts that in the Change To option.
- Ignore ignores this word one time. Use this if the word is correct in its context but you do not want to add it to a user dictionary.
- Ignore All causes the Spelling command to ignore this word throughout the document. This differs from the Ignore button in that Word won't stop if it sees the word again.
- Change changes the word in your document to the one in the Change To option one time.

Figure 19-2. Spelling dialog box

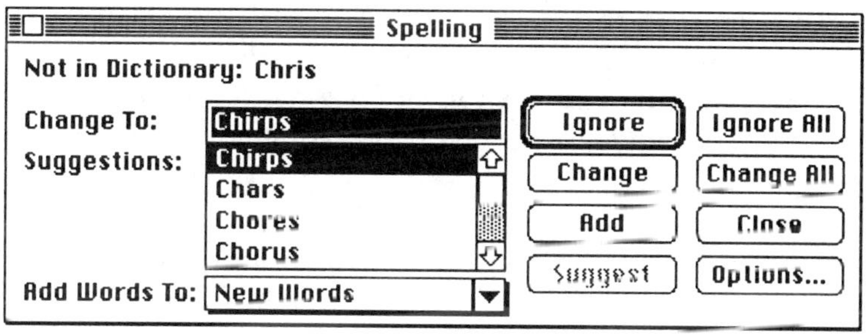

- Change All causes the Spelling command to change the word to the one in the Change To option automatically if it comes to the misspelled word again.
- Add adds the word to the selected user dictionary. You select the user dictionary to add to in the drop-down list at the bottom of the dialog box.
- Close stops the spelling checker.
- The Suggest button is only active if the Always Suggest choice is turned off.
- The Options button brings up the Preferences dialog box with the spelling settings showing.

After you take care of the first word that was not in the dictionary, the spelling checker quickly jumps to the next one. This keeps happening until you reach the end of the document or you click the Close button.

The first few times you run the spelling checker, you will find yourself adding a slew of words to the user dictionary. You will probably add dozens of proper names (including street and city names) as well as jargon from your industry. Within a week or so, you will add fewer words to the user dictionary and will mostly be finding actual spelling mistakes.

Lesson 92: Using the Thesaurus

As you are writing, you may get stuck thinking about a word. It is often hard to come up with just the "right" word for a particular thought. The thesaurus can be helpful in this case.

If you want to find a synonym for a particular word in your document, select the word and give the Thesaurus command from the Tools menu. The dialog box shows the synonyms for that word. Figure 19-3 shows the dialog box if you selected the word "pleased".

To replace the word in your document with one of the choices in the list on the right, click the new word and click the Replace button. For example, click the word "delighted" in the window and click Replace. Word puts that word in your document in place of "pleased".

Figure 19-3. *Thesaurus dialog box for "pleased"*

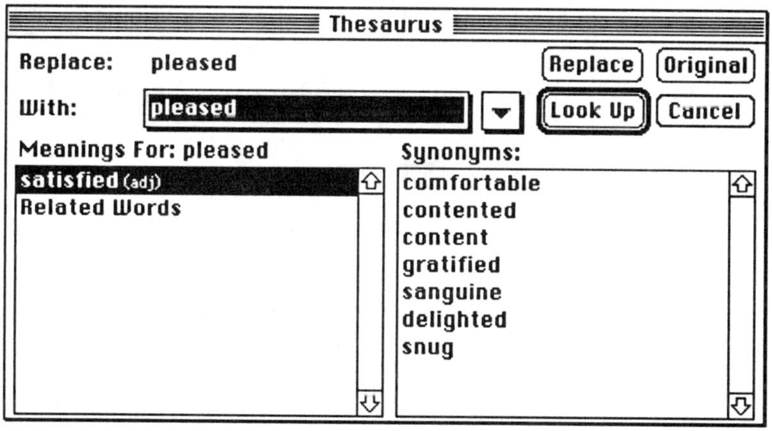

If you see a word in the list at the right that seems close but not exact, select it and click the Look Up button. This brings up a list of synonyms that may be closer to what you want. For example, click "comfortable" and click the Look Up button; you see the choices shown in Figure 19-4. If you click Antonyms, the Synonyms list on the right is replaced by a list of words meaning the opposite of "comfortable". Some words don't have opposites, in which case "Antonyms" doesn't appear on the left.

Lesson 93: Grammar Checking

Spelling errors are often the easiest to pick out in writing. However, grammar errors such as the wrong verb tense ("I will ran the race") and poor writing style ("I never want to stay away from there again in my life") can also mar a document. The grammar checker finds many writing mistakes in your document and even suggests how to change them to sound better.

Before running the grammar checker, you should check the grammar settings in the Preferences command, shown in Figure 19-5.

Figure 19-4. *Result of looking up "comfortable"*

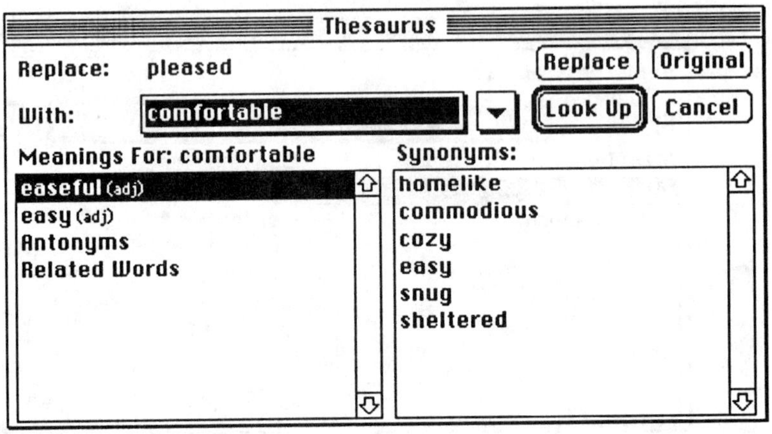

Figure 19-5. *Grammar preferences*

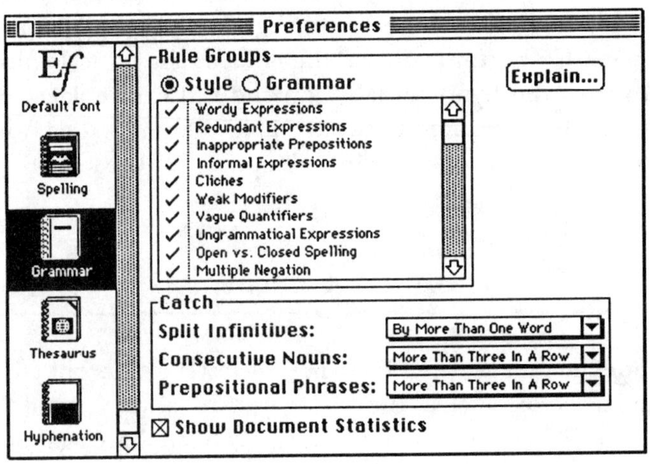

There are two "Rule Groups" at the top of the dialog box. The first rule group is for style—that is, words and phrases that are technically correct but can be improved. The second rule group is for grammatical mistakes. You can turn off any of the rules by clicking (unchecking) the rule in the list. You would only want to turn off a rule if you find that the grammar checker stops at too many instances of that rule in your document and you generally ignore the checker's advice.

The Catch options specify how far the grammar checker should look to catch split infinitives and multiple prepositional phrases. The default settings are usually fine.

The Show Document Statistics choice lets you see a summary of your document after you check the grammar.

To start checking a document, put the insertion point at the place where you want to start, such as before the first text paragraph of a letter, and give the Grammar command from the Tools menu. When the checker finds a possible mistake, you see the dialog box shown in Figure 19-6.

Figure 19-6. *Grammar dialog box*

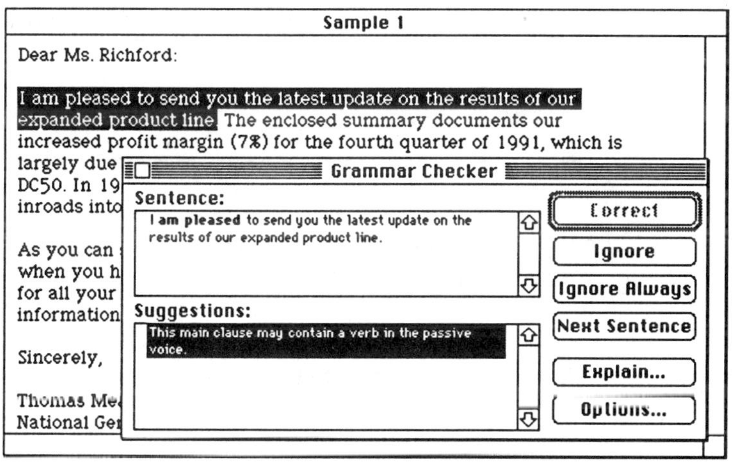

In this example, the grammar checker questions whether you want to use the passive voice in "I am pleased". It is often better to use the active voice, as in "It pleases me", although that sounds too personal in a business letter such as this. The buttons at the right of the dialog box show your choices:

- Correct changes the phrase in question to the suggested phrase, if there is one. In this case, there is no suggestion so the button is not available.
- Ignore causes the checker to skip this problem in this one instance.
- Ignore Always causes the checker to skip this type of error throughout the document.
- Next Sentence indicates that you know that there are problems with the sentence that you will correct later, so the checker should ignore the entire sentence.
- The Explain button brings up a dialog box that tells a bit more about the suggestion. In this case the dialog box shows the following:

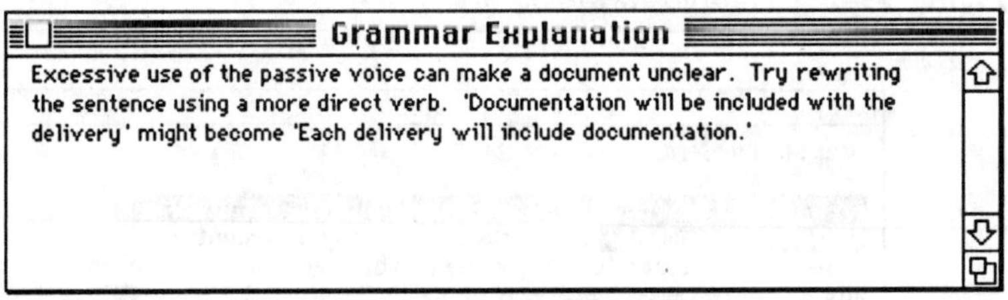

- The Options button brings up the Preferences dialog box with the grammar settings showing.

When you have finished checking the document, the grammar checker displays the dialog box shown in Figure 19-7 if you have chosen the Show Document Statistics choice.

Although the grammar checker can help find problems in your writing, you should certainly not rely on it. The rules in it are general and are not a replacement for you spending time editing your writing or finding an editor to help you. For documents where writing is not critical, you will find the grammar checker to be a good quick guide to finding problems.

Figure 19-7. *Grammar statistics dialog box*

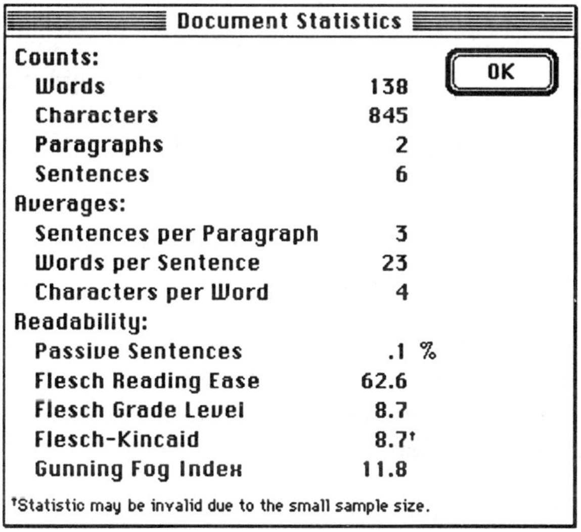

Lesson 94: Hyphenation

You may think that there is only one kind of hyphen, but Word has three: normal, nonbreaking, and optional hyphens. Each time you hyphenate a word, you can indicate the kind of hyphen you want so that word wrap produces the effect you want.

A *normal* hyphen is one that is always printed. For example, the phrase "self-reliant" contains a normal hyphen, since you always want the hyphen to appear in the printed text.

A *nonbreaking* hyphen is like a normal hyphen, except that Word never breaks the hyphenated word if it occurs at the end of a line. For instance, if you use a normal hyphen, you may get a paragraph that looks like this:

> There are many different spreadsheets that perform "what-
> if" calculations.

Since there was a normal hyphen between "what" and "if", Word broke the line there. In many cases, this is all right, but in this case it looks a bit clumsy. If you want to prevent Word from breaking a word at its hyphen, use a nonbreaking hyphen, which you enter by holding down the ⌘ key and the grave accent (`). The result of using a nonbreaking hyphen is the following:

> There are many different spreadsheets that perform
> "what-if" calculations.

If a paragraph contains many long words, word wrap causes the paragraph to look very uneven. For instance:

> His telecommunications discussion was
> significantly sidetracked as he started
> expostulating about interplanetary associations of
> antediluvian civilizations.

To make the lines more even, you need to hyphenate some of the words. If you want Word to hyphenate a word, you can enter an *optional* hyphen. You usually do this only when you notice that a particular set of lines is broken unevenly. You can also let Word help you hyphenate your document.

An optional hyphen is not used until it is needed. You can include optional hyphens anywhere in a word. To enter an optional hyphen, use ⌘-- (hold down the ⌘ key and press the - key). You do not see these hyphens unless they are necessary for proper word wrap. If you use optional hyphens in the previous example, the result is as follows:

> His telecommunications discussion was significant-
> ly sidetracked as he started expostulating about
> interplanetary associations of antediluvian civili-
> zations.

Deciding which words to hyphenate and adding the optional hyphens can be very tedious and time-consuming. Word can help you hyphenate by automatically putting optional hyphens in every word that is at the end of a line and might be split. The Hyphenation command from the Tools menu lets you decide where the hyphen goes in each word at the end of a line or gives you the option of hyphenating without confirmation.

The Hyphenation command from the Tools menu adds hyphens from the location of the insertion point. If you want to hyphenate only part of the document, select that part before giving the command. The Hyphenation dialog box looks like this:

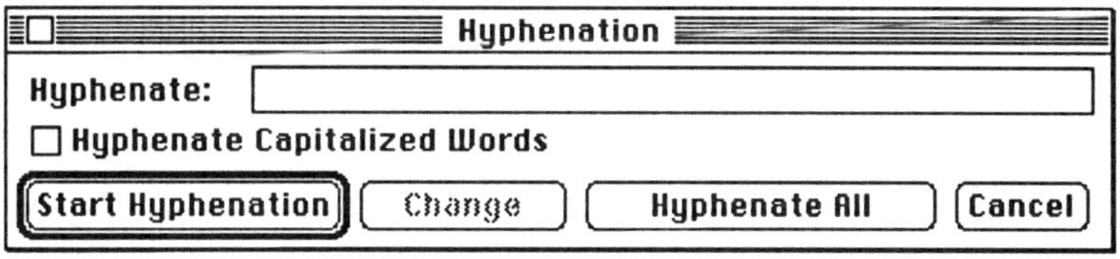

It is unlikely that you will want to have Word confirm hyphenation for each word, especially in a long document. However, if you do choose to have Word confirm each hyphenation, click the Start Hyphenation button.

For each word, the program shows you where it thinks the hyphen should go and asks you to enter a response:

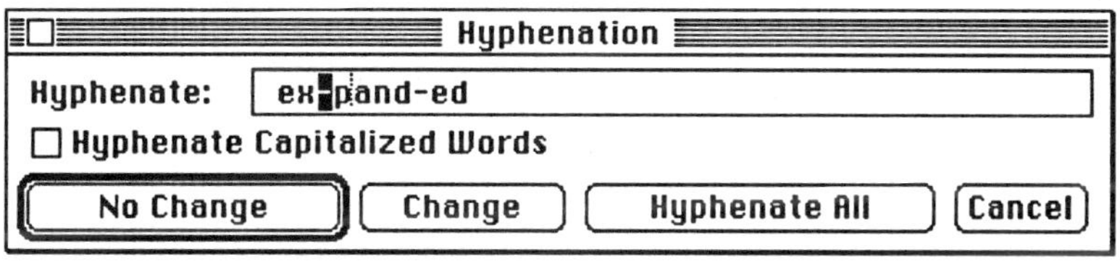

Click Change to confirm the choice or No Change to move to the next word. If you don't want to confirm the hyphenation, click Hyphenate All.

Review

Run the spelling checker on other letters that you may have typed in Word. What type of words does it not recognize?

Type the word **running** into a document, select it, and give the Thesaurus command. Investigate the synonyms and note the difference in meanings of each.

Run the grammar checker on a letter that you may have typed in Word. Consider each suggestion that it makes and see if you can rewrite your letter to incorporate the suggestions.

Type a few paragraphs of your choice and format them to be very narrow. Give the Hyphenation command and note how different they look.

20

Sorting

There are often times when you want to sort a list inside one of your documents. If the list is only five or ten lines long, it is fairly easy to sort by hand, but sorting long lists by hand is extremely inconvenient. The Sort command makes sorting any list easy.

Word can sort both text and numbers. This distinction may seem trivial, but most word processing programs cannot sort numbers the same way they sort words.

Computers think in terms of numbers, not in terms of characters such as letters, punctuation, numerals, and so on. Early computer scientists got around this problem by assigning an internal numeric value to each character. Most computers use a specific system called ASCII to relate characters to internal numbers.

Word sorts international letters in with standard letters so that a word that starts with "ö" is sorted with words that start with "o."

This order, dating back to the 1960s, presents some problems, most of which Word overcomes.

The first problem is that sorting numerals is very different than sorting numbers. Look at the following list:

23
142
5

You would sort this list numerically as "5, 23, 142." However, in ASCII code, 1 comes before 2, and 2 before 5. Thus, an unintelligent sorter (the kind most word processing programs use) would sort the list as

142
23
5

Fortunately, Word can sort numerics as numbers, rather than as ASCII characters.

A second problem is that upper- and lowercase letters are separated in the ASCII sorting sequence. Because of this, many word processors sort words that start with uppercase letters before all words that start with lowercase letters. ("Zebra" would come before "aardvark.")

Most of the time you want your lists sorted in alphabetical order, regardless of case. Word sorts upper- and lowercase words together.

A third, minor, problem is that not all punctuation comes before all numerals in the ASCII system. Some characters, such as the equal sign, fall between the numerals and the letters; others, such as the circumflex, fall between the upper- and lowercase letters; and some, such as the vertical bar, follow the lowercase letters. In general, avoid sorting lists that include punctuation as the first character. The ASCII sort order is shown here:

Spacebar
! " # $ % & ' ( ) * + , - . /
0 1 2 3 4 5 6 7 8 9
: ; < = > ? @
A B C D E F G H I J K L M N O P Q R S T U V W X Y Z
[\ ] ^ _ ‘
a b c d e f g h i j k l m n o p q r s t u v w x y z
{ | } ~

Lesson 95: Sorting Text

The most frequent use for the sorter is sorting lists that are formatted as individual paragraphs. Usually, you want to sort based on entire lines.

Using the Sort command from the Tools menu is easy. First, select the range of paragraphs you want to sort (Word only sorts paragraphs, not lines separated by newline). For this example use the following list:

```
Chicago
New York
Detroit
Dallas
Houston
New Orleans
Buffalo
```

Select the paragraphs, give the Sort command from the Tools menu, and Word sorts the list:

```
Buffalo
Chicago
Dallas
Detroit
Houston
New Orleans
New York
```

You can tell Word whether you want to sort from A to Z (*ascending*), which is the default, or from Z to A (*descending*). To choose descending, hold down the SHIFT key when giving the Sort command. This produces the following list:

```
New York
New Orleans
Houston
Detroit
Dallas
Chicago
Buffalo
```

In addition to sorting lists, you can sort text that runs many lines. Word simply sorts full paragraphs in this case, based on the first letters of the paragraphs.

Lesson 96: Sorting Numbers

You can use the Sort command to sort numbers in their correct sequence. For example, this list,

```
509
22.7
448
100
1000.
17
```

would be sorted as

```
17
22.7
100
448
509
1000.
```

You can also sort numbers in either ascending or descending order.

Lesson 97: Sorting in Tables

So far you have learned only how to sort based on the first letter in a paragraph. While this is usually what you want, there are some circumstances where you might want to sort a table by a column other than the first one. For instance, you may want to sort the following table by the number in the "Amount" column:

Name	Age	Type	Amount
Terrence	88	Regular	88.00
Connors	150	Senior	125.00
Long	130	Regular	130.00
Yee	50	New	67.50

Word lets you sort a table by any column if you select just that column. To do this, use the column selection methods discussed in Chapter 11 (if the table is created with (TAB) characters) or in Chapter 15 (if the table was created with the Insert Table command). After selecting the numbers in the column but not the heading, give the Sort command. For example, if you select the numbers in the "Amount" column, sorting produces the following table:

Name	Age	Type	Amount
Yee	50	New	67.50
Terrence	88	Regular	88.00
Connors	150	Senior	125.00
Long	130	Regular	130.00

Review

Create a list of names of people with whom you work. Sort it both ascending and descending.

Make a two-column table with the names of the same people and their ages. Sort the table by name, then sort it by age.

21

Retrieving Documents

You have probably noticed that the names of the files used in this book are somewhat descriptive of their contents. The name "Summary of Funding", for example, was used for a summary funding proposal. However, Macintosh file-naming conventions limit how much you can indicate in a filename. If you have more than a few dozen files (as you are sure to after using Word for a few weeks), it is hard to remember what each file contains. When you have hundreds of files, opening and closing each one to find a particular file is really time-consuming.

Since Word is designed for use in business, where efficiency is a primary concern, Microsoft has devised a method for scanning rapidly through a large number of files. Each Word file has a *summary sheet* where you can list information that is helpful when you search. For example, to search for a letter, you might include the recipient, the subject, and a few keywords about the contents. Word automatically stores the dates when the letter was created and last updated, so you can also use those in your search.

When you search, Word scans the summary sheets of all the documents on the disks and directories that you specify. You can devise very specific searches (such as one for a file written after January 15, 1992 that lists the keywords "timing" and "starter") or general searches (such as one for all letters to a certain person). This flexibility is very convenient when you are working with dozens or hundreds of files.

You can also have Word search for specific text in the files. For instance, you can locate every letter in which you mentioned "new manufacturing". Note, however, that searching for text in a file is slower than searching for words listed in the summary sheet, especially if you have long documents.

To fill in or search summary sheets, give the Summary Info command from the File menu. Note that this command works only on Word documents, and not on the other files on your system. Also, you can create summary sheets only for files saved with Word's formatting (not for text-only files). The Find File command from the File menu searches through summary sheets as well as through the text in files.

Lesson 98: Filling Summary Sheets

Up to now, when Word has prompted you to fill in a summary sheet, you have simply clicked OK and skipped over the sheet (or you may have guessed about how to fill it out). When you save a file for the first time you fill in the summary information. Here is how to fill in the summary sheets.

Open the Sample 1 file and give the Summary Info command from the File menu. Figure 21-1 shows the same dialog box you see when you save documents.

Figure 21-1. *Summary Info dialog box*

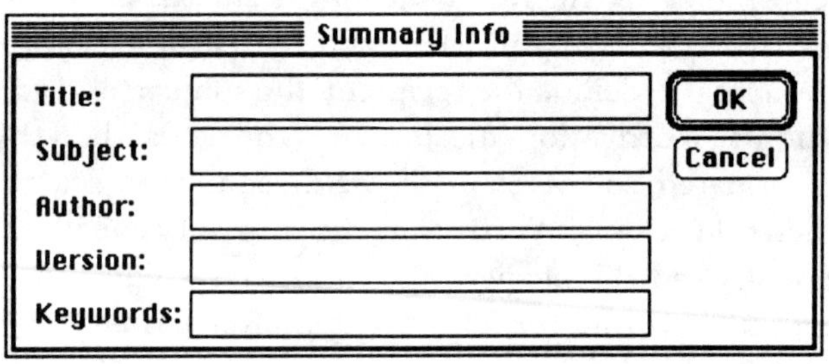

The options in the Summary Info dialog box are described in Table 21-1.

You might use the field entries shown in Figure 21-2 for the Sample 1 and the Summary of Funding documents.

Lesson 99: Searching for Documents

The Find File command lets you search for documents based on criteria you set, such as the drive on which to look and what to look for. The initial dialog box is shown in Figure 21-3.

Table 21-1. *Description of Fields in Summary Info Dialog Box*

Field	Description
Title	A title for the document such as "Request for information on new parts" or "Second notice on overdue accounts".
Subject	The document's subject. This is often similar to the title but might have additional information.
Author	The name of the person who wrote the document. It is good to use both your first and last names, since the person searching the summary sheets may not know both. Word automatically uses the name you entered in the Preferences command, but you can change the name if you wish.
Version	The revision number of the document. Many companies keep each version on disk so that it is easier to go back and look at what a document looked like at each step in the revision process.
Keywords	Words or phrases that are likely to be searched for. Examples are "accounts payable", "urgent", "third notice", and "final".

Figure 21-2. *Summary Info dialog boxes for Sample 1 and Summary of Funding*

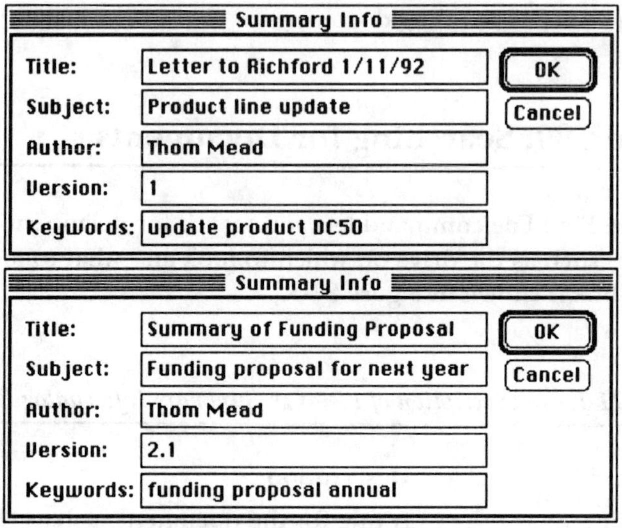

Figure 21-3. *Find File dialog box*

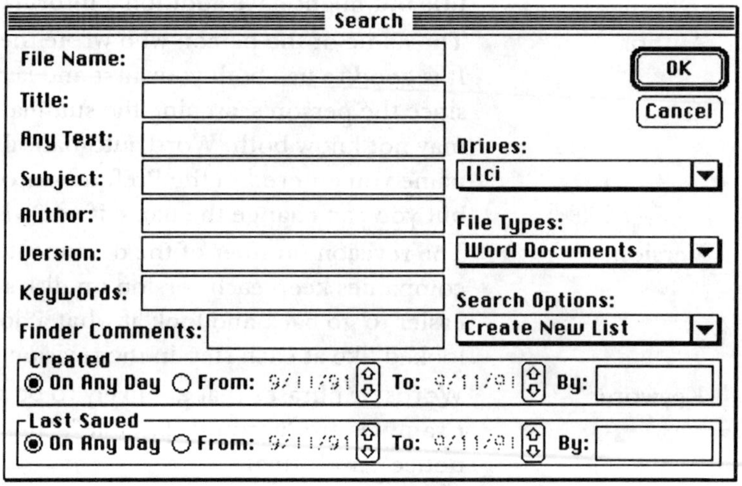

To find specific files, you first narrow the list by specifying *search criteria* in the dialog box:

- File Name is the name of the file (or part of the name) you want to find.
- Title, Subject, Author, Version, and Keywords are the fields from the summary sheet.
- Any Text is text to be searched for in the documents.
- Finder Comments are comments that are stored in the Macintosh Get Info dialog box for the file in the Finder.
- Created and Last Saved specify a range of dates when the file was started or saved on disk. The By option lets you specify the name (or part of the name) of the person who created the file.
- Drives tells the command where to look. It can only look at one drive at a time.
- File Types are the types of files you want to look for. You can specify to look for just Word files, all files (the default), text files, and so on.
- Search Options tells what to do with previous searches, described next.

To start the search, enter the desired criteria and click OK. For instance, to find every file with the keyword "prosecute" in it, type **prosecute** in the Keywords field and click OK. Figure 21-4 shows this dialog box.

If you fill in more than one field, Word finds only files that match the entries in all the filled fields. For example, the set of entries shown in Figure 21-5 would find only documents whose author field contains "Thom" and whose Keywords field contains "loan".

After Word looks where you specify, it shows the dialog box in Figure 21-6. The list on the left contains all the files that match the criteria, and the box on the upper-right is the text from the file. You can scroll through the text with the scroll bar, and you can search for specific text in the Search Text box by typing that text in the box and clicking one of the two arrow buttons.

Figure 21-4. *Finding the keyword "prosecute"*

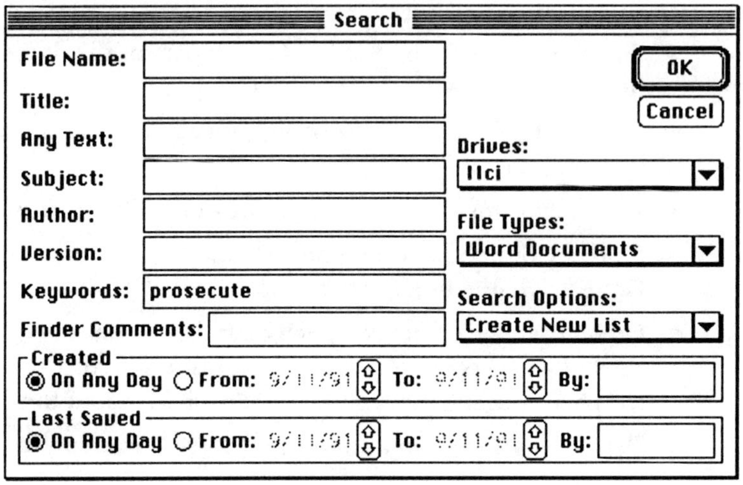

Figure 21-5. *Finding both "Thom" in the Author field and "loan" in the Keywords field*

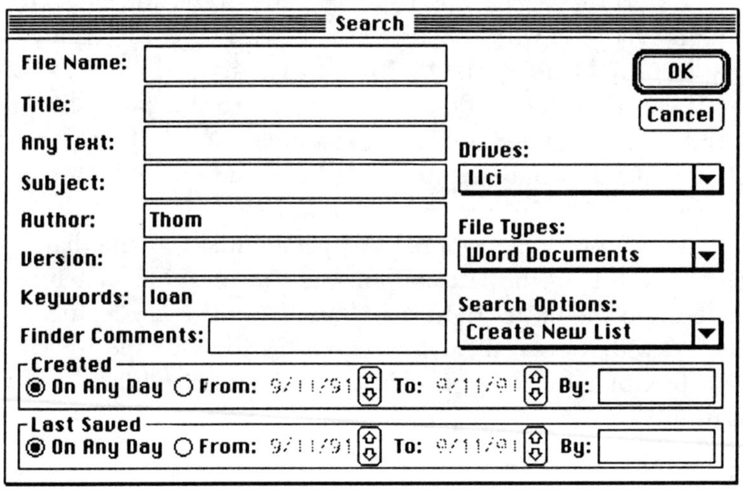

Figure 21-6. *Found files dialog box*

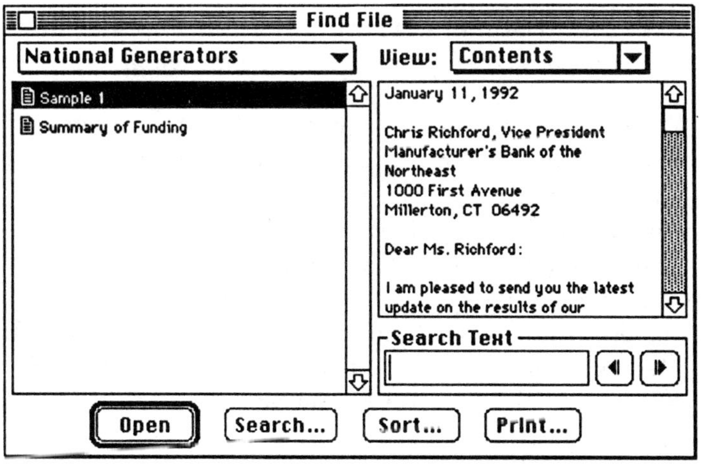

The View drop-down list lets you see different information about the file. The View choices are listed here:

Statistics	Description of the file, such as the file type and size, as shown in Figure 21-7
Comments	Finder comments from the document's Get Info dialog box
Summary Info	Contents of the Summary Info dialog box for the file

The four buttons at the bottom of the dialog box let you decide what to do next. If you find the file that you were interested in, select it in the list at the left and click the Open button. You print the file with the Print button. The Sort button lets you sort the files in the list by name, size, type, or date.

The Search button lets you go back and search again. When you go back to search more, you have three choices in the Search options:

- Create New List ignores the results of the previous search. Use this option when you want to start over.

- Add Matches to List expands the previous search, adding files to the list of files found before.
- Search Only in List narrows the previous search. It only looks in the files you already found for the new search criteria.

For example, assume that you searched for all letters from Thom to a particular customer. You discover that there are 70 letters. You want to narrow the search using a keyword. Click the Search button, enter the keyword in the Keywords field, and select Search Only in List.

There are a few handy features to the Find File command that are not apparent from looking at the dialog boxes. You can add found files to the Work menu (described in Chapter 16) by pressing (⌘)-(OPTION)-(+) and choosing the files from the found file list. You can also save the selected file under a new name by giving the Save As command from the File menu.

Figure 21-7. *Example of statistics*

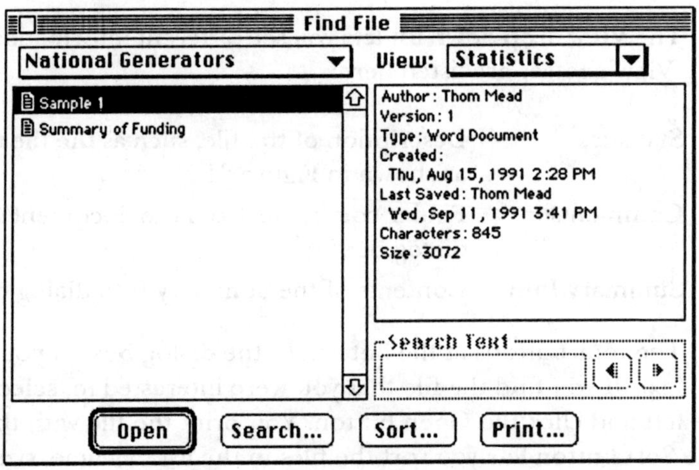

Review

Go back to the files you have created before and add better summary information to the files. With this new information entered, search for files using different keywords and other criteria.

22

Using Word with Other Macintosh Programs

In Chapter 4, you learned how to use the Clipboard to copy and move text in a file. Often, however, you want to incorporate a copy of an entire file into a file that you are editing. For instance, you may keep important charts in separate files so you can include them in a variety of memos.

The simplest way to bring information into Word or to pass information out of Word is to use the Cut, Copy, and Paste commands. You use these commands in other programs just as you do in Word. For example, to copy a picture from a graphics program into Word, you would create the picture, select it, give the Copy command, switch to Word, and give the Paste command.

You can have much more interaction than this, however. You can save files in ways that other programs can read them (since most programs cannot read Word files). You can also read files created by other programs. This chapter describes how to perform these tasks.

Lesson 100: Opening Non-Word Files

So far, you have only used the Open command from the File menu for Word files. However, the Open command is much more powerful than that. It can open the following types of word processing documents:

- Microsoft Word for the Macintosh versions 1, 3, and 4
- Microsoft Word for the PC versions 1, 2, 3, 4, 5.0, and 5.5
- Microsoft Word for Windows versions 1 and 2
- Microsoft Works for the Macintosh version 2
- MacWrite versions 4.5 and 5.0
- MacWrite II
- WordPerfect for the Macintosh version 2
- WordPerfect for the PC versions 4.1, 4.2, 5.0, and 5.1
- Text-only files created by any Macintosh program
- Text files stored with the RTF specification

In addition, Word can open the following graphics documents:

- MacPaint documents
- Encapsulated PostScript (EPS) files
- TIFF files
- PICT files

Many programs can store files in at least one of these formats. For example, almost every graphics program can store documents in either MacPaint or PICT (like MacDraw) format.

You can specify which files are visible in the list when you give the Open command. The List Files of Type drop-down lets you specify the types of files that appear in the list. The choices are listed here:

Choice	Description
All Files	All files, regardless of whether Word can open them
All Readable Files	All files that Word can open normally (default)
Word Documents	Only documents created in Word for the Macintosh
Text Files	Only text files
Apple File Exchange Binary	Files that were moved by the Apple File Exchange (AFE) program
Stationery	Word stationery files
Graphics Files	Graphics files, such as pictures

The File command from the Insert menu works like the Open command except that it puts a copy of the contents of the specified file in the current document at the insertion point. You can use this command if you want to read another file into your current file.

Lesson 101: Saving Files in Non-Word Formats

Word also lets you save files in different formats. This is useful for transferring formatted information to other word processing programs. The formats you can save in are the same as the ones you can open.

When you save a Word document in another format, it is likely that some formatting information will be lost. For example, when you save a Word file in the format of another word processor, you lose the styles you may have attached. Word adds direct formatting to the output instead of styles. Word features, such as tables, may also be lost. Remember that many of the formats you can save in do not have all of the capabilities of Word, so you almost always lose formatting information.

Word allows you to save formatted text as a picture. This might be useful to you if your drawing program (like MacPaint) does not give you as many choices about how to handle text as Word does. To save formatted text as a picture, select the text and press ⌘-OPTION-D. This copies the text as a picture to the Clipboard.

Lesson 102: Using Publish and Subscribe

If you work with other people on a project, you may have come across a common problem: how do many people work on one file at the same time? Apple's new System 7 software supports a unique concept called "publish and subscribe" that lets many people work on different parts of a document without contention. Word fully supports publish and subscribe in a very easy fashion.

Instead of many people working on one document, you create a master document that is made up of pieces of other documents. Instead of using the Cut, Copy, and Paste commands to put together the pieces from other documents, you use publish and subscribe.

Cut, Copy, and Paste do not work well when many people are working on a project. If you collected pieces from the other users and put them into the master document from the Clipboard and then later changed the original documents, the master document would have out-of-date information in it. There is no way for the person who put together the master document to know that one of the original documents was updated.

Publish and subscribe prevents this problem by creating *editions*, documents that are linked from the original document to the master document all the time. If someone updates an original document, that change is reflected in the edition. When you open the master document, it automatically gets the latest version of the pieces through the editions, thereby assuring that the master document is as up to date as possible.

The steps for using publish and subscribe are fairly simple. You first create the editions that are used in the master document; this is called *publishing* editions.

1. When you want to contribute pieces to the master document, create normal Word files. These files can contain more than just the designated pieces, such as other text or graphics.
2. Select the information that will become one piece and give the Create Publisher command from the Edit menu. You use this command to create an edition. Word displays the dialog box shown in Figure 22-1.
3. Give a name to the edition and click the Publish button. This stores the edition on your disk.

You can now make whatever changes you want to the document. Each time you save those changes, Word updates the edition so that it is always up to date.

Incorporating editions into a Word document, called *subscribing*, is also quite easy.

1. Put the insertion point in the master document at the place where you want the edition.
2. Give the Subscribe To command from the Edit menu. You see the dialog box shown in Figure 22-2.
3. Choose the edition you want and click the Subscribe button.

Figure 22-1. *Create Publisher dialog box*

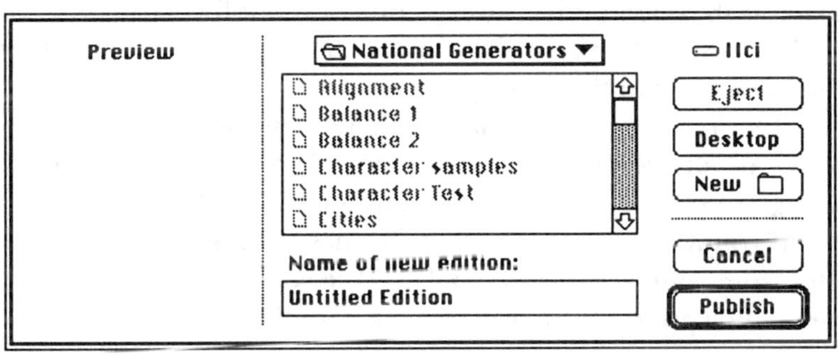

Figure 22-2. *Subscribe To dialog box*

You do not need the editions to come from Word; you can publish them from any Macintosh program that supports publish and subscribe. For example, if someone in your art department is updating a chart using a program, they can publish the chart as an edition that you can use in your Word document. Many programs support publish and subscribe features, so you can use editions from them in Word.

Review

Look at the list of formats that Word can open. See if you have a Macintosh program that saves in one of those formats and try opening a file in that format. Look carefully at the contents and compare them to the way the file looked in the other program.

Save a file in a format that another Macintosh program can read and look at the results. Experiment with various Word features such as styles, tables, and graphics and see how they translate when Word saves the file.

If you work in an office that also has PCs, find out how you can transfer files from your Macintosh to a PC. Save some Word files in formats that can be read by programs on the PC and note the results.

IV

Appendixes

A

Keyboard Reference

This appendix shows the commands that have keyboard equivalents. Table A-1 is arranged by command, and Table A-2 is arranged by keys.

Table A-1. *Commands with Keyboard Equivalents*

Command	Keys
Activate Keyboard Menus	. (keypad) or ⌘-TAB
Add to Menu	⌘-OPTION-= or ⌘-SHIFT-OPTION-=
All Caps	SHIFT-F10 or ⌘-SHIFT-K
Assign to Key	⌘-OPTION-+ (keypad) or ⌘-SHIFT-OPTION-←
Backspace	DELETE
Bold	⌘-B or ⌘-SHIFT-B or F10
Calculate	⌘-=
Cancel	⌘-. or CLEAR
Centered	⌘-SHIFT-C

Table A-1. *Commands with Keyboard Equivalents (continued)*

Command	Keys
Change Font	⌘-SHIFT-E
Change Style	⌘-SHIFT-S
Character	⌘-D or F14
Close	⌘-W
Commands	⌘-SHIFT-OPTION-C
Context Sensitive Help	⌘-/ or HELP
Copy	⌘-C or F3
Copy as Picture	⌘-OPTION-D
Copy Formats	SHIFT-F4 or ⌘-OPTION-V
Copy Text	⌘-OPTION-C or SHIFT-F3
Cut	F2 or ⌘-X
Delete Forward	DELETE or ⌘-OPTION-F
Delete Next Word	⌘-OPTION-G
Delete Previous Word	⌘-OPTION-DELETE
Document	⌘-F14
Dotted Underline	OPTION-F12 or ⌘-SHIFT-\
Double Space	⌘-SHIFT-Y
Double Underline	SHIFT-F12 or ⌘-SHIFT-[
Edit Link (QuickSwitch)	⌘-, or OPTION-F2
Extend to Character	- (keypad) or ⌘-OPTION-H
Find Again	= (keypad) or ⌘-OPTION-A
Find	⌘-F
First Line Indent	⌘-SHIFT-F
Flush Left	⌘-SHIFT-L
Flush Right	⌘-SHIFT-R
Footnote	⌘-E
Footnotes	⌘-SHIFT-OPTION-S
Glossary	⌘-K
Go Back	0 (keypad) or ⌘-OPTION-Z
Go To	⌘-G

Table A-1. Commands with Keyboard Equivalents (continued)

Command	Keys
Hanging Indent	⌘-SHIFT-T
Hidden Text	OPTION-F9 or ⌘-SHIFT-V or ⌘-SHIFT-X
Hyphenation	SHIFT-F15
Insert Formula	⌘-OPTION-\
Insert Glossary Entry	⌘-DELETE
Insert Nonbreaking Hyphen	⌘-`
Insert Nonbreaking Space	⌘-SPACEBAR or OPTION-SPACEBAR
Insert Optional Hyphen	⌘--
Insert Tab	TAB or OPTION-TAB
Insert Paragraph Above Row	⌘-OPTION-SPACEBAR
Italic	F11 or ⌘-SHIFT-I
Justified	⌘-SHIFT-J
Larger Font Size	⌘-SHIFT-. or ⌘-SHIFT->
Line Break	SHIFT-RETURN
Move Keyboard Prefix	⌘-OPTION-'
Move Down One Text Area	⌘-OPTION-2 (keypad)
Move Left One Text Area	⌘-OPTION-4 (keypad)
Move Right One Text Area	⌘-OPTION-6 (keypad)
Move Text	SHIFT-F2 or ⌘-OPTION-X
Move to Bottom of Window	END
Move to End of Document	⌘-3 (keypad) or ⌘-END
Move to End of Line	1 (keypad)
Move to First Text Area	⌘-OPTION-7 (keypad)
Move to Last Text Area	⌘-OPTION-1 (keypad)
Move to Next Character	6 (keypad) or ⌘-OPTION-L or →

A

Table A-1. Commands with Keyboard Equivalents (continued)

Command	Keys
Move to Next Line	⌘-OPTION-, or 2 (keypad) or ↓
Move to Next Page	⌘-PAGE DOWN
Move to Next Paragraph	⌘-2 (keypad) or ⌘-OPTION-B or ⌘-↓
Move to Next Sentence	⌘-1 (keypad)
Move to Next Text Area	⌘-OPTION-3 (keypad)
Move to Next Window	⌘-OPTION-W
Move to Next Word	⌘-6 (keypad) or ⌘-OPTION-; or ⌘-→
Move to Previous Cell	SHIFT-TAB
Move to Previous Character	4 (keypad) or ⌘-OPTION-K or ←
Move to Previous Line	8 (keypad) or ↑
Move to Previous Page	⌘-PAGE UP
Move to Previous Paragraph	⌘-8 (keypad) or ⌘-↑ or ⌘-OPTION-Y
Move to Previous Sentence	⌘-7 (keypad)
Move to Previous Text Area	⌘-OPTION-9 (keypad)
Move to Previous Word	⌘-4 (keypad) or ⌘-OPTION-J or ⌘-←
Move to Start of Document	⌘-9 (keypad) or ⌘-HOME
Move to Start of Line	7 (keypad)
Move to Top of Window	⌘-5 (keypad) or HOME
Move up One Text Area	⌘-OPTION-8 (keypad)
Nest Paragraph	⌘-SHIFT-N
New	F5 or ⌘-N
New Paragraph	ENTER or RETURN
New Window	SHIFT-F5
New Paragraph after Ins. Point	⌘-OPTION-RETURN

Table A-1. Commands with Keyboard Equivalents (continued)

Command	Keys
New Paragraph with Same Style	⌘-RETURN
No Paragraph Border	⌘-OPTION-1
Normal	⌘-OPTION-N
Normal Paragraph	⌘-SHIFT-P
Numeric Lock	CLEAR (keypad)
Open any File	SHIFT-F6
Open Spacing	⌘-SHIFT-O
Open	F6 or ⌘-O
Outline (Format)	⌘-SHIFT-D or SHIFT-F11
Outline (View)	SHIFT-F13 or ⌘-OPTION-O
Outline Command Prefix	⌘-OPTION-T
Page Break	SHIFT-ENTER
Page Layout	F13 or ⌘-OPTION-P
Page Setup	SHIFT-F8
Paragraph	SHIFT-F14 or ⌘-M
Paste	F4 or ⌘-V
Paste Link	OPTION-F4
Paste Special Character	⌘-OPTION-Q
Plain Text	SHIFT-F9 or ⌘-SHIFT-Z
Print Preview	OPTION-F13 or ⌘-I
Print	F8 or ⌘-P
Quit	⌘-Q
Remove from Menu	⌘-OPTION--
Renumber	⌘-F15
Repeat	⌘-Y
Replace	⌘-H
Revert to Style	F9 or ⌘-SHIFT-SPACEBAR
Ribbon	⌘-OPTION-R
Ruler	⌘-R

A

Table A-1. Commands with Keyboard Equivalents (continued)

Command	Keys
Save	F7 or ⌘-S
Save As	SHIFT-F7
Scroll Line Down	+ (keypad) or ⌘-OPTION-/
Scroll Line Up	* (keypad) or ⌘-OPTION-[
Scroll Screen Down	⌘-OPTION-. or 3 (keypad) or PAGE DOWN
Scroll Screen Up	9 (keypad) or PAGE UP
Section Break	⌘-ENTER
Section	OPTION-F14
Select All	⌘-A or ⌘-OPTION-M
Shadow	OPTION-F11 or ⌘-SHIFT-W
Show/Hide Paragraph	⌘-J
Small Caps	OPTION-F10 or ⌘-SHIFT-H
Smaller Font Size	⌘-SHIFT-, or ⌘-SHIFT-<
Spelling	F15 or ⌘-L
Split Window	⌘-OPTION-S
Strikethru	⌘-SHIFT-/
Style	⌘-T
Subscript 2 pt	⌘-SHIFT--
Superscript 3 pt	⌘-SHIFT-=
Symbol Font	⌘-SHIFT-Q
Unassign Keystroke	⌘-OPTION-- (keypad)
Underline	F12 or ⌘-U or ⌘-SHIFT-U
Undo	F1 or ⌘-Z
Unnest Paragraph	⌘-SHIFT-M
Update Link	OPTION-F3
Word Count	OPTION-F15
Word Underline	⌘-F12 or ⌘-SHIFT-]

Table A-2. Keys with Command Equivalents

Keys	Command
⌘-OPTION-'	Move Keyboard Prefix
* (keypad)	Scroll Line Up
⌘-OPTION-+ (keypad)	Assign to Key
+ (keypad)	Scroll Line Down
⌘-,	Edit Link (QuickSwitch)
⌘-OPTION-,	Move to Next Line
⌘-SHIFT-,	Smaller Font Size
⌘--	Insert Optional Hyphen
⌘-OPTION--	Remove from Menu
⌘-OPTION-- (keypad)	Unassign Keystroke
⌘-SHIFT--	Subscript 2 pt
- (keypad)	Extend to Character
⌘-.	Cancel
⌘-OPTION-.	Scroll Screen Down
⌘-SHIFT-.	Larger Font Size
. (keypad)	Activate Keyboard Menus
⌘-/	Context Sensitive Help
⌘-OPTION-/	Scroll Line Down
⌘-SHIFT-/	Strikethru
0 (keypad)	Go Back
⌘-1 (keypad)	Move to Next Sentence
⌘-OPTION-1	No Paragraph Border
⌘-OPTION-1 (keypad)	Move to Last Text Area
1 (keypad)	Move to End of Line
⌘-2 (keypad)	Move to Next Paragraph
⌘-OPTION-2 (keypad)	Move Down One Text Area
2 (keypad)	Move to Next Line
⌘-3 (keypad)	Move to End of Document
⌘-OPTION-3 (keypad)	Move to Next Text Area
3 (keypad)	Scroll Screen Down

Table A-2. *Keys with Command Equivalents (continued)*

Keys	Command
⌘-4 (keypad)	Move to Previous Word
⌘-OPTION-4 (keypad)	Move Left One Text Area
4 (keypad)	Move to Previous Character
⌘-5 (keypad)	Move to Top of Window
⌘-6 (keypad)	Move to Next Word
⌘-OPTION-6 (keypad)	Move Right One Text Area
6 (keypad)	Move to Next Character
⌘-7 (keypad)	Move to Previous Sentence
⌘-OPTION-7 (keypad)	Move to First Text Area
7 (keypad)	Move to Start of Line
⌘-8 (keypad)	Move to Previous Paragraph
⌘-OPTION-8 (keypad)	Move Up One Text Area
8 (keypad)	Move to Previous Line
⌘-9 (keypad)	Move to Start of Document
⌘-OPTION-9 (keypad)	Move to Previous Text Area
9 (keypad)	Scroll Screen Up
⌘-OPTION-;	Move to Next Word
⌘-SHIFT-<	Smaller Font Size
⌘-=	Calculate
⌘-OPTION-=	Add to Menu
⌘-SHIFT-=	Superscript 3 pt
⌘-SHIFT-OPTION-=	Add to Menu
= (keypad)	Find Again
⌘-SHIFT->	Larger Font Size
⌘-A	Select All
⌘-OPTION-A	Find Again
⌘-B	Bold
⌘-OPTION-B	Move to Next Paragraph
⌘-SHIFT-B	Bold
⌘-C	Copy

Table A-2. *Keys with Command Equivalents (continued)*

Keys	**Command**
⌘-OPTION-C	Copy Text
⌘-SHIFT-C	Centered
⌘-SHIFT-OPTION-C	Commands
CLEAR	Cancel
CLEAR (keypad)	Numeric Lock
⌘-D	Character
⌘-OPTION-D	Copy as Picture
⌘-SHIFT-D	Outline (Format)
DELETE	Delete Forward
DELETE	Backspace
⌘-DELETE	Insert Glossary Entry
⌘-OPTION-DELETE	Delete Previous Word
↓	Move to Next Line
⌘-↓	Move to Next Paragraph
⌘-E	Footnote
⌘-SHIFT-E	Change Font
END	Move to Bottom of Window
⌘-END	Move to End of Document
ENTER	New Paragraph
⌘-ENTER	Section Break
SHIFT-ENTER	Page Break
⌘-F	Find
⌘-OPTION-F	Delete Forward
⌘-SHIFT-F	First Line Indent
F1	Undo
F10	Bold
OPTION-F10	Small Caps
SHIFT-F10	All Caps
F11	Italic
OPTION-F11	Shadow

A

Table A-2. Keys with Command Equivalents (continued)

Keys	Command
SHIFT-F11	Outline (Format)
F12	Underline
⌘-F12	Word Underline
OPTION-F12	Dotted Underline
SHIFT-F12	Double Underline
F13	Page Layout
OPTION-F13	Print Preview
SHIFT-F13	Outline (View)
F14	Character
⌘-F14	Document
OPTION-F14	Section
SHIFT-F14	Paragraph
F15	Spelling
⌘-F15	Renumber
OPTION-F15	Word Count
SHIFT-F15	Hyphenation
F2	Cut
OPTION-F2	Edit Link (QuickSwitch)
SHIFT-F2	Move Text
F3	Copy
OPTION-F3	Update Link
SHIFT-F3	Copy Text
F4	Paste
OPTION-F4	Paste Link
SHIFT-F4	Copy Formats
F5	New
SHIFT-F5	New Window
F6	Open
SHIFT-F6	Open any File
F7	Save

Table A-2. *Keys with Command Equivalents (continued)*

Keys	Command
SHIFT-F7	Save As
F8	Print
SHIFT-F8	Page Setup
F9	Revert to Style
OPTION-F9	Hidden Text
SHIFT-F9	Plain Text
⌘-G	Go To
⌘-OPTION-G	Delete Next Word
⌘-H	Replace
⌘-OPTION-H	Extend to Character
⌘-SHIFT-H	Small Caps
HELP	Context Sensitive Help
HOME	Move to Top of Window
⌘-HOME	Move to Start of Document
⌘-I	Print Preview
⌘-SHIFT-I	Italic
⌘-J	Show/Hide Paragraph
⌘-OPTION-J	Move to Previous Word
⌘-SHIFT-J	Justified
⌘-K	Glossary
⌘-OPTION-K	Move to Previous Character
⌘-SHIFT-K	All Caps
⌘-L	Spelling
⌘-OPTION-L	Move to Next Character
⌘-SHIFT-L	Flush Left
←	Move to Previous Character
⌘-←	Move to Previous Word
⌘-SHIFT-OPTION-<	Assign to Key
⌘-M	Paragraph
⌘-OPTION-M	Select All

Table A-2. Keys with Command Equivalents (continued)

Keys	Command
⌘-SHIFT-M	Unnest Paragraph
⌘-N	New
⌘-OPTION-N	Normal
⌘-SHIFT-N	Nest Paragraph
⌘-O	Open
⌘-OPTION-O	Outline (View)
⌘-SHIFT-O	Open Spacing
⌘-P	Print
⌘-OPTION-P	Page Layout
⌘-SHIFT-P	Normal Paragraph
PAGE DOWN	Scroll Screen Down
⌘-PAGE DOWN	Move to Next Page
PAGE UP	Scroll Screen Up
⌘-PAGE UP	Move to Previous Page
⌘-Q	Quit
⌘-OPTION-Q	Paste Special Character
⌘-SHIFT-Q	Symbol Font
⌘-R	Ruler
⌘-OPTION-R	Ribbon
⌘-SHIFT-R	Flush Right
RETURN	New Paragraph
⌘-RETURN	New Paragraph with Same Style
⌘-OPTION-RETURN	New Paragraph after Ins. Point
SHIFT-RETURN	Line Break
→	Move to Next Character
⌘-→	Move to Next Word
⌘-S	Save
⌘-OPTION-S	Split Window
⌘-SHIFT-S	Change Style
⌘-SHIFT-OPTION-S	Footnotes

Table A-2. *Keys with Command Equivalents (continued)*

Keys	Command
⌘-SPACEBAR	Insert Nonbreaking Space
⌘-OPTION-SPACEBAR	Insert Paragraph Above Row
⌘-SHIFT-SPACEBAR	Revert To Style
OPTION-SPACEBAR	Insert Nonbreaking Space
⌘-T	Style
⌘-OPTION-T	Outline Command Prefix
⌘-SHIFT-T	Hanging Indent
TAB	Insert Tab
⌘-TAB	Activate Keyboard Menus
OPTION-TAB	Insert Tab
SHIFT-TAB	Move to Previous Cell
⌘-U	Underline
⌘-SHIFT-U	Underline
↑	Move to Previous Line
⌘-↑	Move to Previous Paragraph
⌘-V	Paste
⌘-OPTION-V	Copy Formats
⌘-SHIFT-V	Hidden Text
⌘-W	Close
⌘-OPTION-W	Move to Next Window
⌘-SHIFT-W	Shadow
⌘-X	Cut
⌘-OPTION-X	Move Text
⌘-SHIFT-X	Hidden Text
⌘-Y	Repeat
⌘-OPTION-Y	Move to Previous Paragraph
⌘-SHIFT-Y	Double Space
⌘-Z	Undo
⌘-OPTION-Z	Go Back
⌘-SHIFT-Z	Plain Text

Table A-2. Keys with Command Equivalents (continued)

Keys	Command
⌘-OPTION-[	Scroll Line Up
⌘-SHIFT-[	Double Underline
⌘-OPTION-\	Insert Formula
⌘-SHIFT-\	Dotted Underline
⌘-SHIFT-]	Word Underline
⌘-`	Insert Nonbreaking Hyphen

B

Word Commands

This appendix shows the commands that are on the Word menus.

Figure B-1. *Word's menus*

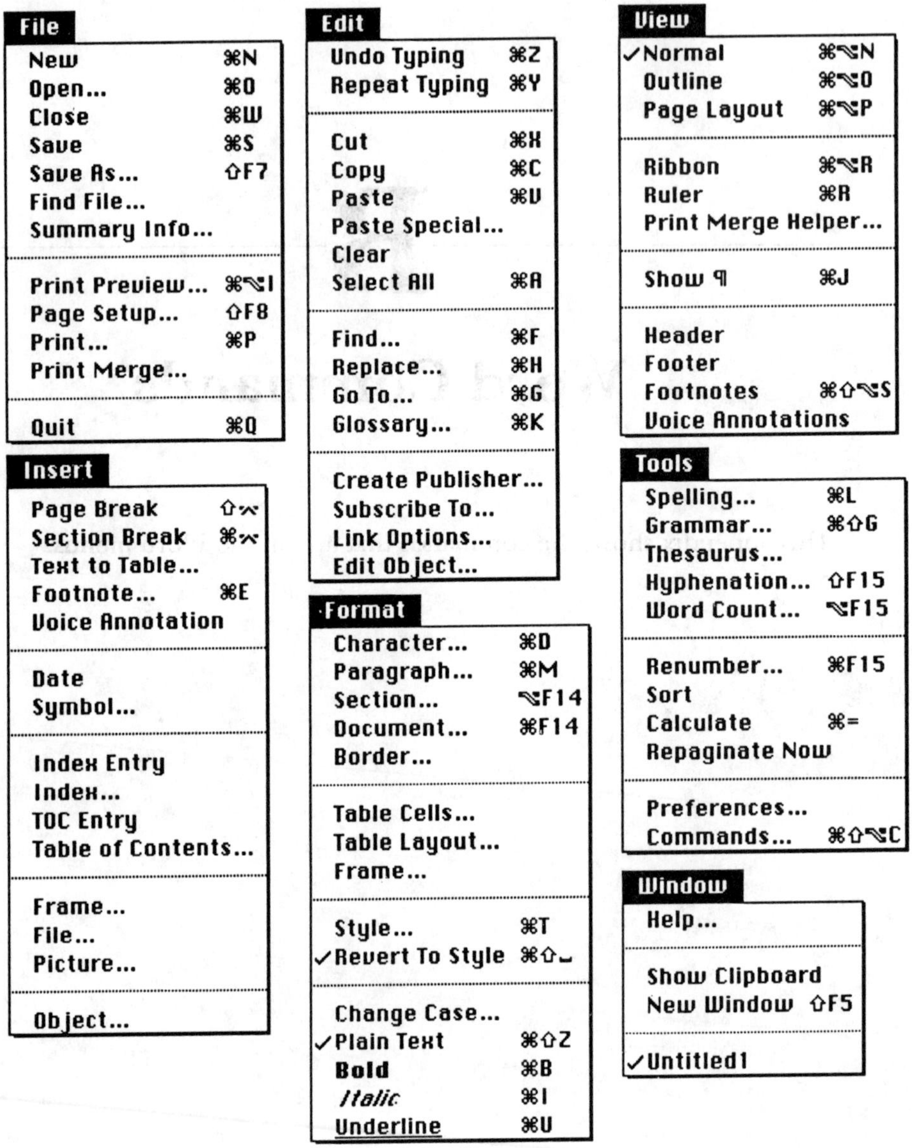

Index

A

B

C

J

K

L

M

N

O

P

Q

R

S

T

Osborne McGraw-Hill

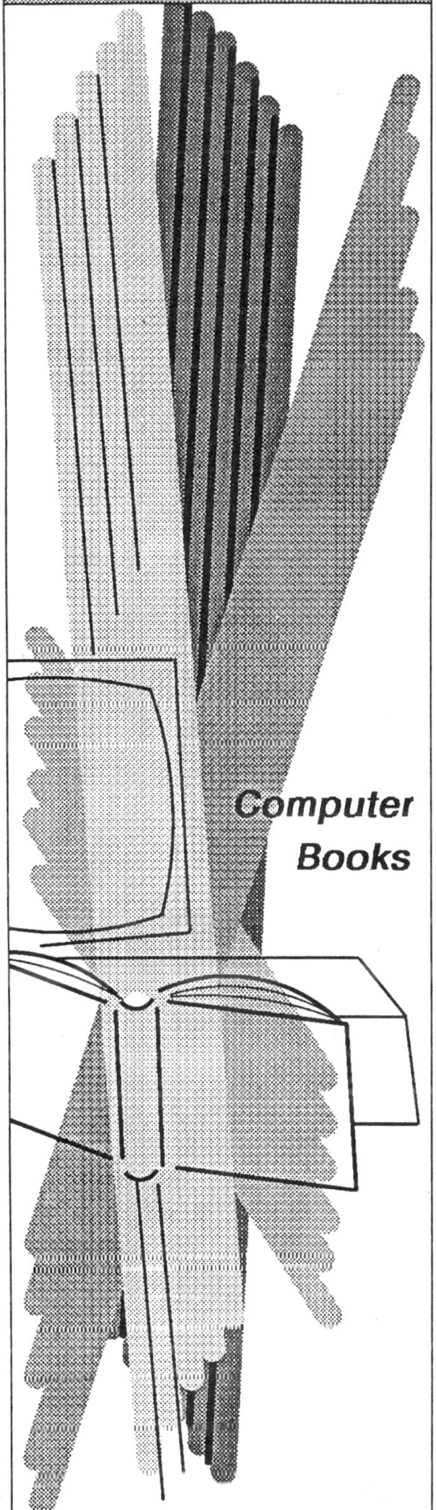

(800) 227-0900

Bookmarker Design — Lance Ravella

Tear off for Bookmark

You're important to us...

We'd like to know what you're interested in, what kinds of books you're looking for, and what you thought about this book in particular.

Please fill out the attached card and mail it in. We'll do our best to keep you informed about Osborne's newest books and special offers.

YES, Send Me a FREE Color Catalog of all Osborne computer books
To Receive Catalog, Fill in Last 4 Digits of ISBN Number from Back of Book (see below bar code) 0-07-881 _ _ _ – _

Name: ________________ Title: ________________

Company: ________________

Address: ________________

City: __________ State: ______ Zip: __________

I'M PARTICULARLY INTERESTED IN THE FOLLOWING *(Check all that apply)*

I use this software

- ☐ WordPerfect
- ☐ Microsoft Word
- ☐ WordStar
- ☐ Lotus 1-2-3
- ☐ Quattro
- ☐ Others ____________

I use this operating system

- ☐ DOS
- ☐ Windows
- ☐ UNIX
- ☐ Macintosh
- ☐ Others ____________

I rate this book:

☐ Excellent ☐ Good ☐ Poor

I program in

- ☐ C or C++
- ☐ Pascal
- ☐ BASIC
- ☐ Others ____________

I chose this book because

- ☐ Recognized author's name
- ☐ Osborne/McGraw-Hill's reputation
- ☐ Read book review
- ☐ Read Osborne catalog
- ☐ Saw advertisement in store
- ☐ Found/recommended in library
- ☐ Required textbook
- ☐ Price
- ☐ Other ____________

Comments ________________

Topics I would like to see covered in future books by Osborne/McGraw-Hill include:

____

IMPORTANT REMINDER

To get your FREE catalog, write in the last 4 digits of the ISBN number printed on the back cover (see below bar code) 0-07-881 _ _ _ – _

NO POSTAGE
NECESSARY
IF MAILED
IN THE
UNITED STATES

BUSINESS REPLY MAIL

First Class Permit NO. 3111 Berkeley, CA

Postage will be paid by addressee

Osborne **McGraw-Hill**
2600 Tenth Street
Berkeley, California 94710–9938

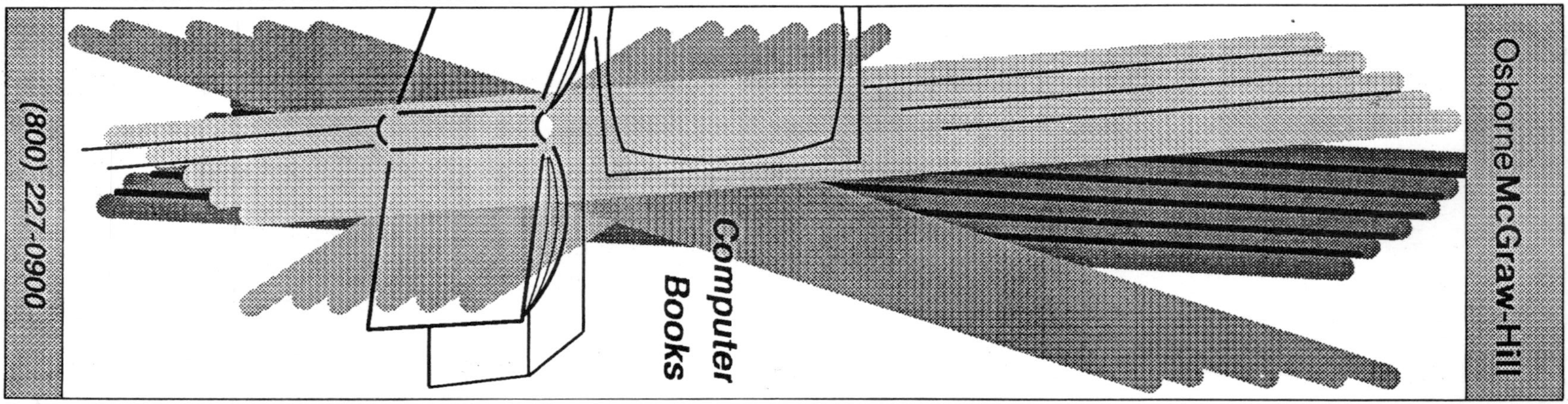